Materials Development for TESOL

Materials Development for TESOL

Freda Mishan and Ivor Timmis

EDINBURGH
University Press

Edinburgh University Press Ltd
The Tun – Holyrood Road
12(2f) Jackson's Entry
Edinburgh EH8 8PJ

www.euppublishing.com

Typeset in 10/12 Minion by
Servis Filmsetting Ltd, Stockport, Cheshire,
and printed and bound in Great Britain by
CPI Group (UK) Ltd, Croydon CR0 4YY

A CIP record for this book is available from the British Library

ISBN 978 0 7486 9135 7 (hardback)
ISBN 978 0 7486 9137 1 (webready PDF)
ISBN 978 0 7486 9136 4 (paperback)
ISBN 978 0 7486 9138 8 (epub)

CONTENTS

ACKNOWLEDGEMENTS

The authors and publishers acknowledge the following sources of copyright material and are grateful for the permissions granted:

Chapter 2 (on web page): Extract from LCIE (Limerick Corpus of Irish English), Farr, F. and O'Keeffe, A.

Chapter 3, Figure 3.1: p. 14 from *New Headway Intermediate Student's Book*, Soars, L. and Soars, J. (2009), Oxford University Press.

Chapter 6, Figure 6.1: p. 15 from *New English File: Upper-Intermediate – Student's Book*, Oxenden, C. and Latham-Koenig, C. (2008), Oxford University Press.

Chapter 6, Figure 6.4: From Dellar/Walkely. *Innovations Advanced*. 1E. © 2007 Heinle/ELT, a part of Cengage Learning, Inc. Reproduced by permission. www.cengage.com/permissions.

The authors wish to acknowledge the contribution and support of the following:
Ivor Timmis would like to thank Heather Buchanan, Felicity Parsisson, Philip Prowse, Sarah Skelton and Jane Templeton for comments on chapter drafts.
Freda Mishan would like to thank the University of Limerick Faculty of Arts, Humanities and Social Sciences and the School of Languages Literature, Culture and Communication for giving her study leave to work on this book. Sincere thanks also to colleagues in the TESOL/Linguistics section for their patience and support during this time. On a personal level Freda extends huge thanks to Kevin and Reuben for their tolerance and support. Finally a dedication to her late father, Ezra, 'in whose academic shadow I remain'.

ABBREVIATIONS

BANA	Britain, Australasia and North America
BNC	British National Corpus
CALL	computer-assisted language learning
CEFR	Common European Framework of Reference (also known as CEF)
CL	corpus linguistics
CLIL	content and language integrated learning
CLT	communicative language teaching
CMC	computer-mediated communication
CoBuild	Collins Birmingham University International Language Database
COCA	Corpus of Contemporary American English
C-R	consciousness-raising
DDL	data-driven learning
EAP	English for academic purposes
EFL	English as a foreign language
EIL	English as an international language
ELF	English as a lingua franca
ELT	English language teaching
ER	extensive reading
ESL	English as a second language
ESOL	English for speakers of other languages
ESP	English for specific purposes
EUROCALL	European Association for Computer-Assisted Language Learning
FFI	form-focused instruction
HLT	humanistic language teaching
IATEFL	International Association of Teachers of English as a Foreign Language
ICT	information and communications technologies
IELTS	International English Language Testing System
IWB	interactive whiteboard
L1	first language
L2	second language
MALL	mobile-assisted language learning
MICASE	Michigan Corpus of Academic Spoken English
NES	native English speaker

NLP	neuro-linguistic programming
NNES	non-native English speaker
NNEST	non-native English-speaking teacher
OLPC	One Laptop per Child
PPP	present, practise, produce
RP	Received Pronunciation
SACODEYL	System Aided Compilation and Open Distribution of European Youth Language
SLA	second language acquisition
SNS	social networking site
TBLT	task-based language teaching
TESOL	teaching English to speakers of other languages
TL	target language
TLC	target language culture
TPR	total physical response
USPs	unique selling points
VLE	virtual learning environment

Online resources, indicated in the text with a 🖥 and a task number are available at: www.euppublishing.com/page/TESOL/AdditionalResources/MishanTimmis

SERIES EDITORS' PREFACE

Editors Joan Cutting, University of Edinburgh and Fiona Farr, University of Limerick

This series of textbooks addresses a range of topics taught within **TESOL programmes** around the world. Each volume is designed to match a taught 'core' or 'option' course (identified by a survey of TESOL programmes worldwide) and could be adopted as a prescribed text. Other series and books have been aimed at Applied Linguistics students or language teachers in general, but this aims more specifically at students of ELT (English Language Teaching – the process of enabling the learning of English), with or without teaching experience.

The series is intended primarily for college and university students at third or fourth year undergraduate level, and graduates (pre-service or in-service) studying TESOL on Masters programmes and possibly some TESOL EdDs or Structured PhDs, all of whom need an introduction to the topics for their taught courses. It is also very suitable for new professionals and people starting out on a PhD, who could use the volumes for self-study. The **readership level** is **introductory** and the tone and approach of the volumes will appeal to both undergraduates and postgraduates.

This series answers a need for volumes with a special focus on **intercultural awareness**. It is aimed at programmes in countries where English is not the mother tongue, and in English-speaking countries where the majority of students come from countries where English is not the mother tongue, typical of TESOL programmes in the UK and Ireland, Canada and the US, Australia and New Zealand. This means that it takes into account physical and economic conditions in ELT classrooms round the world and a variety of socio-educational backgrounds. Each volume contains a number of tasks which include examples from classrooms around the world, encourage comparisons across cultures and address issues that apply to each student's home context. Closely related to the intercultural awareness focus is a minor theme that runs throughout the series, and that is language analysis and description, and its applications to ELT. Intercultural awareness is indeed a complex concept and we aim to address it in a number of different ways. Taking examples from different cultural contexts is one way, but the volumes in the series also look at many other educationally relevant cultural dimensions such as sociolinguistic influences, gender issues, various learning traditions (e.g. collectivist vs individualistic) and culturally determined language dimensions (e.g. politeness conventions).

TESOL students need **theory clearly related to practice**. This series is practical and is intended to be used in TESOL lectures and workshops, providing group tasks and independent activities. Students are invited to engage in critical thinking and to consider applications of concepts and issues to their own particular teaching contexts, adapting the tendencies and suggestions in the literature to their own countries' educational requirements. Each volume contains practical tasks to carry out individually, in small groups or in plenary in the classroom, as well as suggestions for practical tasks for the students to use in their own classrooms. All the concepts and issues encountered here will be translatable into the ELT classroom. It is hoped that this series will contribute to your improvement as a teacher.

The series presents ELT concepts and research issues **simply**. The volumes guide students from the basic concepts, through the issues and complexities, to a level that should make them alert to past and recent teaching and research developments in each field. This series makes the topics accessible to those unaccustomed to reading theoretical literature, and yet takes them to an exam and Masters standard, serving as a gateway into the various fields and an introduction to the more theoretical literature. We also acknowledge that **technology** is a major area within TESOL and this series is aware of the need for technology to feature prominently across its volumes. Issues of technological integration and implementation are addressed in some way in each of the volumes. The series is based on state-of-the-art research. The concepts and issues raised are intended to inspire students to undertake their own research and consider pursuing their interests in a PhD.

Editorial Advisory Board

As well as the two editors, the series has an Editorial Advisory Board, whose members are involved in decisions on commissioning and considering book proposals and reviewing book drafts. We would like to acknowledge and thank members of the Board for all of their work and guidance on the Textbooks in TESOL series:

- Prof. David Bloch, University of London, UK
- Dr Averil Coxhead, Victoria University of Wellington, New Zealand
- Prof. Donald Freeman, University of Michigan, USA
- Mr Peter Grundy, Northumbria University, UK
- Dr Annie Hughes, University of York, UK
- Prof. Mike McCarthy, University of Nottingham, UK
- Dr Liam Murray, University of Limerick, Ireland
- Dr Anne O'Keeffe, Mary Immaculate College, University of Limerick, Ireland
- Dr Jonathon Reinhardt, University of Arizona, USA
- Prof. Randi Reppen, North Arizona University, USA
- Assoc. Prof. Ali Shehadeh, UAE University, United Arab Emirates

- Assoc. Prof. Scott Thornbury, the New School, New York, USA
- Prof. Steve Walsh, Newcastle University, UK

Edinburgh Textbooks in TESOL

Books in this series include:

Changing Methodologies in TESOL	Jane Spiro
Mixed Methods Research for TESOL	James Dean Brown
Language in Context in TESOL	Joan Cutting

INTRODUCTION

1.1 WHY DO WE NEED A BOOK ABOUT MATERIALS DEVELOPMENT?

The first question we need to ask is, 'Why do we need an academic book, even a practice-oriented book, about materials development?' It could, after all, be argued that materials development is essentially a practical rather than a theoretical exercise and that there is no shortage of expertise in this area of practice. There are professional materials writers, backed by all the resources available to publishers, who have produced a wealth of materials for English language teaching (ELT) over many years, including specialised materials for particular skills, contexts or purposes. This wealth of materials also provides a model or template for teachers who want to produce their own materials to supplement those already available. On the surface, then, the area of materials development appears to be well catered for. On closer inspection, however, we can argue that the weight of established practice is a double-edged sword: while it ensures that a wide range of materials is available and that there is a steady stream of new materials, it can lead to a situation where existing materials are the *only* reference point for the development of new materials. In other words, there can be a tendency for materials to be cloned from previous examples of practice and to be geared to the perceived demands of the market. Published materials are typically the result of 'mediated' materials development where stakeholders such as publishers and ministries of education might strongly influence the final product; this can be contrasted with 'unmediated materials' development where the materials writer can engage directly with language learning principles without intervention from intermediaries (Timmis 2014). Tomlinson (2001: 6) provides the following definition of materials development as a field: 'Materials development is both a field of study and a practical undertaking. As a field it studies the principles and procedures of the design, implementation and evaluation of language teaching materials.'

In similar vein, McGrath (2002: 217) argues that 'materials represent the first stage in which principles are turned into practice'. This emphasis on principles is one we share: this book is about principled materials development, i.e. materials development which takes into account current practice, but goes beyond it to consult first principles drawn from second language acquisition (SLA) and language teaching theory. One of the authors of this book, Ivor Timmis, recalls his first encounter with principled materials development:

My own first experience of principled materials development came when my PhD supervisor suggested that I write a unit of materials as part of my thesis. My first reaction was, 'Dull'; my second reaction was, 'Easy'. I was wrong on both counts. The process turned out to be both far more interesting and far more challenging than I had anticipated.

The purpose of this book about materials design, then, is to help readers to evaluate current practice in materials design critically; to consider principled ways in which they could design materials for particular skills, particular aspects of language and particular contexts; and to provide some practical guidelines on the kinds of resources available and the materials production process. We began with a simple question: 'Why do we need a book on materials development?' We consider two other (deceptively) simple questions in the introduction:

- What are materials?
- What do we need materials for?

1.2 WHAT ARE MATERIALS?

Tomlinson (2011a: 2) provides a very interesting answer to this question when he defines materials thus:

[Materials are] anything which is used by teachers and learners to facilitate the learning of a language. Materials could obviously be videos, DVDs, emails, YouTube, dictionaries, grammar books, readers, workbooks or photocopied exercises. They could also be newspapers, food packages, photographs, live talks given by invited native speakers, instructions given by a teacher, tasks written on cards or discussions between learners.

There are a number of observations we can make about this thought-provoking definition. Firstly, it begins by pointing us towards electronic media (videos, DVDs, emails, YouTube), and we should acknowledge that the ever-changing nature of electronic media will continue to broaden the scope of what we consider to be materials (see Chapter 5). Secondly, it points us to the more traditional realm of paper-based materials (dictionaries, grammar books, readers, workbooks or photocopied exercises), and thirdly it considers realia (newspapers, food packages, photographs). These first three categories are all artefacts or products, but the fourth category, with the exception of tasks written on cards, includes processes (live talks given by invited native speakers, instructions given by a teacher, discussions between learners), a category which would probably not be included in materials by most teachers (but it is one we discuss in Chapter 5). Tomlinson's (2011a) definition, whether you agree with it or not, has the merit of opening the discussion of what constitutes materials, and encouraging us to think of non-traditional examples. Tomlinson (2011a) specifies that materials are anything which is *used* by teachers and learners to facilitate the learning of a language, and we could take this further by arguing that the defining characteristic of materials is that the materials designer builds in a pedagogic purpose. On this basis, it is possible to draw a distinction between resources and materials. A YouTube video, for example, remains a resource until we add a pedagogic purpose to it, which might range from something as simple as a single question to some elaborate extended project or task. By the same token, learner talk remains a resource until you do something with it: to convert it from a resource to material, you might ask learners to record and transcribe their own talk; you might listen to learners' talk and highlight some good examples of language use, or elicit correction of a couple of interesting errors. Learner talk is a very good example of an under-used resource, but can it be regarded as material if it simply disappears into thin air? The positive point to take from this argument is that resources are limitless and the potential to convert them into materials is limited only by our pedagogic imagination.

1.3 WHAT DO WE NEED MATERIALS FOR?

We tend to take it for granted that materials are needed for language teaching, but if we are to develop materials in optimally purposeful ways, it is worth asking a funda-mental question, 'What do we need materials for?' A good starting point for answer-ing this question is an article by Thornbury (2000b) where he argues that, in fact, we do *not* need materials, or at least not to the same extent that we currently make use of them. Thornbury (2000b) took as his inspiration for a materials-free or materials-light approach to teaching the Dogme school of film-makers, who began to produce films using a minimum of technical 'trickery'. Thornbury (2000b: 2) wanted to apply the same approach to ELT:

> My belief is that it is high time Dogme-type principles were applied to the classroom. While EFL [English as a foreign language] may seem to have little in common with Hollywood, it is certainly true that EFL teaching has never been so copiously resourced. Along with the quantity (I hesitate to use the word variety) of coursebooks in print, there is an embarrassment of complementary riches in the form of videos, CD-ROMs, photocopiable resource packs, pull-out word lists, and even web-sites, not to mention the standard workbook, teacher's book, and classroom and home study cassettes. Then there is the vast battery of supplementary materials available, as well as the authentic material easily downloadable from the Internet or illegally photocopied from more conventional sources. There are the best-selling self-study grammar books, personal vocabulary organisers, phrasal verb dictionaries, concordancing software packages – you name it. But where is the story? Where is the inner life of the student in all this? Where is real communication? More often as [*sic*] not, it is buried under an avalanche of photocopies, visual aids, transparencies, MTV clips and Cuisenaire rods. Somewhere in there we lost the plot.

Adapting the Dogme principles to the ELT classroom, Thornbury (2000b) argues that the most important resources in the classroom are learners and teachers. He complains about teachers' obsession with grammar and materials-driven lessons where the materials actually act as an obstacle between learners and teachers and bury the 'inner life' of the learners. For Thornbury, it is the quality of talk between teachers and learners that is paramount (an interesting departure from the mantra of pre-service training courses: reduce teacher talking time): 'Teaching – like talk – should centre on the local and relevant concerns of the people in the room, not on the remote world of coursebook characters, nor the contrived world of grammatical structures' (Thornbury 2000b: 2).

Finally, Thornbury (2000b) describes this rejection of conventional materials and the conventional use of materials as 'a vow of chastity' and urges us to join him in this vow. We need to keep in mind that Thornbury is probably playing devil's advocate to some extent, but his arguments do highlight two potential problems with materials: they can drive lessons rather than support them; teachers can teach the materials rather than the learners.

Thornbury's (2000b) rather dismissive approach to materials naturally provoked a reaction from other practitioners, and Gill (2000: 18–19) wrote an interesting response in which he argued against this rejection of materials, particularly if applied to inexperienced teachers:

I . . . think it's much easier to adopt a 'chaste' classroom policy if you've actually had a chance to use, assess, and then decide to reject the sort of resources Scott [Thornbury] is concerned about. Such a rejection needs to be an informed choice, based on experience; now, with twenty years' teaching behind me, I'm quite happy to go, as it were, naked into the classroom when my professional judgement tells me it is appropriate for the situation, but for the less experienced teacher, who is still seeking to establish their repertoire of styles, a process of experimentation, of trial and error, is surely a key element of the process of learning to be a good teacher. (Gill 2000: 19)

Gill's (2000) comment about the need to use and assess resources before rejecting them points to an irony in Thornbury's (2000b) Dogme approach: teachers are often in a better position to improvise in class after they have internalised procedures, routines and repertoire from published materials. Gill (2000) also makes a crucial point about the need to match an approach to the context, and presents a number of scenarios from his own experience which required either lighter or heavier use of materials according to factors such as the availability of resources, learner expectations and school policy. We should note here McGrath's (2006, cited in McGrath 2013: 152) observation on *learners'* views of coursebooks, based on a study when he asked them to come up with metaphors for the coursebook:

It will be clear from the positive images that learners respect coursebooks . . . and value them both for what they contain and for the benefits they can bestow. In some cases, the book is even anthropomorphized (e.g. 'my mother', 'my friend'; but note also negative equivalents, for example, 'a devil', 'a professional killer').

We can also add that Thornbury's suggested focus on the 'inner life' of the learners seems to be very much a Western notion of education (Gadd 1998).

In this introduction, we have stressed the need for principled materials development, and Gill (2000: 19) makes a similar point about the need for materials to be *used* in a principled way:

> I believe that all the tools we use, from the humblest piece of chalk to the mightiest multimedia centre, have the potential to be valuable *if used in a principled way*, and that my duty to trainees is to introduce them to as wide a range of tools as possible and to guide them in developing their own principles for the assessment and use (or otherwise) of these tools.

Gill's (2000) emphasis on principled use of materials echoes our earlier discussion of principled materials development. Indeed, we could argue that Thornbury's (2000b) teacher talk is material if the teacher has a pedagogic plan about what to do with it. Gill (2000) provides an interesting defence of the need for materials, but does not go into detail about *why* we need materials, other than to say that learners generally expect them and teachers find them useful. We still need to go into more depth about what we need materials for. This question, 'What do we want materials for?', was put to a group of British Council teachers working in Southeast Asia on a short materials development course which took place in Bangkok in 2011. Here are some of their answers (the grouping of the answers is explained below).

We want materials to:
a. arouse our learners' interest
b. be challenging enough
c. make the students feel that they are having a properly planned class
d. support and guide both the students and the teacher, and provide structure and progression (even if this is not explicit)

e. provide a variety of experience in terms of texts

f. be a resource that introduces and/or reinforces areas of lexis or grammar.
g. teach new skills and strategies that our learners really need
h. provide knowledge about other cultures

i. be a 'springboard' that stimulates students to engage with the language and use it
j. stimulate interest in non-linguistic issues
k. guide learners to be more autonomous
l. be flexible for other teachers to use or for teachers to personalise

m. provide teachers with sound teaching principles

We would argue that these answers encapsulate five key purposes of materials:

1. Materials **meet a psychological need** (a, b, c, d). Firstly, through texts, topics, tasks and visuals, materials can provide motivation for the learner which it is difficult

for the teacher alone to sustain. Secondly, in the case of a set of course materials, they give learners and teachers at least *a sense of* ordered progression and, indeed, meet their expectation that learning involves materials. While there is a good deal of evidence that progress in a language is not steady and systematic, the belief that one is making steady and systematic progress can itself can be important.

2. Materials **provide exposure to the language** (e). Teachers themselves are, of course, important sources of exposure to the target language (TL), but they cannot provide the *range* of exposure – different spoken and written genres and styles, different accents and so on – which can be achieved through carefully selected listening and reading texts and through visual media.

3. Materials **are vehicles of information** (f, g, h). Materials can provide information about grammar and vocabulary and about the TL culture/s and other cultures which may be more accurate and comprehensive than the teacher's alone. They can also provide learner training in different skills and strategies.

4. Materials **provide a stimulus for other activities** (i, j, k, l). Materials – texts or tasks, for example – can elicit an oral or written response from learners. This might be in the form of an immediate reaction to a text or a more extended discussion, debate or project. Materials can also be of broader educational value in introducing learners to topics beyond their own experience and by fostering more independent learning. Materials can also stimulate teachers to think of their own ideas of how best to exploit them.

5. Materials **can act as teacher education** (m). Materials, particularly those with an accompanying teacher's book, can provide good models of practice for teachers, especially if the teacher's book gives a clear rationale for the approach.

As we have shown above, materials can have a range of purposes, and the way they are used will vary from context to context depending on factors such as the aim of the course, the experience and confidence of the teacher, the requirements of the institution and the expectations of the learner. Richards (2001: 251, cited in McGrath 2013: ix) stresses the importance of materials in language teaching:

> Teaching materials are a key component in most language programs. Whether the teacher uses a textbook, institutionally prepared materials, or his or her own materials, instructional materials generally serve as the basis for much of the language input learners receive and the language practice that occurs in the classroom. In the case of inexperienced teachers, materials may also serve as a form of teacher training.

1.4 THE PURPOSE OF THIS BOOK

We began this introduction with the question, 'Why do we need a book about materials development?' We end it with the question, 'Why do we need *this* book about materials development?' Tomlinson (2011b) has argued that in the last twenty to thirty years, materials development has been taken more seriously as a field of study rather than simply a practical undertaking. More and more teaching English to speakers of other languages (TESOL) courses are offering modules in materials development – indeed, this may be why you have this book in front of you – and there have been a number of publications focusing on materials evaluation and/or materials development (e.g. Harwood 2010, 2014; McGrath 2002, 2013; Mishan and Chambers 2010; Tomlinson 2011b, 2013a). This book, however, offers a *course* in materials development. It aims for comprehensive coverage of the main theoretical and practical issues in materials development rather than a focus on specialist issues. By the end of the book, we hope you will be equipped to evaluate, adapt and develop materials in principled and effective ways – and we hope you enjoy the journey too.

1.5 THE STRUCTURE OF THE BOOK

This course in materials development covers within its eight core chapters (Chapters 2–9) all the essential areas that make up the field that we have noted above. The call for 'principled materials development' above is met in the first core chapter, **Chapter 2**, where we seek to establish core materials development principles drawing on our current knowledge of SLA. **In Chapter 3** we consider the materials–culture interface, examining the implications of the global diversification of the English language for teaching materials as well as the relationship between the ELT publishing industry and the diversity of cultural contexts it serves. ELT publishing features in the following chapter too; given the predominance of coursebook teaching in the field of TESOL, we demonstrate in **Chapter 4** that the development of informed criteria for systematic evaluation of these materials is an indispensable component of materials development. In **Chapter 5** we turn to technology, where we explore how our traditional concept of language learning materials can be broadened to include the digital environment. Chapters 6 and 7 focus on materials for what are conventionally known as 'the four skills': developing materials for reading and listening skills is covered in **Chapter 6** and for speaking and writing skills in **Chapter 7**. Developing materials for vocabulary and grammar teaching follows in **Chapter 8**, and we note the influence of corpus linguistics research in establishing corpora as important resources for these. The book culminates in a chapter (**Chapter 9**) on materials production, exploring the notoriously elusive processes of creating materials but also offering sets of materials and frameworks.

The core chapters have the following structure:

- **Introduction**
- **Three input sections** (note that Chapters 6, 7 and 8 contain only two as they cover two skills each)
  - ☐ Each input section includes three tasks to be used in class and outside for self-study. These vary to include tasks such as:
    - ☐ Evaluating language learning materials and/or principles relating to their development
    - ☐ Trying out concepts and materials within and with respect to your teaching contexts
    - ☐ Mini research or materials development projects

- **Two Further Reading sections**
  - ☐ Each consists of:
    - ☐ A research-based article or chapter summary, with bite-size chunks from the article
    - ☐ Two tasks:
      - ☐ Trying out concepts in your teaching contexts
      - ☐ Mini research projects
- **Conclusion**
- **Additional reading**, with guiding comments.

PRINCIPLED MATERIALS DEVELOPMENT

2.1 INTRODUCTION

There is no specific 'theory' of materials development itself. This is because, as we will argue and illustrate in this chapter, materials development draws – or, we maintain, should draw – directly on what we know about how learners acquire a second language (L2): 'every time teachers make pedagogic decisions about content or methodology they are in fact making assumptions about how learners learn' (Ellis 1994: 4). The field that investigates SLA is vast and diverse, with a plethora of theories; an overview by Long in 1993 identified between forty and sixty, and this number has expanded in the years since. This diversity and the hesitation as to whether the findings of SLA research are 'sufficiently robust to warrant application to language pedagogy' (Ellis 2010: 34), or indeed precisely how they might be applied, has meant a slower than desirable influence on teaching approaches, and an even slower one on materials development (ibid.). Nevertheless, we would agree with Tomlinson's assertion that it is time to take the plunge; 'this should not stop us from applying what we *do* know about second and foreign language learning to the development of materials designed to facilitate this process' (Tomlinson 2011a: 7, italics in original).

With an eye to applying findings from research and theories to materials development, then, the approach taken here has been to trawl through the myriad factors that affect language learning to isolate those in which clear correspondences with learning materials can be perceived. These include factors internal to the learner, within both the 'affective domain' (concerned with emotions) and the 'cognitive domain' (concerned with rationality). They also include external factors, of course; the language input itself (the 'materials'), the teacher and the learning environment. Discussion of these factors will allow us to extract a set of usable 'SLA-based principles for materials development' to form benchmarks for principled development of language learning materials. Sets of principles should not, of course, be misread as rules and need to be combined with the variables relevant to each particular learning context, such as sociocultural issues, curricular constraints and materials developers' own beliefs, preferred teaching styles and so on.

Finally, it is important to flag here that we take the 'back to SLA basics' approach, as we do not think materials development principles can be usefully informed by teaching methodologies (such as the communicative approach, task-based language teaching (TBLT) and so on). This is because these methodologies are themselves 'interpretations' into pedagogy of beliefs around SLA (see Spiro 2013). They are informed, what is more, by the conventions of language pedagogy of the cultures in which they were conceived (see more on this in Chapter 3). This chapter is in no way a complete overview of SLA research; the reader is therefore referred to comprehensive works on the area such as the writings of Rod Ellis (e.g. 1997 and 2008) and Ritchie and Bhatia (2009).

2.2 THE IMPORTANCE OF AFFECTIVE AND COGNITIVE CHALLENGE IN LANGUAGE LEARNING MATERIALS

MOTIVATION

In this section, we explore that strongest predictor of learning success, motivation: '*Given motivation, it is inevitable that a human being will learn a second language if he is exposed to the language data*' (Pit Corder 1974: 72, our italics), and consider how we can design language learning materials which stimulate aspects of motivation.

Motivation is a multi-faceted construct conceived as a spectrum covering affective as well as cognitive dimensions. Dörnyei, one of the principal figures in the area, characterises it as an '"engine" made up of effort, will and attitude' (1998: 122). Despite – or perhaps because of – being one of the most 'intensely investigated' variables in SLA (Dewaele 2009: 634), it remains 'one of the most elusive concepts in the whole of social sciences' (Dörnyei 2001: 2). A generally agreed description of motivation as being 'responsible for determining human behaviour by energizing it and giving it direction' (Dörnyei 1998: 117) belies the 'bewildering array of theoretical positions' (Ellis 2004: 538) as to how it does this.

For our purposes we will attempt to cut through the complexities of the theoretical debate to draw out core concepts that we see as relevant to the design of language learning materials. The first involves the conceptualisations of what 'drives' motivation, and it is interesting to note the evolution of these concepts to reflect increasing influence from the field of psychology. One of the earliest and perhaps best-known distinctions in motivation theories in SLA is between *integrative* and *instrumental* motivation. The former is driven by 'a sincere and personal interest in the people and culture represented by the language group' (Lambert 1974: 98). This contrasts with instrumental motivation where language learning is considered 'a means to an end' in terms of leading to improved job or educational prospects and the like, or even just pleasing parents or family. These original terms made way (from the mid-1980s) for the notions of *intrinsic* motivation – 'behaviour performed for its own sake in order to experience pleasure and satisfaction such as the joy of doing a particular activity or satisfying one's curiosity' (Dörnyei 1998: 121) – and *extrinsic* motivation, which, like instrumental motivation, is driven by some external reward. These two apparent 'poles' of motivational impulse were reconciled through Deci and Ryan's notion of 'self-determination' (see, for example, 1985), whereby motivation is seen as first and foremost a self-propelling act. In more recent research, motivation for L2 learning stretches into the realm of psychology, being bound ever more tightly to the notion of developing an L2 'identity' (for further reading on this, see Dörnyei 2009), which links to the sociolinguistic aspects of language learning (see, for example, Coupland 2001). Dörnyei's theories resonate with another concept on the SLA–psychology border, that of the permeable 'language ego' (Guiora, Beit-Halllahmi, Brannon, Dull and Scovel 1972): in lay terms, the often-reported sensation of being 'a different person' when speaking another language.

Affective aspects of motivation in language learning: 'Language Orientation Questionnaire' by Zoltan Dörnyei

2.1

These affective aspects of motivation bring us to the second area we wish to explore. Although, as we have noted above, motivation involves aspects of both the affective and cognitive domains, what emerges from the literature is how vulnerable it is to affective factors – and ones which can be directly impacted/stimulated by the language materials used.

These factors include some already discussed above and others which we consider particularly susceptible in this regard, to be discussed below:

- intrinsic interest
- (linguistic) self-confidence and self-esteem
- anxiety (see discussion of 'affective filter' below)
- intrinsic value attributed to the activity i.e. its 'worthiness'

The notion of 'intrinsic interest' is a particularly important one for materials developers, as well as for teachers, since in the pedagogical context, showing interest is generally considered a sort of 'external manifestation' of motivation. Indeed, 'enthusiasm, attention, action and enjoyment [are considered] referents for and components of motivation' (Peacock 1997: 145–6) to such an extent that motivation might be defined in these terms; 'for this study, "motivation" is defined [as] interest in and enthusiasm for the materials used in class' (ibid.: 145). While we cannot ultimately control motivation, as it is internal to the learner, we can seek to provide materials which are likely to stimulate intrinsic interest.

If motivation can be equated with intrinsic interest, it might as easily be equated with notions of *enjoyment* (Gardner 1995) and *engagement*: 'teachers would describe a student as motivated if s/he becomes productively engaged on learning tasks and sustains that engagement' (Crookes and Schmidt 1991: 480). Engagement with the learning task is in a sense both a symptom and a cause: not only is it an indicator of motivation but it is an essential factor for language acquisition: 'We know that affective engagement is vital for long-term learning' (Tomlinson 2003a: 234).

Engagement, of course, is an aspect of the cognitive domain as well as the affective – 'learners . . . need to be engaged both affectively and cognitively in the language experience' (Tomlinson 2011a: 7) – and is one we will look at further when considering language input.

AFFECT

In this section we emphasise the importance of affective factors in language acquisition and ask you to consider the implications for language learning materials. The concept of 'affect' refers to 'aspects of emotion, feeling mood or attitude which condition behaviour' (Arnold and Brown 1999: 1). Nowadays, affect is given a high priority in the context of language learning, as well as in other spheres such as health and education in general, acknowledging the interrelationship between the emotional, the physical and the cognitive. In this context, affect refers to the feelings, ranging from positive to negative, which impact on learning. Positive emotional factors which do this include pleasure, happiness, confidence, self-esteem and empathy, while negative factors include ones unfortunately common to the educational context: stress and anxiety, as well as fear, anger and depression (Arnold and Brown 1999).

It is noticeable that in the literature where the impact of affect and language learning is discussed, preoccupation with negative affect predominates (as noted by Arnold and Brown 1999 and Shanahan 1997, for instance). Of all the affective factors, it is a negative one, anxiety, which is 'quite possibly the [one] that most pervasively obstructs the learning process' (Arnold and Brown 1999: 8) and which has consequently, according to Ellis (2008), attracted the most research. This suggests that the language learning context itself is (often perceived as) an intrinsically negative one in terms of the emotional 'blocks' it can cause (see, for example, Arnold and Brown 1999). Indeed, the influence of affect on language learning has been conceptualised, by Krashen (e.g. 1982), as an affective 'filter' to learning, lowered by positive emotions but raised by negative ones, thereby 'obstructing' learning. 'Grim determination and struggle', Krashen asserts, 'are not part of the language development process' (Krashen 2009: 184). The affective filter concept, while somewhat ignored in some of the more academic works on SLA (Ellis 2008 and Ritchie and Bhatia 2009, in their comprehensive volumes on SLA, scarcely mention the theory), has a strong commonsense appeal to practitioners and acts as a convenient 'shorthand' acknowledging the importance of affective responses in learning.

But affect does not only impact on language learning; it is crucial to it. 'If learners do not feel any emotion while exposed to language in use, they are unlikely to acquire anything from their experience' writes Tomlinson (2010: 89). He stresses that this applies to a range of emotions, even, controversially, ones that materials developers and teachers conventionally steer clear of: 'laughter, joy, excitement, sorrow and anger can promote learning' (Tomlinson 2003b: 18).

Others would point out the risks in sparking such 'negative' factors as anger and sorrow in the name of affective involvement: 'in the presence of overly negative emotions such as anxiety, fear, stress, anger or depression our optimal learning potential may be compromised' (see box p. 13; Arnold and Brown 1999: 2). Arguably, though, feeling something, to paraphrase the famous song, is better than feeling nothing at all: 'neutrality, numbness and nullity cannot [promote learning]' (Tomlinson 2003b: 18).

Teachers' and materials writers' decisions on taking affective risk by dealing with provocative or taboo topics need of course to be informed by learners' ages, backgrounds, level of emotional sophistication and so on.

> The ELT resource book *Taboos and Issues* (MacAndrew and Martinez 2002) includes units on:
> torture – prostitution – gun crime – AIDS – euthanasia – depression

The key point is to recognise how much can be gained by creating materials which exploit affect. Invoking positive affect, indeed, was the ethos of the so-called 'humanistic' language teaching approaches which appeared in the 1970s and 1980s. Suggestopedia, for instance (Lozanov 1978), uses music to induce a relaxed state conducive to language acquisition. Humanistic language teaching (HLT), associated with practitioners such as Moskowitz (e.g. 1978) and Rinvolucri (e.g. 2002), places language learning in the holistic context of individual personal development and self-awareness. Neuro-linguistic programming (NLP) (Bandler and Grinder 1979) uses multiple intelligences principles (see Gardner 1983 and elsewhere) and principles of whole-brain learning (e.g. Ellison 2001) in an effort to maximise learning potential by stimulating different senses, through imagination, creativity and physical activity.

In practice, these methodologies tend to be used less in isolation than in combination with others. Nevertheless, they can certainly infuse pleasure, relaxation and enjoyment into the learning experience and thereby enhance learning – as long as they are critically selected for, and appropriately applied to, the particular language teaching situation (see Gadd's 1998 article 'Towards less humanistic English teaching').

Among the affective factors which we noted above as having an interplay with that crucial SLA factor, motivation, are *self-esteem*, *self-confidence* and *empathy*. We will briefly examine what part our language learning materials can play in nurturing these.

Self-esteem, 'a self-judgment of worth or value, based on feelings of efficacy, a sense of interacting effectively with one's environment' (Oxford 1999: 62), can be affected by language learning situations in that these can 'deprive learners of their normal means of communication . . . and their ability to behave like normal people' (ibid.). If we link this to linguistic *self-confidence* (belief in one's ability to learn the L2) and note how this confidence can stem from frequent contact with the TL (Ellis 2008: 684, reporting on a study by Clement 1986), we come up with the common denominator of *familiarity*.

Familiarity can also be seen as having an impact on that other important emotional factor, *empathy*. We might 'translate' empathy in the language learning context as identifying with, or 'disposition' towards, the TL and its culture. It therefore embraces the learner's attitude to the TL and to the target language culture (TLC). Familiarity (as opposed to 'the alien') is thus an important consideration in the selection and design of language learning materials (this emerges as an issue in Chapter 3 on materials, methods and contexts).

2.2

Another affective factor noted as impacting on motivation is the 'intrinsic value attributed to the activity' (Williams and Burden 1997 in Dörnyei 1998: 126); what might be called (perceived) 'worthiness'. This might be described as an aspect of *face validity* (in simple terms, whether something does what it claims to do) in that it is the learner's evaluation of whether the material/task is intrinsically rewarding in terms of interest and investment of affective/cognitive effort. It would therefore seem vital for materials developers to consider worthiness when developing materials, as without it, there is a risk of learners carrying out tasks at a very superficial level, with the only motivation (essentially extrinsic) being task completion. It is, moreover, an aspect somewhat overlooked in some published teaching materials, to judge by the findings of three overviews of coursebooks of the last fifteen years or so, in 2001 (Tomlinson, Dat, Masuhara and Rudby), 2008 (Masuhara, Hann, Yi and Tomlinson) and 2013 (Tomlinson and Masuhara).

COGNITIVE CHALLENGE

'Materials should maximize learning potential by encouraging *intellectual*, aesthetic and emotional involvement' (Tomlinson 2011: 21, our italics).

As we leave the affective domain, turning to the cognitive, this is not to imply that cognition is the antithesis of affect. On the contrary, it is a necessary complement to it, as Arnold and Brown emphasise (1999: 1), reminding us that ' whole-brain' learning, the concept of 'uniting' the 'rational' left brain with the 'emotional' right side, has had quite an influence in language learning and learning in general (see, for example, the HLT movement, mentioned above).

The importance of cognitive involvement for learning, at least as conceived in terms of long-term memory retention, has its roots in the field of psychology: 'It is now generally accepted that memory performance is directly and strongly linked to the nature of the processing underlying the original experience', conclude Lockhart and Craik (1990: 109) in their review of research on the influence on memory of levels of processing. This has been transferred to language acquisition and materials development research; materials which make 'analytic, creative, evaluative . . . demands on processing capacity can lead to deeper and more durable learning' (Tomlinson 2011a: 21). This involvement helps maximise learning potential by activating the 'conscious and unconscious cognitive processes of inquiry that help . . . discover and assimilate patterns and rules of linguistic behaviour' (Kumaravadivelu 1996: 243). The essential characteristic of such materials is that they are intellectually demanding. Put simply, this amounts to the equation 'meaningful material is learned faster and remembered better than information that is less meaningful' (Ghosn 2013: 64).

If we look at published materials we note that they have often been found lacking with regard to the level of intellectual challenge they provide. Only four of the eight coursebooks reviewed in Tomlinson et al.'s survey review of EFL courses for adults (2001) were assessed as offering sufficient challenge. A later review by Masuhara et al., in 2008, noted a fall (to three of the eight books reviewed) in 'adult content and tasks which require intellectual and/or affective investment from the learners' (2008: 309), falling to only one coursebook (of six) in the latest review at the time of writing (Tomlinson and Masuhara 2013) (see Tomlinson et al. 2001, Masuhara et al. 2008 and Tomlinson and Masuhara 2013 for details of the evaluation criteria and procedure). This can be a particular issue in coursebooks for lower levels: 'Despite their very limited proficiency in the language, students need the challenge and stimulation

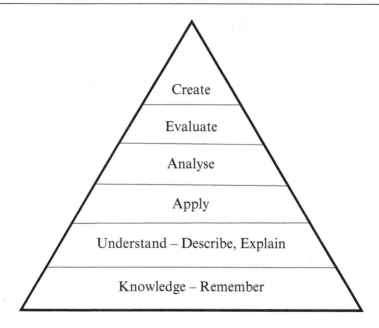

Figure 2.1   Bloom's taxonomy as revised by Anderson and Krathwohl (2001)

of addressing themes and topics that have adult appeal' (Lazar 1994: 116). This is not to imply the exclusion of young language learners either; challenge is all the more important to children because they are still developing cognitively. This requires teachers to cater to their developmental needs in tandem with teaching them the TL (Hughes 2013).

Our intent here, then, is to consider how to create challenge by deploying the cognitive domain in our learning materials. The cognitive domain refers to the use of our mental skills and to how we process knowledge. Bloom's taxonomy, originally 1956 (Bloom, Engelhart, Furst, Hill and Krathwohl 1956) and regularly revised since (the Anderson and Krathwohl 2001 revision is given in Figure 2.1), remains the default reference on cognitive skills in education. Bloom's taxonomy illustrates the successive degrees of cognitive engagement in terms of how we deal with knowledge and can be simplified as shown in Figure 2.2.

It would seem clear that cognitive engagement can only really be invoked by making our language materials work at the higher levels of Bloom's taxonomy and minimising work at the lower levels: 'it is . . . very important that learners are cognitively engaged by the texts and tasks they are given to use' (Tomlinson 2013a: 12) (and we would stress that such 'tasks' include language-focused activities; see Chapter 8). Tomlinson continues: 'they need to use such higher level mental skills as inferencing, connecting, predicting and evaluating' (ibid.).[1] So what can we extract from the higher-order thinking skills, as Tomlinson has done here, to feed into materials design? Bloom's taxonomy has been endlessly interpreted in the literature in terms of learning activities.[2] Extrapolating from the 2001 version (as revised by

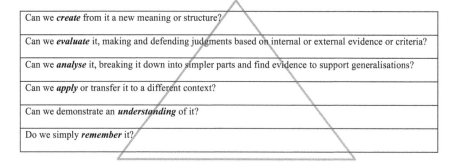

Can we *create* from it a new meaning or structure?

Can we *evaluate* it, making and defending judgments based on internal or external evidence or criteria?

Can we *analyse* it, breaking it down into simpler parts and find evidence to support generalisations?

Can we *apply* or transfer it to a different context?

Can we demonstrate an *understanding* of it?

Do we simply *remember* it?

Figure 2.2   How we deal with knowledge, based on revised version of Bloom's taxonomy, Anderson and Krathwohl (2001)

Anderson and Krathwohl), we offer sample learning activities that can be designed to invoke the range of cognitive processes (working 'down' from the peak of the skills pyramid) in Figure 2.3. (Another version of this figure appears in Chapter 6, Figure 6.3, with reference to listening and reading materials.)

The concept of cognitive involvement will be extended to include that of 'noticing' in Section 2.4. Meanwhile, we will see how 'challenge' became a vital construct in language acquisition research in relation to that vital ingredient for language learning – input.

Task 2.1

'While we cannot ultimately control motivation, as it is internal to the learner, we can seek to provide materials which are likely to stimulate intrinsic interest.'

- List materials/topics that might be of 'intrinsic interest' to your teaching or learning context.
- Are there materials/topics that are inherently 'interesting'?
- What is 'interest' determined by?

Task 2.2

- Reflecting on the section on 'affective factors' and your own language learning and/or teaching experiences, what are some of the implications for the design of materials?

Use these implications as criteria to evaluate a piece of language learning material (perhaps your own, or a coursebook).

Task 2.3

Below we look very briefly at the psychological concept known as ' flow' (Csikszentmihalyi 1997 and elsewhere). Read the quotations and the brief outline and consider the relationship of 'flow' to language learning materials; then do the 'debate' activity at the end.

Cognitive skill level	Processes	Prompts	Sample activities
Creating	Based on given information; reformulating, extending, building, planning, hypothesising, generating new patterns/structures	*create, compose, predict, design, devise, formulate, imagine, hypothesise*	Devise/perform role plays, advertisements, games or mazes using the input as a launching point Compose a sequel or prequel to the input – genre/media-switch, e.g. written input transferred to aural/graphic output or newspaper article transferred to dialogue, poem, blog
Evaluating	Making/defending judgements and arguments based on evaluation of criteria Linking to own values/ideas Critiquing/reviewing	*judge, debate, justify, critique, review, argue*	Write a set of rules or conventions relating to conduct in a particular situation or context, e.g. school rules, hospitality conventions in a specific culture Conduct a debate Write a critique or review
Analysing	Separating information into its component parts to identify how the parts relate to each other and the overall structure Inferencing (and distinguishing between facts and inferences) Differentiating Organising Deconstructing	*compare, contrast, categorise, deconstruct*	Conduct a mini-research project (design a survey, gather and analyse data)
Applying	Abstracting and reapplying to a different situation Selecting and/or connecting information/ideas Implementing, changing	*illustrate, interpret, transfer, infer, change, complete*	Recast input as a different genre/medium, e.g. rewrite a newspaper article as a dialogue, or write a description of a photograph
Understanding	Determining the meaning of written/audio/graphic communication, i.e. interpreting the message	*explain, paraphrase, summarise, exemplify, categorise, predict*	Re-tell or summarise input (in written, oral or graphic form)
Remembering	Recalling data or information	*tell, list, draw, locate, recite*	Make a list, timeline or fact chart Answer list of factual questions

Figure 2.3   Cognitive processes and sample activities for TESOL adapted from Bloom's taxonomy as revised by Anderson and Krathwohl (2001) and web resources

Access the link below for further information on flow:
Karen The Librarian: http://www.karenthelibrarian.com/wp-content/uploads/2010/04/cawley.a1.flow_.pdf

2.3

Flow experiences are described as 'moments … when what we feel, what we wish and what we think are in harmony ... Athletes refer to it as "being in the zone"' (Csikszentmihalyi 1997: 29). Its relevance to learning emerges from Csikszentmihalyi's descriptions of the flow experience: 'flow tends to occur when a person faces a clear set of goals that require appropriate responses' (ibid.: 29); 'flow tends to occur when a person's skills are fully involved in overcoming a challenge that is just about manageable' (ibid.: 30) (this gives a psychological dimension to the SLA notion of 'comprehensible input' – input that is manageably above the current proficiency level of the learner – which will be discussed later).

Csikszentmihalyi describes the flow experience as 'a magnet for learning' (ibid.: 30).

- In two groups, take sides and debate the following statement:

  Flow is the ultimate in engagement and materials developers should aspire to it when creating their materials.

2.3 INPUT AND OUTPUT IN LANGUAGE LEARNING MATERIALS

INPUT

'Given motivation, it is inevitable that a human being will learn a second language *if he is exposed to the language data*' (Pit Corder 1974: 72) (our italics). Pit Corder's words, which we quoted earlier, point to the two essential requirements for L2 learning: motivation – which we examined earlier – and language input. While input is unquestionably the vital ingredient for language learning, the amount and degree of challenge are subjects of continued and prolific research in the SLA field with direct implications for materials development.

A good launching point here is the work of Stephen Krashen. As with his affective filter hypothesis, Krashen captured the pedagogical imagination of many teachers years ago with his input hypothesis (Krashen 1985 and elsewhere). In this he posited that all that was needed for language acquisition was 'comprehensible' input (one step beyond the learner's current proficiency level), which he configured as 'i + 1', along with suitable affective conditions (a 'low affective filter'). Like the affective filter, the (i + 1) formula is memorable and has commonsense, practical appeal to teachers and materials developers. It should be noted, however, that the comprehensible input hypothesis has been regularly challenged by other researchers in the field (e.g. Greg 1984; Grigg 1986).

The main bone of contention, insofar as the concept impacts on materials development, is the identifying of comprehensibility with acquisition. Gilmore, for example, points out, with reference to Leow (1993), that there is no 'causal link' (Gilmore 2007: 110) between understanding input and acquiring language. If comprehensibility does not necessarily make for acquisition, then the practice of making it a main concern in materials design surely needs to be questioned.

Chief among the strategies used to make materials 'comprehensible' is, of course, 'simplification'. This is a complex issue and one that goes to the very heart of language learning materials development: let us therefore examine this practice to see its impact on language acquisition.

Task 2.4

List some 'modifications' or 'simplifications' evident in published materials with which you are familiar – or ones that you have carried out on materials you have developed yourself. Modifications might involve (and add to this list):

- Shortening sentences.
- Replacing unusual words with more common ones.

As you draw up this list, reflect on the impact on the texts as language input.

Task 2.5

Compare the two extracts on the web page – the original from *The Guardian newspaper online*, the second simplified for inclusion in the coursebook *New English File: Upper-Intermediate – Student's Book* (Oxenden and Latham-Koenig 2008b) – with regard to the simplification strategies used in the latter. Speculate on the rationale for the simplifications and reflect on their possible impact on language acquisition.

2.4

An earlier work by one of the authors (Mishan 2005) discussed the treatment of authentic input in language learning materials and coursebooks with regard to the 'to simplify or not to simplify' issue, justifying the latter position with reference to a body of SLA research. Seminal studies by Yano, Long and Ross (1994), Leow (1993) and Long and Larsen-Freeman (1991), for instance, were cited to demonstrate that linguistic simplification does not necessarily improve comprehensibility or promote intake (intake refers to elements of the input that learners notice and which thus become available for acquisition). Of significance among their conclusions was that simplification:

- may actually impede comprehension (Blau 1982, describing work measuring learner understanding of short versus complex sentences)
- 'does not have a facilitating effect on intake' (Leow 1993: 333)

It is with bittersweet satisfaction that we reaffirm this position with reference to subsequent research and overviews of research (see below) while noting that despite all the counter-evidence, 'commercially published teaching materials continue the practice of linguistic simplification as the primary modification strategy' (Gor and Long 2009: 446). Gor and Long and Yano et al. (1994) are among the many researchers to argue that simplification impoverishes input, reducing its potential for acquisition. Gor and Long cite studies suggesting, first of all, that simplified materials such as textbook dialogues and other pedagogic materials, while arguably more comprehensible to learners, 'often constitute stilted, fragmented, unnatural, and psycholinguistically inappropriate target-language samples' (2009: 447). As Crossley, Louwerse, McCarthy and McNamara confirm, 'atypical' 'short, choppy' sentences resulting from simplification (2007: 27) can actually complexify the syntax, constitute unnatural models and impede comprehension (ibid.). What is more, in educational settings – and we should note this application to English for academic purposes (EAP) and content and language integrated learning (CLIL) contexts – Gor and Long note that 'simplification of language in teacher speech, written texts, homework assignments and so on . . . tends to dilute curriculum content' (2009: 447).

Comprehensibility, then, can be at the price of 'L2 samples largely bled of the very items to which learners must be exposed if they are to progress' (Gor and Long 2009: 447) and furthermore 'bled' of semantic content. Acquisition, as Gor and Long emphasise here, is only possible with meaningful exposure to previously *unknown* forms (ibid., italics in the original). This is not to deny any place to simplification in language learning, but to say that this is in general better restricted to language practice activities than applied to language input. The distinction between a 'simplified' text (involving the sort of 'reductive' processes described above) and a 'simple' one is essential to flag here too. With young learners, for example, teachers naturally use 'simpler' books, graded readers and so on, designed to be developmentally as well as level-appropriate.

Much of the research on simplification has been in conjunction with examining the sorts of changes which do appear to enhance comprehension and acquisition, and has looked to interaction studies on the Interaction Hypothesis (Long 1996 and elsewhere) as their starting point (see also Section 2.4). The Interaction Hypothesis (which has undergone a number of permutations since it first appeared in 1983) is based on the process of 'negotiating for meaning', in which learners work together to achieve mutual understanding. As learners do this, the strategies they use and the input they receive all facilitate language acquisition.

Using interaction studies as a point of departure here would seem to make a good deal of sense. Identifying ways in which learners arrive at mutual comprehensibility via 'negotiation of meaning' is not only valuable from the perspective of SLA research; it also tests the SLA basis for a pedagogical practice that is intrinsic to communicative language teaching (CLT). On another level, it offers materials writers patterns for the creation of dialogues that are realistic and attuned for acquisition, as well as, more generally, ways of modifying texts that prime them for acquisition.

One aspect of interaction that is of particular relevance to materials development is the modifications made by interactants (see, for example, Larsen-Freeman and Long 1991, and Yano et al. 1994). Overall, rather than simplification strategies such as those we have discussed above, studies revealed that speakers tend to use linguistically *elaborative* changes.

These include:

- increased redundancy: using full noun phrases rather than pronouns or anaphoric referents (so, for example, 'your phone's on the desk' rather than 'it's there')
- paraphrasing: 'he's out' recast as 'he's not here'
- inserting conjunctions to clarify conceptual relations between clauses: ('next', 'therefore', 'however')
- topic saliency: (for instance, 'did you like the film?' recast as 'the film – did you like it?')
- clarifications checks and requests: ('do you mean . . .?')

Some of these elaborative changes, it will be noticed, tend actually to extend or lengthen input – as opposed to what is done in many text simplification techniques. You might like to compare the above to the list made for Task 2.4 above.

As an illustration of elaborative changes, we give below a sample of learners 'negotiating for meaning' in an information gap activity in which they are describing a room.

Task 2.6

- In the extract, mark any instances of the types of elaborative changes described above.
- What are the implications for the design of learning materials, in particular for the creation of dialogues?

A longer dialogue for the same task can be found on the web page.

2.5

111 Donna: Do you have a cobweb next to the clock on the wall?
112 Mika: Yes. A cobweb?
113 Donna: A spider makes a cobweb.
114 Mika: Spider!
115 Donna: Spider web. A Spider's web.
116 Mika: Web aa
117 Donna: You have that?
118 Mika: yes
119 Donna: er you know a cobweb or spider web.
120 Mika: (??) the spider's the making spider made it.
121 Donna: Right, it's called a web.
122 Mika: um . . . what can I say? Under the clock. Pee coo clock?
123 Donna: Cuckoo clock?
124 Mika: Cuckoo clock, um . . There's two drawerr . .
125 Donna: Oh. Umhum I think it's a filing cabinet.
126 Mika: Cabinet. There's cabinet with two draw . .
127 Donna: drawers
(Nakahama, Tyler and van Lier 2001: 398–9)

Input and materials: some food for thought

As a final word on 'comprehensible input', we would like to float the perhaps controversial idea that comprehensibility is now a concept that is over-rated and outdated. In the West at least, today's 'digital native' learners (the term is from Prensky, 2001; see Chapter 5), born into a society where technology is normalised to a large degree, are unfazed by 'non-comprehension'. Web pages, social networking platforms and digital interfaces bristle with terms meaningless to many of us (*cache, feed, hub* etc.) which we recognise as being incidental to the message and simply ignore (as we do when dealing with the enormous numbers of 'hits' generated by any search term), only getting acquainted with them perhaps on a 'need to know' basis. Given the 'transferable skills' contention – that skills and strategies honed in language learning can be extended as 'life skills' – the reverse is surely also true. The preoccupation with achieving comprehensibility might, therefore, be seen as over-cautious today, as learners have all the skills required to deal with this – not least that of 'ignoring' unfamiliar terms (see Mishan 2010a). Might it be time, we suggest, to think about revising Krashen's 'i + 1' as i + 2, i + 3, i + 4 ...?

Input serves not only to *provide* language but to *release* it (Tomalin 2000)
Given the enormous range of input resources at our disposal from a huge variety of media – from YouTube clips to newspapers, from magazines to Facebook – what can be very fruitful for materials design is to turn on its head our conventional pedagogical practices, and think of input in terms of the language it can release rather than the language data it can provide. On the principle of the old adage 'a picture paints a thousand words', if we think of what learners might have to say about the resource, rather than considering it as language input that needs to be processed, we open it up exponentially. It does away, first of all, with the obsession with matching material to proficiency level. A 'difficult' text, for instance, can be discussed by lower-level learners at whatever level they are able to engage with it – even if from the title alone, or an accompanying illustration. Conversely, a 'simple' text might prompt debate or launch creativity with more advanced students.

2.6

OUTPUT

Learner output is central to language teaching pedagogies such as CLT and TBLT with their emphasis on peer interaction. In this section we will briefly explore the basis for this in SLA research and the implications for the design of materials. The two theories most relevant here are the Interaction Hypothesis (Long 1996), which we looked at in the previous section, and the Comprehensible Output Hypothesis (Swain 1985). This, in essence, holds that output is both a product and part of the process of language acquisition. The output hypothesis maintains that learners learn from being 'pushed' into producing output in a form comprehensible to their interlocutor. This, first of all, forces learners to attend to language form: 'production requires learners to process syntactically' (Ellis 2008: 261). Production, significantly, engages syntactic processing in a way that comprehension alone does not (ibid.): 'learners . . . can fake it, so to speak, in comprehension, but they cannot do so in the same way in production' (Swain 1995: 127). Secondly, producing output in this way helps learners to 'automatise their linguistic and discourse knowledge' (Ellis 2008: 261). Validation from the field of SLA research – a major review of research on the comprehensible output hypothesis by de Bot, for instance, concludes that 'output plays a direct role in enhancing fluency' (de Bot 1996: 553) – serves also to validate the practices of teachers and materials developers for whom promoting interaction is one of the main parameters for lesson and materials design.

2.4 AWARENESS-RAISING AND LANGUAGE LEARNING MATERIALS

'THE IMPORTANCE OF NOTICING'

CLT, introduced in the late 1970s, famously (or notoriously) gave such primacy to learner interaction as the stimulus for 'unconscious' language acquisition that it effectively banished grammar teaching for over a decade (in its 'strong' (original) form at least). By the late 1980s there had grown a resistance to CLT from learners, from teachers, from materials developers and, not least, from applied linguists. With timely research from Schmidt (1990), the role of consciousness was abruptly reinstated in language pedagogy as a result of his seminal work on 'noticing'. Analysing the complex notions of 'unconscious versus conscious' learning in terms of awareness, effort, level of understanding, ability to articulate knowledge and, most importantly, noticing, Schmidt concluded that while no one could deny an unconscious aspect to language learning (after all, we are still far from being able to peer inside the black box of the language learner's mind), 'subliminal language learning is impossible . . . noticing is the necessary and sufficient condition for converting input to intake' (Schmidt 1990: 129). This was a rebuttal of the role of an unconscious learning effect which seriously undermined the SLA research basis of communicative pedagogy.

As this research trickled down into language teaching practice and materials development, we saw the pedagogical interpretation of noticing as 'awareness-raising' and 'consciousness-raising' (C-R) activities. C-R encourages learners to notice for themselves, that is, 'induce', conventions of grammar, lexical patterns, pragmatics (the relationship between context and language meaning) and phonology (Schmidt explicitly applied 'noticing' broadly, across all of these four aspects; 1990: 149). C-R can be seen creeping into coursebook materials from the late 1990s onwards, adhering to the intrinsic principle of inductive learning rather than explicit exposition with varying degrees of success (see Mishan 2013b for a critique on this). The following extract gives a taste of how C-R is interpreted in coursebooks.

> Which of the verb forms can change from simple to continuous or vice versa?
> What is the change in meaning?
> 1. What did you do in New York?
> 2. I know you don't like my boyfriend.
> 3. I had a cup of tea at 8.00.
> 4. Someone's eaten my sandwich.
> 5. I'm hot because I've been running.
> (Soars and Soars 2005: 16)

The SLA concept of 'noticing' came in the same era that saw the field of corpus linguistics (CL) 'break into' pedagogy. It is little surprise really that this field that depended on the 'noticing' of patterns (lexical, grammatical, discourse, pragmatic etc.) in corpus data conceived pedagogical applications that were a perfect 'fit' with this SLA theory. An early application was data-driven learning (DDL) (e.g. Johns 1991), probably the closest pedagogically to CL research itself, which saw learners mining raw data (in the form of concordances) in order to expose grammatical patterns from which they could infer rules of use. (See more on DDL in Chapter 5.)

FEEDING RESEARCH ON FORM-FOCUSED INSTRUCTION INTO MATERIALS AND SYLLABUS DESIGN

Form-focused instruction (FFI), i.e. the explicit teaching of grammar and lexis, still remains the defining feature of the syllabus in the majority of ELT coursebooks (see, for example, Tomlinson 2013a: 11). In this section we look briefly at the vital intersection between SLA research on FFI, language materials and the syllabus in order to assess how far this emphasis is justified. For this, we draw chiefly on meta-analyses (summaries) of studies on FFI, found in Ellis (2008).

In these, FFI was in general found to be effective for accelerating and increasing accuracy of acquisition, by making knowledge explicit, i.e. teaching rules ('explicit' FFI, done via traditional 'present, practise, produce' (PPP) or permutations of it) or helping learners discover them ('implicit' FFI, done via C-R activities, as just discussed). However, *how* and *why* FFI seems to work, and when the effects on acquisition emerge, are still being explored. Instruction may work by raising learners' consciousness of a feature (i.e. promoting 'noticing') for later reference and acquisition, with some delay in manifesting; or FFI may appear to 'teach' a feature which is subsequently forgotten. Some language features are more 'teachable' than others; some features can be acquired 'naturally'. Perhaps the most telling finding, as far as devising syllabi is concerned, is that 'grammar instruction may prove powerless to alter the natural sequence of acquisition of developmental structures' (Ellis 2008: 863). At the heart of all this is the uncontrollable variable that is the learner, whose learning is affected by a host of factors ranging from aptitude to attitude and affective state.

On the whole, these conclusions from applied linguistic research do not offer definitive parameters for syllabus design. This can be seen, we would argue, as an opportunity for innovation. One approach is to make the syllabus 'responsive', as in Tomlinson's text-driven approach to syllabus development (e.g. 2003c) – a retroactively constructed 'checklist' of what has been covered in a collection of input texts and activities – rather than a prescriptive one. This would acknowledge the rather pointless preoccupation with 'coverage' in syllabus design; 'as if teaching materials can encapsulate the whole of the language, rather than offer a series of snapshots of it' (Prowse 2011: 158). Discarding attempted coverage as a factor does, of course, put the onus on informed selection of syllabus items; this is discussed in Chapter 8 with reference to corpus-based criteria for building vocabulary and grammar syllabi.

APPLYING SECOND LANGUAGE ACQUISITION RESEARCH TO MATERIALS DEVELOPMENT

In this chapter, we have endeavoured to identify what materials development can draw from SLA research. Combining four key concepts we have explored above, namely *input*, *interaction*, *output* and *noticing*, and taking into account the importance of *affective* and *cognitive engagement* discussed earlier, it would seem that we have identified the perfect conditions for language acquisition to build into materials; *meaningful, purposeful interaction*. That is, *meaningful* affectively and cognitively and *purposeful* intellectually and/or in terms of incentive or motivation. This, not insignificantly, vindicates the basic paradigm of communicative pedagogy; activity which gives a genuine 'reason' for communication and which creates conditions for negotiating meaning to achieve it.

Task 2.7

input + output (interaction) + affect + cognition → meaningful purposeful interaction → language acquisition

- Find some 'interactive' tasks set for learners in coursebooks or in materials you have designed yourself.
- Evaluate to what extent the tasks are 'meaningful' and 'purposeful' for students in your learning context. To do this, extract criteria from what we have discussed so far in this chapter, such as the following (and add to this list):
  □ Is the task interesting/relevant to students in my learning context?
  □ Is the task (intellectually) challenging for my students?
  □ Does the task give an incentive for communication (such as a genuine information gap)?

Task 2.8

- Drawing on this discussion of factors essential for SLA and on your own readings, experience and reflections, extrapolate principles for the design of materials to promote acquisition, continuing the list below.

  'In order for materials to promote acquisition they need to:
  □ stimulate positive affect (happiness, pleasure etc.).'

- Look at chapter 1 in *Materials Development in Language Teaching* (Tomlinson 2011a) (see Further Reading One below), and compare your set of principles to his.

Task 2.9

Looking back at the set of principles you drew up in Task 2.8, the next logical step is to use these to devise guidelines for materials development. Our sample principle above might be expanded as follows:

In order for materials to promote SLA they need to:	*How?? By devising:*
– stimulate positive affect (happiness, pleasure etc.)	materials that are relevant and appealing to learners

2.5 FURTHER READING ONE

Tomlinson, B. (2011a). Introduction: principles and procedures of materials development. In B. Tomlinson (ed.), *Materials Development in Language Teaching,* **2nd edn (pp. 1–31). Cambridge: Cambridge University Press.**

The objective of our chapter was to establish SLA-based principles to underpin materials development. The reading recommended here will give you an idea of how this has been done by arguably the most active and influential materials development practitioner in the field, Brian Tomlinson. In chapter 1 of his edited book *Materials Development in Language Teaching* (2011a: 1–31) – the second edition of his seminal 1998 work – Tomlinson offers a 'compilation of learning principles and procedures' (p. 7) considered to contribute to successful language learning, based on the recommendations of teachers and SLA researchers. The thrust of Tomlinson's chapter, then, like ours, is to move from 'what we know' about SLA from the field of SLA research, to extrapolate findings that are directly relevant to materials development – and finally to formulate principles for applying these to materials development. 'What we know' of SLA is, of course, that there is 'considerable' and, in Tomlinson's view, 'stimulating' disagreement amongst SLA researchers. However, he concludes: 'I believe that there is now sufficient consensus of opinion for SLA research to be used as an informative base for the formulation of criteria for the teaching of languages' (p. 8).

Tomlinson's 'informative base' consists of six core principles for language acquisition.

1. A prerequisite for language acquisition is that the learners are exposed to a rich, meaningful and comprehensible input of language in use.
2. In order for the learners to maximise their exposure to language in use they need to be engaged both affectively and cognitively in the language experience.
3. Language learners who achieve positive affect are much more likely to achieve communicative competence than those who do not.
4. L2 language learners can benefit from using those mental resources which they typically utilise when acquiring and using their L1 [first language].
5. Language learners can benefit from noticing salient features of the input and from discovering how they are used.
6. Learners need opportunities to use language to try to achieve communicative purposes. (p. 7)

The implications of these for the development of materials are then given as summarised here, each with brief 'how to . . .' suggestions. As you are reading, you might like to compare these with those you drew up in Task 2.8 above:

Materials should:
1. achieve impact
2. help learners feel at ease
3. help learners to develop confidence

4. be perceived by learners as relevant and useful
5. require and facilitate learner self-investment
6. take into account that learners must be ready to acquire the points being taught
7. expose learners to language in authentic use
8. draw learners' attention to linguistic features of the input
9. provide the learners with opportunities to use the target language to achieve communicative purposes
10. take into account that the positive effects of instruction are usually delayed
11. take into account that learners differ in learning styles
12. take into account that learners differ in affective attitudes
13. permit a silent period at the beginning of instruction
14. maximise learning potential by encouraging intellectual, aesthetic and emotional involvement
15. not rely too much on controlled practice
16. provide opportunities for outcome feedback. (summarised/adapted from pp. 8–23)

Tomlinson intersperses discussion of his principles with accounts of materials development experiences internationally. Inevitably, he contrasts these with coursebook practices – with regard to which he is characteristically forthright:

> In a recent analysis of new low level coursebooks I found that nine out of ten of them contained many more opportunities for controlled practice than they did for language use. It is possible that right now all over the world learners are wasting their time doing drills and listening to and repeating dialogues. (p. 22)

For the reader wishing to get acquainted with the fundamentals of the field, therefore, this chapter is highly recommended reading. Tomlinson is strenuously loyal to his own principles (as can be seen in his 2003a, 2010, 2013a, 2013b, among other works), giving a strong cohesiveness to his contribution to the field in this regard.

Task 2.10

The extract from *New Cutting Edge Upper Intermediate Students' Book* (Cunningham and Moor 2005) in Figure 2.4 has been annotated to indicate its fit with Tomlinson's SLA-based principles for materials development from Further Reading One. Analyse a short piece of coursebook material in a similar way.

Task 2.11

Materials development is still seen in applied linguistics circles as 'an essentially atheoretical activity'. (McGrath 2013: xi, citing Samuda 2005: 232)

From your reading of Tomlinson's chapter and Chapter 1 of this book, and from your own research in this area, make the arguments in favour of, or against, this position.

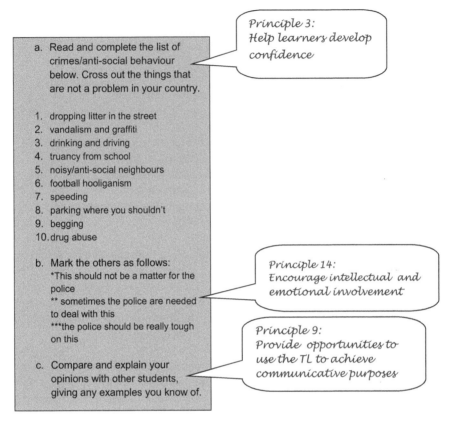

Figure 2.4   Annotated extract from New Cutting Edge Upper Intermediate
Students' Book *(Cunningham and Moor 2005: 30)*

2.6 FURTHER READING TWO

Gilmore, A. (2007). Authentic materials and authenticity in foreign language learning. *Language Teaching,* **40 (2): 97–118.**

The issues covered in this article are in fact broader than its title suggests and it has proved a seminal contribution to the field of materials development. It covers four areas which relate to this chapter as well as to other chapters in the book.

Gilmore's attitude is clear right from the title of the first main section, *the gap between authentic language and textbook material.* Here he assesses textbook material from the perspective of communicative competence (broken down into linguistic, pragmalinguistic and discourse competence, referring to learners' competence in language structure, politeness and genre/register variation respectively). Gilmore is particularly critical of the failure of textbook materials to take account of the findings of CL or to heed the substantial research revealing textbook gaps in areas such as the range of spoken genres and turn-taking patterns. He concludes, with reference to Schiffrin (1996): 'The contrived materials of traditional textbooks have often presented learners with a meagre, and frequently distorted, sample of the target language to work with and have failed to meet many of their communicative needs' (p. 103).

The next section of the article, the *English-as-a-world-language debate*, addresses issues treated in Chapter 3 of this book. These include the positioning of the native speaker as 'model' of the language as opposed to lingua franca models, and the thorny issue of the TLC (Gilmore discusses the proposition of a 'cultura franca', with reference to writers such as Cortazzi and Jin 1999).

The following section of the article is more central to the concern of this chapter, *authenticity and motivation*. Here, Gilmore challenges the twin assumptions that authentic materials are 'a motivating force' (p. 106) and 'inherently more interesting than contrived ones' (pp. 106–7), on the grounds that (a) the term 'authentic materials' is used inconsistently in the research and (b), as a consequence, results of research in this area are not trustworthy. One detects a note of disappointment in these findings: 'A consensus amongst researchers on this issue [a link between motivation and authenticity] could have major implications for materials design' (pp. 107–8).

The next two sections, *text difficulty and task design* and *text modification, comprehensibility and SLA*, also complement our chapter. In the second, Gilmore sifts through the mass of research on the effects of text modification on comprehensibility and on acquisition, and looks at the different independent variables used here: simplification, modification via elaboration and so on. For 'conclusions' he turns in fact to interactionist and constructivist notions, citing Mariani's (1997) argument that effective learning depends on the level of classroom *support* combined with the level of challenge. This would seem to place the responsibility for learning on task design and implementation, rather than on any text manipulation.

In his conclusions, Gilmore examines reasons for resistance to change in curriculum and materials publication. Among these are the perceived rift between applied linguistics and language practice; one which, we would like to think, we have worked at addressing in this chapter.

Task 2.12
Accessing the full article if possible, find some further research (journal articles or books) on one of the areas covered in Gilmore's paper, choosing from the following:

- Consider the implication of the gaps between coursebook material and authentic materials.
- Explore the research on the relationship between authentic materials and motivation.
- Explore the research on the relationship between text manipulation and language acquisition.

Task 2.13
Accessing the full article if possible, focus on *Section 6, Text difficulty and task design*:

- Synthesise the factors given by the author which contribute to text difficulty. Add your own factors, for example:

☐ idiomatic language
☐ cultural references
- On the basis of Gilmore's article as well as of your own experience, suggest the implications of these 'difficulties' for task design; for example:
  ☐ the requirement to balance a sufficient degree of challenge with a sufficient degree of support

2.7 CONCLUSION

The main drive of this chapter has been the drawing up of SLA-based principles for materials development with reference to the importance of the following factors for language acquisition:

- affect, e.g. motivation, engagement
- cognitive challenge
- rich samples of language input in authentic use
- opportunities for meaningful language use
- focus on judiciously selected language structures encountered in input and output

It is fitting to conclude this chapter with Ellis's confirmation about the relationship between SLA research and materials development: 'SLA [is] a source of ideas for fine-tuning materials options that have originated from elsewhere' (he gives the example of tasks); 'the proposals for materials development that emanate from SLA are research- and theory-based' (2010: 52).

While reading the chapter, you may well have asked yourself whether these sorts of SLA-based principles actually underlie the development of coursebooks, given that the coursebook is the default learning material for many teachers (as we discuss further in Chapter 3). In order to pursue this, you may wish to refer to Chapter 4, which discusses processes for evaluating materials in terms of these factors and others. Meanwhile, however, we will turn to the other determining factors underlying development of our language learning materials: the cultural and pedagogical contexts in which they function.

2.8 ADDITIONAL READINGS

Arnold, J. (ed.) (1999). *Affect in Language Learning*, Cambridge: Cambridge University Press.
This remains, as at the time of writing, the most comprehensive work on affect and language learning. Establishing the centrality of affect to language acquisition after years as 'the Cinderella of mental functions' (p. 1), this is an essential reference for those involved in developing language materials.

Dörnyei, Z. (1998). Motivation in second and foreign language learning. *Language Teaching*, 31: 11735.
A summary of research on, and an overview of, what constitutes motivation, that

'complex, multifaceted construct' that is so vital to learning, from the pre-eminent researcher on it in the field.

Ellis, R. (2008). *The Study of Second Language Acquisition*, 2nd edn. Oxford: Oxford University Press.
A comprehensive work on L2 acquisition research which should serve as a core reference for materials developers in linking their materials design to sound principles of language learning.

Schmidt, R. (1990). The role of consciousness in second language learning. *Applied Linguistics*, 11(2): 129–58.
The seminal work marking an about-turn from the theories supporting the communicative approach, namely that language acquisition is 'subconscious'. Schmidt's claim that 'subliminal language learning is impossible', and that 'intake' depends on learners consciously noticing aspects of language, resonated in applied linguistics and pedagogy alike. Schmidt's theories transferred to pedagogy as C-R, which has been steadily integrated into pedagogy and learning materials.

Spiro, J. (2013). *Changing Methodologies in TESOL*. Edinburgh: Edinburgh University Press.
This first volume in the series *Edinburgh Textbooks in TESOL*, to which the current volume belongs, is a valuable complement to this one. As its title suggests, *Changing Methodologies* looks at how language teaching has evolved in time and space: it establishes where we are in language teaching in the twenty-first century, in terms of methodologies, our attitudes to teaching and learning and to the teacher and the learner, the added dimension of cultural competences, and the impact of technology on literacy and learning. Covering a lot of ground in a very 'hands-on' interactive format – it is full of thought-provoking questions, tasks and case studies – the book is highly readable, with sections designed to be free-standing to increase accessibility.

Tomlinson, B. (2012). State of the art review: materials development for language learning and teaching. *Language Teaching*, 45(2): 143–79.
An overview of the current status of materials development, this comprehensive article gives a brief history of what is a relatively new field, reviews current literature and looks at aspects of materials development, such as coursebook evaluation and adaptation. It stresses the importance of tying in the development of materials to research in applied linguistics, and goes on to comment on contemporary issues in materials development ranging from the place of published materials vis-à-vis electronic ones, to ideology, authenticity and humanising textbooks. The article closes by reviewing current materials development projects and research, and flagging future developments.

NOTES

1. It can be noted here that an analysis of question types in coursebook material (Freeman 2014) revealed a significant number that still call on the two lower levels. This is reported in more detail in Chapter 6.
2. One useful reference (of many) for questions and activities referenced to Bloom's taxonomy is http://www.utar.edu.my/fegt/file/Revised_Blooms_Info.pdf (retrieved 6 August 2013).

MATERIALS, METHODS AND CONTEXTS

Task 3.1

Consider the piece of material from the coursebook *New Headway Intermediate Student's Book* (Soars and Soars 2009: 14) in Figure 3.1 in relation to the following questions.

- What are the setting(s) or context(s) for the various situations shown in the materials?
- Can you identify with the situations/contexts?
- Are these settings and contexts 'universal'?
- Can you identify the language variety used (British English, American English etc.)?
- Which teaching approach(es) is/are implicit in the materials?

3.1 INTRODUCTION

Task 3.1 anticipates the issues to be discussed in this chapter: the cultural and contextual variables at work in ELT materials. At the heart of these issues is the global diversification of the English language. We explore the ramifications of this for ELT materials, addressing the following questions with respect to their content and design:

- Which English?
- Which culture?
- Which pedagogy?

We then analyse where ELT coursebooks are positioned with respect to these. Finally, we look at the range of production of ELT materials in the world, and zoom in on the growing international practice known as 'localisation', that is, developing materials within and for specific geographical contexts.

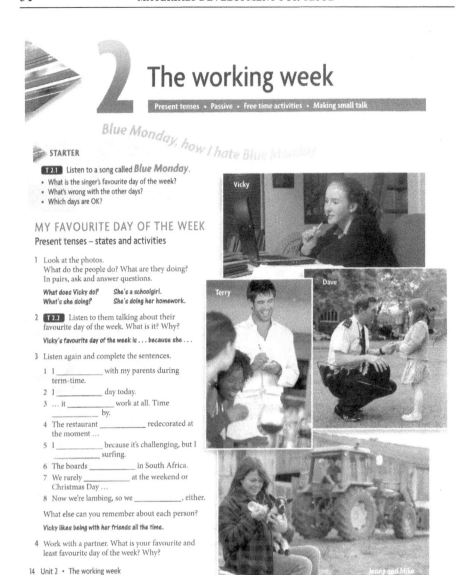

Figure 3.1   *Extract from* New Headway Intermediate Student's Book *(Soars and Soars 2009: 14)*

3.2 ENGLISH LANGUAGE TEACHING AND THE GLOBAL DIVERSIFICATION OF ENGLISH

Although much-covered ground, the logical starting point for positioning language learning materials in cultural contexts is the global landscape of English into which the ELT industry was born in the 1960s (the ELT coursebook industry is covered in Section 3.4). The breadth of the English language 'map' was due to the twin powers of Britain and the USA, the first already declining along with its dwindling colonial possessions, the second enjoying a post-war economic boom. This made for an extensive English language 'footprint' on the globe. Today, well over a third of the world's population (2,214 million people) are 'routinely exposed' to English, according to Crystal's figures (2003: 108). Almost half of these are using it as a foreign language, in countries aspiring to internationalisation for economic and/or political reasons – Russia, China and Japan, for instance. The former British Empire gives us the next group of English speakers, those who speak it as an L2; this is in countries such as India, Singapore and Hong Kong, and totals approximately 422 million, depending on what degree of proficiency is used as a criterion for L2 speaker. When we finally reach the traditional centres where English is the first language (L1) – Britain, North America, Australia and so on – we see that, estimated at about 323 million, L1 speakers are outnumbered by non-L1 speakers by about three to one. Statistically, therefore, English is spoken most commonly among *non*-native speakers. This has been acknowledged in the descriptions of English as an international language (EIL) and English as a lingua franca (ELF) (see below). In a famous model, Kachru (1985) schematised this world 'map' of the language (see Figure 3.2) as three concentric circles, with the traditional bases as the 'Inner Circle' of English; countries where it is an L2 as the 'Outer Circle'; and an 'Expanding Circle' of countries using English as an international language (EIL). Kachru's conceptualisation signalled a break from the commonality implied in the term 'world English' (e.g. Crystal 2003) to 'world Englishes' (e.g. Kachru and Nelson 2006) or 'global Englishes'[1] – a significant step towards decoupling the language from its 'Inner Circle' roots and giving it more 'local' identities. It should be stressed here that in the literature in this area, the terminology around 'Englishes' is weighted by sociopolitical agendas and we need to be aware of these underpinnings (useful references in this regard include Galloway and Mariou 2014; Gagliardi and Maley 2010; McKay 2002).

The clarity of Kachru's model made it a useful 'shorthand' (Bruthiaux 2003: 159) for the different status English holds in different territories (and it remains an influential reference point for research in the field). However, the growing awareness of the diversity of global Englishes which it illustrated also saw the growth of an anti-imperialist movement in ELT, consisting of such writers as Pennycook, Phillipson, Holliday and Canagarajah, among many others. These 'anti-imperialists' saw the identifying of those in the 'Inner Circle' as native speakers of the language, and by implication not attributing native speakership to those in the other circles, as problematic. First of all, a perceived 'Inner Circle' 'ownership' of the language implicitly disempowers the 'Outer Circle' (e.g. Rubdy and Saraceni 2006). Secondly, from a purely numerical point of view, native speakers so defined are statistically a minority (see figures above), so that native speakership could be classed as 'elitist'. By extension, assuming the native English speaker (NES) variety or varieties to be the prescribed norm for teaching materials can be construed as 'native speaker hegemony' (supremacy) (e.g. Modiano 2000), ignoring the sociocultural reality of a language which holds 'special status' ranging from official L1 to unofficial L2 in

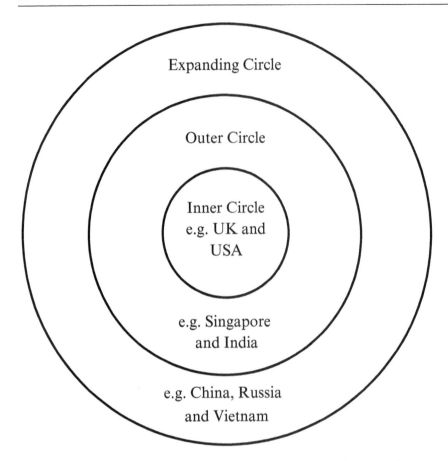

Figure 3.2   The three circles of English, based on Kachru (1985)

seventy-five different territories around the world (Crystal 2003: 106) for up to 880 million people – as well as its role as an international language (see also below). This reality, it was claimed, also called into question the assumption that English language learners' objectives are predicated on (minority) native speaker norms (Howatt and Widdowson 2004). Furthermore, it was argued, since these are norms belonging to those at the 'Inner Circle' 'centre', including Britain, which was responsible for the imperialism that originally spread the language, 'the authoritarian imposition of socio-cultural values . . . consists of a kind of continuing colonisation' (Howatt and Widdowson 2004: 361). This anti-imperialist movement clearly posed an unprecedented challenge to the 'ownership' of English – and to the ELT industry, as we will see later. Even without this sociopolitical angle, the decoupling of the language from its 'Inner Circle' roots into its diverse identities necessarily raised fundamental questions for language educators and materials developers. The first, 'whose English?', has been briefly addressed above. The second, 'which English to model in our materials?',

3.1

is discussed below. Finally, we go to the very heart of language teaching to ask 'which culture?'

WHICH ENGLISH?

We will look briefly here at varieties of English to consider the choices that need to be made when developing language learning materials. Each English-speaking country has its own accepted standard; a prestige variety, often the one used in broadcasting, which is widely understood but not widely produced (Crystal 2003: 110); in effect, a minority variety. The British form Received Pronunciation (RP) falls into this category; having been the model taught in the early days of ELT, it is today spoken by more non-native English speakers (NNESs) than NESs (Crystal 2003). Used by fewer than 3 per cent of British people, it is by now an endangered minority variety of British English – itself 'increasingly a minor dialect of World English' (ibid.: 365).

As we described above, the term 'NES' is one of those that has become somewhat politicised in the climate of awareness of global Englishes created by Kachru's work and that of others. Even from a purely sociolinguistic perspective, native speakership is ever more difficult to define within increasingly multilingual societies: does it refer, for example, to childhood L1, fluency, grammatical intuition and/or communicative range (Davis 2006: 435)? It can in any case refer to the 'native' speaking of a wide range of varieties from within the 'Inner Circle' itself (if this is used as a criterion for native speakership).

Turning next to what is generally known as 'International English', there is a variety of conceptualisations in the academic community: those most commonly used are EIL and ELF. EIL refers to uses of English spanning Kachru's (1985) 'Inner Circle', 'Outer Circle' and 'Expanding Circle' contexts, where it is used for intra-national as well as international communication. The main features of the conceptualisation of EIL are that it is not linked to any one country or culture (McKay, e.g. 2002). ELF, on the other hand, refers to the use of English as a common language between speakers from different non-English-speaking L1 backgrounds: so, for example, a group of students from Italy, China and Sweden might converse in English. It should be stressed that both EIL and ELF refer to situational *use*: neither is a single identifiable 'variety' (despite attempts at the characterisation of ELF in particular; see Jenkins 2007, for example).

What are the implications of the global Englishes paradigm for English language pedagogy and materials? First of all, as noted above, this broadened perspective calls into question the basic assumptions regarding legitimacy – in terms of ownership and native speakership of the language – which forged the original ELT publishing industry; this will be discussed in Section 3.4. Secondly, these new characterisations of the language (as EIL, ELF and so on) have less clearly defined cultural bases, complicating the notion of the 'language–culture bond', as we will see below. Thirdly, as numbers of NNESs so vastly exceed NESs, is the NES model sustainable – or worth teaching/learning? This leads us to examine how the concept of global Englishes sits with the stakeholders themselves: teachers, learners and, of course, materials writers.

GLOBAL ENGLISHES, ENGLISH LANGUAGE TEACHING MATERIALS, LEARNERS AND TEACHERS

As the dominant teaching material in the ELT classroom,[2] the coursebook presumably remains the main influence on which variety is taught. European markets tend to look to British English coursebooks, while Asian markets, e.g. Japan, South Korea, Thailand and Taiwan, tend towards American ones (an overview of materials in use throughout the world is given in Section 3.4). Research on varietal use in 'Inner Circle'-produced coursebooks reveals that there is a gradual increase in representations of global Englishes – though certainly not enough to represent proportionally the English spoken internationally. While more regional varieties are appearing (see, for example, Gray 2010 on the British context), these are often in modified forms. The standard, NES varieties still, therefore, largely prevail in 'Inner Circle'-produced coursebooks (the findings of an analysis of sixty authentic texts used in six coursebooks from British publishing houses published between 2008 and 2011 revealing a continuing preponderance of Britsh English (Clavel-Arriotia and Fuster-Márquez 2014) would thus seem to be representative).

Empirical research with the stakeholders, the learners and teachers of the language, seems to show support for the coursebook status quo. It suggests that the 'native speaker' norm (in the form of a British or American standard) retains a psychological foothold (see, for example, Timmis 2002; Johnstone Young and Walsh 2010; Jenkins 2010; Sifakis and Sougari 2010). In their survey with twenty-six teachers from fourteen different countries, Johnstone Young and Walsh found that:

> Most teacher participants adopted what they felt to be a very practical and pragmatic perspective on varieties of English, suggesting a need to believe in a 'standard' form of the language. This perspective was upheld even when participants acknowledged that it does not really correspond to the reality of Englishes which are in use worldwide. (Johnstone Young and Walsh 2010: 135)

A large-scale study among state school teachers of English in Greece corroborates this. Teachers reveal a 'markedly inner-circle orientation' to variety (Sifakis and Sougari 2010: 312), and while acknowledging 'the reality of world Englishes' (ibid.: 314), they believe 'the EFL teachers' "job" is to teach Standard English' (ibid.). Although there has been less consultation with the learners themselves, some research indicates a preference for native-like fluency (Sybing 2011). Indeed, native-speaker pronunciation can be seen as 'a benchmark of achievement' (Timmis 2002: 242); as one Korean respondent in Johnstone Young and Walsh's study put it, 'most Koreans dream to be [*sic*] an NS' (2010: 132). It appears that many learners still aspire to a notional 'proper' English: to what they consider a 'prestige variety', in other words.

3.2

WHICH CULTURE?

The orthodoxy that language and culture are inextricably interwoven, the importance of teaching 'language-and-culture' (Byram, Morgan and Colleagues 1994) and not treating culture as an 'expendable fifth skill' in language teaching (Kramsch 1993: 1), became more mainstream from the 1990s. Yet set within the geography of global Englishes, with no single cultural 'heart', the principle runs into the question '*which* culture?'

3.3

> When 240 respondents in the Philippines were asked what culture English belonged to, 93.8% felt that English was an international language, 7.5% assumed that it was an Asian language, 12% said that it was owned by the Philippines and . . . no-one indicated that it belonged to Britain or the USA. (Dat 2008: 264)

> English has been acquiring an identity in Europe, has been absorbing and revealing old and new values for decades and thus steadily has been undergoing a process of Europeanization. (Berns 1995: 30)

> If we accept that English today is truly a global language we must also acknowledge its dynamic multicultural backdrop. (Nault 2006: 316)

These quotations give a flavour of the multiple cultural identities of English as a global language and the consequent complexifying of the notion of the language–culture link: 'with English now spoken worldwide, it makes little sense to speak of a "target culture" of the English language', writes Nault (ibid.: 324). 'It would be . . . realistic to speak of one language which is not always inextricably tied to one particular culture' (Alptekin 1996: 58). There is, of course, an opposing view; that this is a problem 'manufactured' by counter-imperialists and that 'native-speaker culture cannot simply be separated from a language that has already left its cultural imprint on non-English-speaking cultures' (Sybing 2011: 467). This is closer to the attitude implicit in the ELT coursebook, as we will see later.

For the purposes of developing ELT materials in the global English context, however, the problem is how to capture the 'moving target' that is culture – how to represent culturally a language with such multiple identities. Attempts at doing this within published ELT materials have a chequered history (see also Section 3.4 below). Early ELT books, from the 1970s, emanated from and reflected the 'Inner Circle', with British or American settings, reference points and implicit cultural values. Oxford University Press's *Streamline English* series (Hartley and Viney 1978, 1979, 1985, 1987) are characteristic of books from that era. The 1990s saw a trend towards 'international' materials (see *International Express Intermediate* (Taylor 1997) as an example). These tried to address this problem by using 'neutral' settings, such as airports, international hotels, business meetings and the like, projecting what Pulverness disparagingly called 'a cultural no-man's land' (1999: 5). This was followed by the so-called 'global coursebook', which went for a more multicultural and cosmopolitan perspective, although dissatisfaction with its perceived superficial treatment of culture persisted (see Section 3.4 below). This led to a growing interest in localisation, i.e. producing materials within and for non-'Inner Circle' contexts in which English is used but which are relatively neglected in global coursebooks – notably the 'Expanding' and 'Outer Circle' (see Section 3.6). Localisation is particularly suited to countries in the latter (such as Singapore and India) where national and local English language materials, e.g. books, newspapers and other cultural products, are available. Localised materials for these contexts can situate English language learning within familiar cultural reference points: concrete notions – national events, landmarks and celebrities – as well as abstract ones – values, ambitions, family relationships and so on (Munandar and Ulwiyah 2012). Versioning (the production of national versions of global coursebooks) uses a similar principle (see Section 3.6 below).

While localisation thus conceived appears to solve the cultural familiarity issue, however, it brings with it its own limitations; 'if all reference to people, places and events outside students' experience is to be replaced or deleted, does this not deprive students of information and knowledge that might possibly be of interest or value to them?' (McGrath 2013: 67). Timmis notes that language learning can be seen as part of students' broader educational development, which includes the development of analytical and other cognitive skills (2014: 257), in the same way that it does, even more crucially, with young language learners. It is essential for materials to include 'culturally "foreign" ideas' in order to 'introduce children to a world outside their ken' (Eapan 2014: 10).

More fundamentally, sticking entirely with the local risks missing out a crucial dimension of language learning; that of broadening horizons and allowing sufficient distance for the native speaker culture itself to be viewed critically; that is, the raising of intercultural awareness. This feeds into that vital skill for the rounded language learner, **intercultural competence**: the ability to interact effectively with people from other cultures. (There exists a large body of work in this area. The interested reader is referred to the works of Byram, e.g. 1997, Deardorff 2009 and Risager 2007, among many others.)

MATERIALS AND THE 'CULTURAL BIND'

How can the materials developer get out of this cultural 'bind', in which stretching cultural horizons and relevance/familiarity are so finely balanced? One solution might be a sort of 'relativism': the culture(s) taught in connection to the TL depend(s) on the geographical contexts of learning and of use. In EIL and ELF situations, the culture(s) need not be referenced to native English-speaking cultures (Saville-Troike 2003; Yuen 2011). Cortazzi and Jin's (1999) categorisations are pertinent here: they distinguish three types of cultural materials: *target culture materials* that use the culture of a country where English is spoken as the L1, *source culture materials* that draw on the learners' own culture as content, and *international target culture materials* that use a mixture of cultures in English and non-English-speaking countries. Adopting this type of approach, the starting point for selecting materials is, crucially, relative to the teaching/learning context. It depends on the students' L1 and learning context, the TL variety and corresponding culture, all balanced with the scope of the needs, wants and, we would add, imaginations of our learner group. Ideally, materials using these reference points can be used to develop language skills as well as nurture intercultural competence.

Task 3.2
- Consider these two opposing stances with regard to language learning and variety:
  - ☐ 'The whole mystique of the native speaker and the mother tongue should probably be quietly dropped from the linguist's set of professional myths about language' (Kachru 1982: vii).
  - ☐ A Russian immigrant resident in Ireland went to Cambridge for an intensive summer course in English. When placed with an Asian host family, she demanded to be moved to a 'native English' family who spoke 'proper' English (personal anecdote).
- Discuss how we as materials developers can reconcile these ambivalent attitudes towards the variety of English to be taught and learned.
- Consider whether this ambivalence can be reconciled in the materials we design, and if so, how.

Task 3.3
Some materials designed for the EIL and ELF context are given on the web page. Identify within them the following issues and concepts discussed above:

3.4

- ELF/EIL
- Which English(es)?
- Which culture(s)?
- The NES and the NNES
- Relationships with English in ELF/EIL contexts
- Intercultural competence

3.3 PEDAGOGY AND ENGLISH LANGUAGE TEACHING MATERIALS

Another facet of the complex sociopolitical, sociocultural and sociolinguistic struggle for the ownership and status of English that we have explored above is, of course, pedagogy. Pedagogy per se is somewhat beyond the scope of this volume (and, indeed, is the topic of another in this series, Spiro's (2013) *Changing Methodologies in TESOL*), but it is another essential element influencing materials development. Brief descriptions of the prevailing approaches on the international ELT scene – the grammar translation method, CLT and TBLT – are provided on the web page for reference. An outline of the TBLT procedure is also given in Chapter 9, Section 9.6. We thus approach pedagogy critically, exploring the value sets such pedagogies embody and the implications for developing materials for use in different parts of the world. Implicit in our approach in this section is the concept of 'critical pedagogy' put forward by Akbari (2007) and others: the idea that educational systems are reflections of societal ones.

3.5

In the West, any English language teacher under the age of 50 has grown up during the communicative era. The communicative ethos has become as embedded within such teachers' educational philosophy as any cultural value system and is as difficult for them to view objectively. The communicative approach has thus become more or less the default teaching methodology for a generation of language teachers and there is a danger in such an uncritical attitude, however unwitting.

CLT and TBLT developed within a Western pedagogical tradition which to a large extent (in language teaching at least) threw off the perception that knowledge is 'transmission-based', 'flowing', as it were, from teacher to learner. These background beliefs and values mean that these approaches accommodate interaction between teachers and learners, and among learners alone. But these are not, as Edge points out (1987), 'value-free' modes of behaviour and may not be in harmony with traditions from other cultures. The Western norms related to hierarchy and respect implicit in these approaches are relatively loose compared to those of other cultures such as the East Asian countries of Japan, Korea and China, which share a Confucian heritage marked by deep respect for elders and teachers (Humphries 2012) and a very clear delineation of teacher–learner roles (Hu 2002). A corollary of this is that in these cultures, value is not necessarily attributed to input from peers in the pedagogical context (see, for example, McGrath 2013), undermining one of the basic precepts of the communicative approach. In the communicative classroom, the removal of the teacher from the central position can be perceived as a slackening of classroom 'control', which can be unsettling for many NNES teachers (who statistically represent the majority of English teachers on the worldwide scale). The non-teacher-directed classroom can be anathema to teachers' cultures and their professional training (e.g. Hu 2002) as well as putting a strain on their linguistic resources (Prodromou and Mishan 2008).

Many Asian cultures are, furthermore, 'collectivist' cultures, whose driving force is the imperative for group consensus – compared to the individualist culture of the West which values personal competitiveness, for example. This can be at odds with communicative activities such as pair and small group activities which invite and value argument as much as collaboration.

Other potentially alien behaviours built into communicative pedagogy stem from what Prodromou and Mishan call the 'cult' of 'emotional frankness' (2008: 201), emanating from North American traditions of psychoanalysis etc. and manifesting in coursebooks in so-called 'personalisation' activities (such as expressing personal opinions and sharing experiences). The communicative approach and TBLT (particularly in its digital incarnation; see also Chapter 5) embed other characteristics that are valued in the West: flat hierarchies and a sort of communicational 'promiscuity'.

HANDLING PEDAGOGICAL MISMATCH

Materials developers and users from non-Western settings react to the sort of pedagogical mismatch described above in diverse ways. In some cases, it is problematised, with practitioners endeavouring to coax learners and teachers into communicative modes of behaviour and practice, a view embodied in this article title:

'Communicative language teaching in China: progress and resistance' (Yu 2001). Implicit here is an unquestioning acceptance of communicative principles – and that they are universally valid and universally applicable.

Others perceive the need for cultural 'intersection'. An action research study from Iran (Modirkhameneh and Samadi 2013), for instance, reports how a communicative slant was put on the traditional grammar translation approach by using a 'diglot-weave' technique. This uses code-switching, the language of a reading text switching between the native language and the TL. A Japanese study (Shimada 2009) also discusses how to combine the approach and style taken in more traditional Japanese textbooks with those taken in overseas products.

Most typical of the literature from Asia, though, is ambivalence; an awareness that traditional methodologies and materials are failing to produce learners who can communicate in the TL, yet a reluctance to abandon them for foreign ones. This can lead to an unsatisfactory compromise, such as recasting communicative materials in a more traditional guise. Two representative case studies, one from Oman (Tasseron, forthcoming), the other from Egypt (Abdul Latif, forthcoming), revealed teachers 'stripping away' the communicative aspects of the coursebook down to the 'bare bones' of grammar, to fit the form-focused approach habitual in those countries. The ultimate extension of this can be materials and pedagogy that pay mere lip service to communicativeness (see, for example, Hu 2002, Li 1998 and Liu, Mishan and Chambers, forthcoming, on the Chinese context, and Humphries 2012 on that of Japan). At the far end of the spectrum are those who openly resent the 'Anglo-phone centre' imposing a so-called 'methodological correctness' (Prodromou and Mishan 2008: 194) which is inconsistent with the local context and the learning needs and wants of students there.

In sum, pedagogical approaches are unavoidably value-laden and implementation of them within the materials we design needs to be carefully positioned in context. Pedagogy is the final issue we have considered in our exploration of the cultural and sociolinguistic underpinnings of ELT materials, so we turn in the following section to the most commonly used product that incorporates these: the ELT coursebook.

Task 3.4

In the light of the above discussions about teaching approaches, consider how far these contrasting quotations are true of the use of materials in your teaching context:

> 'Here we go again . . . we always have the English language teaching methodology coming from another galaxy.' (A Turkish teacher interviewed by Arikan 2004: 46, cited in McGrath 2013: 172)

> Combine . . . 'new' with 'old' to align the communicative approach with traditional teaching structures and . . . modernize not westernize. (Modirkhameneh and Samadi 2013: 17)

Task 3.5

Access the site below to find an online (pdf) version of the following paper:
Littlewood, W. (2006). Communicative and task-based language teaching in East

3.6

Asian classrooms. Revised version of a plenary paper presented at the International Conference of the Korean Association for Teachers of English, June, Seoul, Korea. http://www.zanjansadra.ir/attaches/30062.pdf

While discussing the East Asian context in particular, many of the concerns expressed in the paper can be shared by teachers everywhere, so it is worth reading in its entirety.

Littlewood concludes by saying:

> There is now widespread acceptance that no single method or set of procedures will fit all teachers and learners in all contexts. Teachers can draw on the ideas and experiences of others but cannot simply adopt them as ready-made recipes: they need to trust their own voice and develop a pedagogy suited to their own specific situations.

Consider the implications of Littlewood's recommendations:

- for you as a teacher and materials developer
- for the materials we use, adapt and develop

Task 3.6

> Many teachers on the periphery use the task-based, process-oriented, student-centred pedagogy because it comes stamped with the authority of centre professional circles. But . . . it seems likely that they [students] would prefer a more formal, product-oriented, teacher-centred pedagogy of the sort denigrated by centre professional circles. (Canagarajah 1999: 14)

With reference to this section and to the descriptions of pedagogies given on the web page, consider how far Canagarajah's claim is true of students in your own teaching context.

3.5

3.4 ENGLISH LANGUAGE TEACHING COURSEBOOKS

The history of ELT publication has been well charted elsewhere (e.g. Howatt and Widdowson 2004). The 'boom' in ELT was precipitated by a combination of factors at work in the early 1960s. One was a new interest in language teaching in the nascent 'Common Market' (now the EU) and subsequent work on this by the Council of Europe. Another was the realisation, in the UK and USA, that ELT was an eminently marketable and exportable product in terms of both native-speaking teachers and learning materials. The foci for the new publishing industry in Britain were respected academic publishers based in Oxford and Cambridge, and in the USA publishers like Longman, Macmillan, and Cambridge University Press's American division. Today ELT publishing is a billion-pound growth industry in the UK, still largely dominated by the same core group of British publishers.

ENGLISH LANGUAGE TEACHING COURSEBOOKS: FACTIONISM

As we have described above (Section 3.2), the centralised nature of the ELT industry sowed the seeds of resentment among some of those working in the field, in a world just awakening to the implications of postcolonialism for the English language. This saw the establishment of a strident anti-textbook community – which was inevitably countered by a pro-textbook camp, giving rise to a polarisation in the field that exists to this day. Here we examine the arguments and invite you to reflect on your own position.

Those arguing in favour of the coursebook tend to stress practical factors. From the perspective of the teaching institution, the coursebook offers a ready-made, cost-effective, standardised syllabus that can slot into its English language curriculum. Their long-established international publishers (see above) give coursebooks a certain authority, credibility and guarantee of quality. Most coursebooks today are part of a comprehensive package of print-based and digital materials including the student book, teacher's book, workbooks, CDs, DVDs, an accompanying website or e-learning platform and, increasingly, mobile apps. This cluster of materials serves as a time-saver for the busy teacher and a guide for the inexperienced one. Not to forget the learners, of course, who can chart their progress through such a syllabus and use it for revision. It has been pointed out that arguments based on such practical factors are a 'less than inspiring' defence (Hadley 2014: 206) against the ideological ones of coursebook opponents – even if these, some would observe, are short on constructive ideas.

The early anti-coursebook 'movement' was, as we noted above, avowedly 'counter-imperialist'. Typical of the arguments ranged against the early coursebooks was that materials emanating from an industry with an 'Anglo-American heart', the derogatorily labelled BANA countries (Britain, Australasia and North America; Holliday's term, 1994), approximating Kachru's 'Inner Circle', could not but perpetuate imperialism and the hegemony of the native speaker – and so was effectively a 'new' colonialism. Looking at early ELT materials (such as two series' mentioned earlier, *Streamline English* from Oxford University Press or the *Strategies* series from Longman), it is hard not to sympathise with this interpretation, as in them the language is projected chiefly as a British or American product, within British/American settings. These early coursebooks were accused of having 'a hidden curriculum' (Cunningsworth 1995: 90) which embedded and projected Western values and attitudes (e.g. consumerism, perceptions of beauty and gender roles; see Harwood 2014). These were not only Western, it was pointed out, but mainly white and middle-class (see, for example, Dendrinos 1992, Rossner 1988, Canagarajah 1999 and Gray 2010). In this view, learning a foreign language became, at best, 'a kind of enculturation where one acquires new cultural frames of reference, and a new world view, reflecting those of the target language and its speakers' (Alptekin 2002: 58) and, at worst, a type of ideological 'indoctrination' (Dendrinos 1992) with learners expected to accept and act within the parameters of values and behaviours of another culture. These perceived effects extended to pedagogical traditions too, of course, as we have discussed above.

THE 'GLOBAL' COURSEBOOK

In response to such criticisms and to throw off this 'neo-imperialist' stigma (Pulverness 2003: 426), from the 1990s there evolved what came to be known as 'global' coursebooks which endeavoured to cater better to the diverse varieties, statuses and needs for English. These books were designed with this diversified world market in their sights, portraying wider international and cultural contexts for the language. The global coursebook is now a recognisable brand; 'the all-singing all-dancing, glitzy multimedia package', as Bell and Gower, themselves coursebook authors, describe it (2011: 137). It includes books no doubt familiar to users worldwide, such as Oxford University Press's *New Headway*, *New English File* and *Cutting Edge*, Longman's *Intermediate Matters* and Macmillan's *Inside Out*.

The global coursebook brought with it its own issues and has done little to appease the entrenched anti-coursebook faction. The core criticism remains that it lacks cultural appropriateness and/or relevance for many of its target markets (Harwood 2014 in a synthesis of research on culture in ELT textbooks). The proclaimed 'globalisation' is largely cosmetic, it is claimed, with coursebooks still paying only lip service to cultural relativism or pluralistic representation of English-speaking countries (Pulverness and Tomlinson 2013: 445).

One vital aspect of this which, like the claim about the whole area of culture, 'should not be regarded as an optional extra in a textbook syllabus', is **pragmatics** (Harwood 2014: 7). This concerns what in pedagogy was traditionally called 'functional language': speech acts such as expressing opinion, giving advice, apologising and so on. The problem is that pragmatic norms are not easily transferable; they are keenly culturally determined and thus subject to national and even regional variation (for more on pragmatics, see Cutting 2014). In global coursebooks, the sociological context for such language remains limited to their predilection for British or American English. Furthermore, the in-depth sociocultural context-setting required when teaching speech acts is, researchers note, beyond the scope of most coursebooks (Harwood 2014; Munandar and Ulwiyah 2012; Cohen and Ishihara 2013).

THE ENGLISH LANGUAGE TEACHING COURSEBOOK: THE STAKEHOLDERS

It would seem important to solicit the opinions of the stakeholders themselves in all this. There exists only a limited amount of research on teachers' views on coursebooks, and even less on learners' (McGrath 2013), and it is significant that what there is tends to be carried out by coursebook critics rather than supporters. Its critics would suggest that the high incidence of coursebook use (see note 2) might be a question of pragmatism rather than preference (see also below). Yet teachers, particularly at novice level, often respect the coursebook as a manual written by experts. While adaptation is commonplace (see, for example, studies cited in McGrath 2013), coursebooks still provide the 'skeleton' for the teaching taking place in the classroom. Even in non-'Inner Circle' environments, many teachers still place greater faith in global coursebooks in areas of grammar, listening, pronunciation, general accuracy and quality of production than in local coursebooks (Zacharias 2005, reporting on a study in Indonesia). Learners, similarly, can regard the coursebook as 'essential for knowledge we need to learn' (Shawer, Gilmore and Banks-Joseph 2008: 19). The coursebook is a resource that students can hold in their hands (Hadley 2014: 229) – something that gives them a concrete sense of 'clarity, direction and progress' (Hadley 2014: 229, citing Woodward 2001: 146). A seemingly convincing 'response' to coursebook detractors comes from the findings of a large-scale longitudinal study which followed 700 students in Japan using a global coursebook over a six-year span, which concludes that 'there are strong indications that GTs [global textbooks] can play an important part in helping, *and not harming*, second language learning' (Hadley 2014: 230, our italics).

THE ENGLISH LANGUAGE TEACHING COURSEBOOK: PRAGMATISM

It is important, finally, to maintain perspective. ELT publishing is a multimillion-pound industry which makes a major contribution to the global economy, and it remains relatively impervious to its denigrators from the academic sidelines. While coursebook producers are not unaware of the ever-changing political and sociocultural landscape of the English language and its evolving place and use in the world, the tension between satisfying the demands of culturally diverse international markets and commercial feasibility are largely irreconcilable – with commercialism inevitably winning out. The coursebook 'is the way it is', as Singapore Wala says, 'because of what it has to do' (2003: 60). The (arguably) compromised but practical end-product is one that engenders a sort of 'love–hate' relationship in many teachers who find themselves at the same time dependent on them yet resentful of their dictates. This is where the importance of materials evaluation and adaptation, and, of course, materials creation itself comes in, as we will see in subsequent chapters.

THE ENGLISH LANGUAGE TEACHING COURSEBOOK: 'WASHBACK'

What we are particularly interested in noting in the context of this book is the effect of widespread use of coursebooks on materials writing: 'There may be a closed circle at work here, wherein textbooks merely grow from and imitate other textbooks', wrote Sheldon in 1988 (p. 239) – this is clearly not a new phenomenon. Since Sheldon was writing, the effective 'flooding' of the market has further embedded the global coursebook paradigm, as regards structure, approach and content, in a way that affects both its users, in terms of expectation and face-validity, and coursebook writers: 'Teachers and curriculum developers tend to imitate the approaches of best-selling coursebooks on the assumption that this must be what learners and teachers want' (Tomlinson 2003a: 7). This 'subliminal' influence has been called the 'washback'[3] effect (ibid.). (This will be touched on again when we deal with materials structure in Chapter 9.) The vital 'escape clause' here, however, is that teachers and materials designers need not be subject to such tensions, as we will see later in the section on the trend in 'localisation'.

ENGLISH LANGUAGE TEACHING COURSEBOOKS AROUND THE WORLD

Issues around global ELT coursebooks discussed above need to be relativised to the status and role of these global coursebooks within the worldwide language teaching community. In some places, they constitute the only ELT materials; in others, they have been superseded by locally produced ones. The practices relating to – and stakeholders within – the control and production of ELT materials vary considerably from country to country and continent to continent. Before zooming in on localisation practices, we will take an overview of ELT materials use worldwide.

As we have seen above, in the USA and Britain, ELT materials emanate predominantly from a small number of international publishers – Cambridge University Press, Oxford University Press, Pearson, Macmillan etc. – and these are used in state educational institutions where ELT is conducted and in private language schools alike. Materials in those countries are not centrally controlled by government ministries, unlike the case in many countries, such as Malaysia, Korea, China, Japan, Turkey, Egypt, India and Kenya, where ministries of education control primary- and secondary-level English teaching and produce or commission dedicated materials for this (Tomlinson 2008). Language curricula are also centrally directed in Southeast Asia, in countries including Indonesia, Myanmar/Burma, Singapore and Thailand, as well as in the Middle East (in Egypt and Lebanon, for instance). In most countries in Europe, the Council of Europe influences curricula and materials. In Spain, for example, CLT is built into the Ministry of Science and Education laws for primary and secondary education and a combination of Spanish and British coursebooks is used which integrates it (Criado and Sánchez 2009). Turkey likewise looks to the Council of Europe, to its Common European Framework of Reference (CEFR), as a reference point for its English language curricula and materials (Ates 2012). In a lot of places, private language schools are not constrained by national curricula, though, so British- or American-produced materials are taught in tandem with prescribed ones (as in Lebanon, Kuwait and the United Arab Emirates, for example). Another model is 'versioning', where dedicated national versions of international coursebooks are produced, such as a Spanish version of *New Headway* (Bowler, Cunningham, Moor and Parminter 1999), a Polish version of *face2face* (Tims, Redston and Cunningham 2005) and Spanish and French versions of *Essential Grammar in Use* (Murphy 2011; Murphy and García Clemente 2008). Ministries of education might also commission the production of materials or curricula from international writers or institutions, fund international projects (as in Romania; see Popovici and Bolitho 2003) or receive international funding for materials production (as was the case in Vietnam; see Further Reading Two below). In some countries a tripartite paradigm is represented. In Japan, some materials are produced locally by NESs for the Japanese and Asian markets, and these co-exist with 'indigenously produced', ministry-approved materials and global coursebooks (Smiley and Masui 2008). Similarly, in Southeast Asia, global, local and 'regional' coursebooks co-exist (regional books are those produced on the same continent; Singapore, for example, produces textbooks for surrounding countries such as Malaysia, Thailand and Vietnam) (Dat 2008; see also Further Reading Two below).

LOCALISATION

As this brief overview has suggested, numbers of countries in the 'Expanding Circle' and EFL contexts are involved in the production of local materials (including Greece, Japan, Korea, Brazil and countries in Central and Eastern Europe, Africa, Southeast Asia and the Middle East; see surveys in Tomlinson 2008; Tomlinson and Masuhara 2010). With the diversity in ELT materials' use worldwide, it is unsurprising that the processes of materials development and production within different countries are just as varied. In a lot of cases, where ELT is under government control, the process is instigated by ministries of education; sometimes this is to fit new curricula (as was the case in two Indian states; see Kadepurkar 2009 and Eapan 2014, describing production of materials to fit new second-level and primary-level curricula respectively). In other cases, institutions themselves promote the production of in-house materials (as in university case studies in Venezuelan and Japan, reported in St Louis, Trias and Pereira 2010 and Jenks, Stone and Navarro 2012 respectively). Localisation often calls on international expertise; training from international ELT experts (as was the case in the Romanian project reported in Popovici and Bolitho 2003 and the Turkish one in Ates 2012) or reference to established language teaching parameters such as the CEFR (Ates 2012). Indeed, the need for training in materials development is, we are pleased to report, something of a refrain in the literature in this area (e.g. Bolitho 2008; Dat 2008).

Task 3.7
- Look at the macro unit structures of a selection of coursebooks. Are these and their subsections (e.g. skills) comparable in each book?
- Can you detect evidence of 'washback' as defined above? (Do the structures appear to resemble each other?)

Task 3.8
Access the site below to find an online (pdf) version of the following paper:
Tran-Hoang-Thu (2010). Teaching culture in the EFL/ESL classroom. Paper presented at the Los Angeles Regional Conference, California Teachers of English to Speakers of Other Languages, 11 September, Fullerton, USA.
http://files.eric.ed.gov/fulltext/ED511819.pdf
   This paper discusses a number of concepts associated with language learning and culture which for reasons of space we have not covered in this book, and it is worth reading in its entirety. The section of the paper most directly relevant to this section for you to consider is entitled: 'What are the roles of teachers, curricula, and textbooks in culture learning in second and foreign language learning?' (Tran-Hoang-Thu 2010: 18–20).

Task 3.9
In the light of the issues discussed in this chapter, evaluate some of your coursebooks with an eye on their 'match' to your teaching context. Evaluation factors might include:

- Variety or varieties of English?
- Ethnicity of characters?
- Locations?
- Topics/cultural issues – rate on scale from familiar to unfamiliar.
- Topics – rate on a scale from global to local.
- Pedagogical approach?
- More evaluation factors can be found in Chapter 4.

3.5 FURTHER READING ONE

Harwood, N. (2014a). Content, consumption, production: three levels of textbook research. In N. Harwood (ed.), *English Language Teaching Textbooks: Content, Consumption, Production* (pp. 1–44). Basingstoke: Palgrave Macmillan.

Harwood provides a valuable snapshot of the 'state of the art' in textbook research in this substantial introduction to his 2014 edited volume. He grounds his overview in textbook research in mainstream education which, he argues, 'is more developed, rigorous and sophisticated' (p. 2). His conceptualising of textbook analysis at the levels of *content*, *consumption* and *production* is edifying in itself, as it reveals the uneven treatment of these three areas of research in the field. While there is a long history of (not uncontroversial) analysis of textbook content in ELT, as our chapter has illustrated, and quite a lot of reporting on production (see, for example, three much-referenced chapters: Jolly and Bolitho 2011, Bell and Gower 2011 and Prowse 2011), there is far less on their consumption – how teachers and learners actually use textbooks in the classroom.

Starting with the 'content' dimension, Harwood analyses the treatment of language, culture and pragmatics in ELT coursebooks, looking also at teachers' guides, which have been rather neglected in the research. His content analysis of the language of coursebooks takes the corpus perspective, which is being increasingly applied in teaching and resource materials (as shown in this volume), and not unexpectedly, he finds many coursebooks wanting in aspects of syntax, lexis and pronunciation. Harwood's content analysis of 'culture' in coursebooks raises many of the concerns expressed in this chapter as regards appropriateness and relevance of behaviours, values and attitudes. As he points out, however, coursebooks are open to interpretation, and 'however well-intentioned or politically correct the message of textbook content, there is no guarantee the message will be taken up' (p. 7). Coursebooks are not, after all (or should not be), in the business of 'preaching'.

Harwood's analysis of teachers' guides is very welcome, mainly because, as he points out, citing Coleman (1986), many 'appear to be little more than incidental afterthoughts' (Coleman 1986: 31 in Harwood 2014b: 9). This lack of care is compounded by neglect in the research, and this is a real danger in that 'poorly written guides . . . lead to poor textbook use' (p. 9). An interesting question that arises here is the *role* of teachers' guides. Harwood cites Mol and Tin (2008) complaining (with regard to EAP textbooks) that 'they focus on *what* to teach rather than *how* to teach' (2008: 88 in Harwood 2014b: 9) – with the implication that this (the latter) falls under the remit of the teachers' guide.

Turning to the next section of the chapter, research on textbook consumption is second in importance only to textbook creation itself. This is because *content* does not dictate *use* – so it is essential to investigate what happens in the space between what is 'intended' and what is 'enacted'. Harwood looks at research on this within ELT and mainstream education environments. Among the chief factors which were found to influence coursebook use were teacher experience, training, teaching style and beliefs; institutional constraints (such as examination preparation); and the learners – as well as (a huge consumption variable, this) the characteristics of the textbook itself. Harwood synthesises this as 'teachers shape . . . textbooks in response to their own beliefs, and to their micro- and macro-environments' (p. 16).

The biggest 'consumers' of ELT coursebooks are of course, the learners themselves, and it is 'striking' (p. 17), as Harwood says, that so few consumption studies have been done in this area. Ones that have been done included investigation into learner response to authentic materials (e.g. Peacock 1997 and Gilmore 2011) and learner/teacher attitudes to different activity types (Peacock 1998). In that last study, and quite predictably one might say, learners favoured error correction and grammar exercises over the communicative activities that their teachers preferred. It is useful to add a coda here that although research on textbook use is identified as a gap by Harwood, it is one that is being filled. McGrath 2013 covers this in a fascinating and original chapter, 'Learner perspectives' (2013: 147–66), which we include in the additional reading sections below, and Bolster (2014, 2015) analyses coursebook use and adaptation by teachers in China. At the time of writing, two chapters are forthcoming on coursebook use in Oman (Tasseron, forthcoming) and Egypt (Abdul Latif, forthcoming).

There have been a number of accounts of coursebook production, and a few which give valuable insight into the 'black box' of the mental processes involved in this (see also Chapter 9). Harwood sums up the production studies he describes in this section, which include Bell and Gower's record of writing the *Matters* series (2011), Mares' writing for the *Atlas*, *Interchange* and *Online* series (2003), and Prowse's (2011) account of sixteen textbook writers' practices, as giving a sense of 'the trickiness of writing for such a diverse set of needs' (p. 21). He diplomatically spreads the blame, however: 'there are question marks over some of the writers' practices and of those practices imposed on writers by publishers' (ibid.). Publishers' perspectives in fact add to these concerns. Publishers are changing and reducing piloting processes due to production time and cost pressures (e.g. Amrani 2011, writing about Oxford University Press). This compounds the difficulty of ascertaining 'learners' wants and needs across diverse settings' (p. 25), which is, of course, the classic dilemma of the global coursebook that we have been discussing in this chapter.

Harwood adds a subsection on reports of authors 'engaging (or refusing to engage) with corpora' (p. 21) which includes McCarthy and McCarten (2010, 2012) writing on creating corpus-informed material for their hugely successful *Touchstone* series, and Swales and Feak (2010) on using corpus data for their textbook on abstract writing. Such accounts are balanced by Burton's (2012) research on ELT textbook writers' attitudes towards corpora, which showed some reluctance to use them, and which finds, according to Harwood's summary, 'no evidence that teachers, school administrators, or policy makers currently demand a greater use of corpora in textbooks, meaning publishers have no incentive to move in this direction' (p. 23).

The final section of the chapter emphasises the importance for textbook writers, publishers and teacher educators of paying heed to textbook research. From the other perspective, for this research to be usable, Harwood stresses the need for *constructive* criticism; textbooks 'are far easier to criticise than they are to write' (Mares 2003: 136 in Harwood 2014b: 26).

The tasks below are based on two of Harwood's dimensions of textbook research, **content** and **consumption**.

Task 3.10 Content
Choose one coursebook with which you are familiar and analyse its treatment of **pragmatics** (see also Section 3.4 above).

- What sort of materials are there for raising pragmatics awareness?
- Which 'speech acts' are modelled/practised?
- Are these contextualised within a specific situation/culture?

Task 3.11 Consumption
Design a mini-study on how one of the coursebooks adopted in your institution is actually *used* in the classroom (a good model for this can be found in Bolster 2014 and 2015).

- Explore how the coursebook is *adapted* (e.g. in terms of methodology?) *supplemented* (what sorts of materials are added and why?) and *reduced* (what is omitted and why?).

3.6 FURTHER READING TWO

Dat, B. (2008). ELT materials used in Southeast Asia. In B. Tomlinson (ed.), ***English Language Learning Materials: A Critical Review*** **(pp. 263–81). London: Continuum.**

In keeping with the international scope of this chapter, we are recommending as our second reading a 'representative' piece of research reporting on materials experiences from Southeast Asia. For his materials overview, Dat has looked at the situations in Vietnam, Singapore, Thailand, Laos, Malaysia and the Philippines. The review comes with a weight of educational experience in the region, and offers a 'triangulated' investigative method combining textbook evaluation with in-depth interviews with over forty teachers, as well as wide-ranging secondary research.

Dat documents 'sterling efforts' to upgrade the quality of English materials in the region, driven by economic interests (p. 263). These have not, however, been at the cost of ideological compromise, and the author describes an eclectic approach to combining curricula, pedagogy and local mores, with each country in the region 'trail[ing] its own path of effective learning' (p. 264).

As in many other areas of the world discussed above, a number of types of coursebooks co-exist in Southeast Asia; imported coursebooks (often revealingly called 'foreign coursebooks'), in-country books and, finally, 'regional ones' (Dat gives the example of Singaporean products used in Malaysia, Thailand and Vietnam). The proportional breakdown of these varies from region to region. The number of imported coursebooks seems to be inversely proportional to the use of English as an official language (in the Philippines and Singapore, 60–80 per cent of coursebooks are locally produced). Although perhaps unexpected, this might be seen in the light of perceived cultural identity. In a survey in the Philippines on English language and culture reported in this chapter, none of the respondents identified the English language with the culture of 'Inner Circle' countries (where 'imported' texts would come from); instead, nearly 95 per cent identified it as an international language (Dat 2008: 264; see full quotation in Section 3.2 above).

Evaluating the locally developed materials, positive features to emerge are close cultural knowledge – 'the vigour of the courses lies in their topic content connected with the learner's knowledge and cultural background' (p. 271), albeit with an eye to the globalisation to which Southeast Asia aspires – and a technique frowned upon in communicative methodology: use of the mother tongue. The L1 is used plentifully in local materials, and is seen as 'a way to examine the social distance between L1 and L2, check comprehension, provide feedback, direct complex activities, explain abstract concepts and clarify problematic grammatical structures' (p. 273).

On the other hand, some of the weaknesses condemned in the locally produced materials recall those of the early British/American ELT books: too much 'insider perspective' and an 'excessive' dwelling on the local culture, overlooking the reality of the learners' knowledge of the world (p. 276). These problems and others are seen as rooted in a lack of professional support in materials development, and the article concludes with a 'cry from the heart' on the part of the author:

> I would like to appeal for more interaction and investment among course developers in the region . . . countries seriously lack professional course developers and . . . there has not been adequate training in materials development. (ibid.)

Task 3.12
Conduct a mini-research study about the production of the coursebooks used in your own teaching context:
- Which publishers produce coursebooks for your context?
- Where are the publishers based?
- Are any of the coursebooks 'local' versions of mainstream series' (i.e. published for a different geographical market)? If so:
  - ☐ Where are they published?
  - ☐ Are the authors 'local'? (For example, the *New Headway* series, published by Oxford University Press, has an American version which is published in Britain with the same authors as the English versions.)

Task 3.13
Elsewhere in his chapter, Dat states:

> An overdose of local culture ingredients can easily damage learner curiosity and the novelty effect of many subject matters. In many cases the cultural content seems too familiar and predictable to be interesting to the learners and thus offers little challenge to their creative mind. Some writers pay attention to common cultural practice, settings and occupations in local contexts while ignoring less usual but more fascinating features about the local life. (2008: 268)

- Compare this with arguments we have made in this chapter about local materials and local contexts.
- Consider strategies for designing English language learning materials for 'Outer' or 'Expanding Circle' countries which balance the advantages and disadvantages of 'local' as opposed to 'Inner Circle' cultural content.

3.7 CONCLUSION

Three core questions about language teaching and culture which we see as crucial to materials development formed the basis for this chapter. In our discussions, we have deliberately raised as many further questions as provided answers. We give below a synthesis of these for ongoing consideration:

- **Which English?** The global spread of English casts sociocultural and sociopolitical complexities over the learning of it. With a vast geographical range of NES and NNES varieties, choices of which to teach in our materials depend on context of use.
- **Which culture?** While language cannot be taught in isolation from its culture of use, for English there is a vast diversity in the latter corresponding to the geographical spread of contexts in which the language is spoken. Context-relevant choices regarding cultural materials have to be made which take into account the needs and wants of the learners.
- **Which pedagogy?** The acceptability of teaching approaches is keenly culture-dependent: materials writers and coursebook publishers must take this into account in the materials they offer.

Taking its cue from the final issue, the following chapter, Chapter 4, offers a detailed treatment of evaluating teaching materials.

3.8 ADDITIONAL READINGS

Johnstone Young, T. and Walsh, S. (2010). Which English? Whose English? An investigation of 'non-native' teachers' beliefs about target varieties. *Language, Culture and Curriculum*, 23(2): 123–37.

Johnstone Young and Walsh's article synthesises many of the questions posed in this chapter about ownership of the sprawling language that is English today and, concomitantly, which variety or varieties is or are targeted as teaching/learning models. It is useful to have an empirical study to draw on amidst the many heated theoretical debates in this area, and the authors slyly undercut these by noting that their non-native English-speaking teacher (NNEST) respondents were relatively unconcerned about target models 'in either practical or socio-political terms' (p. 136).

McGrath, I. (2013). Learner perspectives. In I. McGrath, *Teaching Materials and the Roles of EFL/ESL Teachers* (pp. 147–66). London: Bloomsbury.

This chapter helps fill a gap identified by Harwood in the chapter reviewed above, by offering research on the most important consumers of coursebooks: the learners themselves. Research in this chapter gets learners involved at all levels, evaluating coursebooks, authentic materials and activity types, and finally generating materials themselves.

NOTES

1. We use 'global Englishes' as an inclusive term for the worldwide use of English, in a similar way to that of Galloway and Mariou (2014).
2. A British Council poll (2008) revealed that 67 per cent of teachers claim to use the coursebook for part (48 per cent) or all of their teaching (19 per cent).
3. 'Washback' is usually applied to the effect of testing on coursebooks/curricula, but its meaning is extended here to that used by Tomlinson (2003a) and Mishan (2010b).

4

MATERIALS EVALUATION AND ADAPTATION

4.1 INTRODUCTION

Language teachers, as Amrani (2011: 270) notes, are constantly engaged in evaluating materials:

> Materials evaluation is nothing new to teachers. They do it all the time from wandering casually around a bookshop choosing a new book or borrowing a new idea gleaned from a conference presentation or colleague to surfing the internet discussion and resource sites to gather together new materials.

To this list of informal evaluation activities, we could add the well-known 'flick test', which involves no more than a rapid glance through the pages of a coursebook, perhaps taking in the topics, illustrations and the main language points covered in a particular book. Tomlinson notes wryly, 'publishers are well aware of this procedure and sometimes place attractive illustrations in the top right-hand corner of the right-hand page in order to influence the flicker in a positive way' (2013a: 31).

Such activities are, however, basically intuitive. Where this intuition is professionally informed, these activities may be of some value to the person concerned, but the evaluation remains, to use Tomlinson's (2003b: 17) words, 'ad hoc and impressionistic': it is not based on an explicit set of teaching and learning principles articulated before the evaluation. In this chapter we are mainly concerned with the *principled* evaluation to which Tomlinson refers, and we will follow his definition (2003b: 15): 'Materials evaluation is a procedure that involves measuring the value (or potential value) of a set of learning materials. It involves making judgements about the effect of the materials on the people using them.' Tomlinson (2003b) chooses his words carefully in his definition: words such as 'procedure', 'measuring', 'value', 'judgement' and 'effect' combine to suggest a process which is more *systematic*, more considered and more complex than informal, intuitive processes such as browsing the book stalls at an ELT conference or carrying out the 'flick test'.

4.2 THE NEED FOR PRINCIPLED EVALUATION

A question we need to ask at the outset, then, is: '(Why) is *systematic* and *principled* materials evaluation necessary?' The first reason is that, as we established in the introduction to this volume, materials play an important role in the language learning process. Indeed, in some contexts, materials will constitute the main exposure which learners have to the TL. As Littlejohn (2011) argues, the added extras that many publishers now offer (e.g. workbooks, CDs, interactive whiteboard (IWB) resources) potentially mean that materials will occupy an even more prominent role in class than previously. We can add to this that the materials teachers use may even, in practice, constitute teacher education in the hands of inexperienced and/or untrained teachers who rely heavily on materials for guidance on how to conduct their classes. The second reason that systematic and principled evaluation is necessary is that materials potentially represent a significant professional, financial and/ or political investment (Sheldon 1988). This is particularly the case when national or regional governments are providing English language coursebooks for the state school system. To these two strong practical reasons for taking materials evaluation seriously we can add a third, perhaps more academic reason: materials evaluation can be a powerful professional development activity for those who engage in it. Seen in this way, materials evaluation is not an additional component to materials development, but an integral part of it. The argument that materials evaluation is developmental rests on the idea that drawing up evaluation criteria and making judgements based on those criteria reveals much about the assumptions, knowledge and values of the evaluators themselves. It can also broaden the horizons of the evaluators: McGrath (2013: 107), for example, argues that when teachers and supervisors are involved in evaluation, this can prompt 'reflection on aspects of the materials that they might otherwise not have thought about and [offer] an outlet for feelings that might otherwise not have been expressed'. In similar vein, Al Khaldi (2011) reported that many teachers who took part in his coursebook evaluation exercise in Jordan commented that they found it an enlightening experience, as the evaluation criteria they were given and the process of applying those criteria helped them to see more clearly what they wanted from the materials they used.

While we have defined materials evaluation above, we can perhaps delineate it more firmly by also considering what it is *not*. We need to note, then, that Tomlinson (2003b) contrasts evaluation with analysis: whereas evaluation is concerned with judging the effects of the materials in a given context, analysis is concerned with what is in the materials, e.g.

- How many units does the coursebook have?
- Does the coursebook contain authentic texts?

The first question can be answered with a number; the second can be answered yes/ no. We need to acknowledge, however, that evaluation can sometimes be implicit in apparently simple, objective materials analysis questions. In the second point above, for example, we could argue that the very fact of including a question about authenticity shows that the analyst thinks authenticity is important. We might go further and suggest that definitions of authenticity might vary from analyst to analyst. Analysis, as we have defined it here, might, for example, be useful in the 'weeding out' process, i.e. eliminating materials at the selection stage which are clearly unsuitable in terms of straightforward analysis criteria such as level, target age range; number of units, exam focus and so on. The materials which survive the initial analysis can then be subjected to more detailed evaluation.

Task 4.1
Decide on a target learner group, e.g. an International English Language Testing System (IELTS) preparation class. Formulate four or five analysis questions you would ask about potential materials for that group, such as:

- Is the exam format explained?

4.3 THE NATURE OF EVALUATION

Having defined evaluation and distinguished it from analysis, we need to consider the different ways in which evaluation can be carried out. Fundamentally, evaluation can differ along four dimensions:

- What is being evaluated?
- When is the evaluation carried out?
- How is the evaluation carried out?
- Who carries out the evaluation?

In this section, we address these four questions.

WHAT IS BEING EVALUATED?

The assumption in the materials evaluation literature is often that evaluation is applied to coursebooks. Indeed, this is probably the most common form of evaluation, and much of the discussion in this chapter reflects that assumption. We need to note, however, that coursebooks are not the only possible focus of evaluation. Among the materials which could usefully be evaluated are, for example, in-house materials, tests, graded readers or self-access materials. We should note in passing that the evaluation of in-house materials is a clear case in which evaluation can be developmental, as it will almost certainly involve reflection and revision of the materials by practitioners themselves. McGrath (2002) also notes that evaluations have been carried out on specific *aspects* of materials, e.g. illustrations, cultural content and gender stereotypes, while Ellis (2011) reports on 'micro-evaluation', which involves researching in detail the effects of particular classroom tasks included in the materials. The benefit of micro-evaluation, Ellis (2011: 231) argues, is that it 'forces a teacher to examine the assumptions that lie behind the design of a task and the procedures used to implement it. It requires them to go beyond impressionistic evaluation by examining empirically whether a task "works" in the way it intended and how it can be improved for future use.'

WHEN IS THE EVALUATION CARRIED OUT?

The obvious choice in terms of when evaluation takes place is between pre-use, whilst-use[1] and post-use evaluation (Tomlinson 2003b). We need to note, however, that ideally all of these kinds of evaluation will be preceded by a detailed analysis of the context in which the materials will be used (McGrath 2002). This context analysis may involve, depending on the specific circumstances, background information about national educational goals, curriculum goals or the specific aims of language teaching. It may also involve researching documents such as syllabi and examination papers. Information about learners (e.g. motivation and expectations) and teachers (e.g. qualifications and experience) will be of central importance in such context analysis. Armed with this contextual information, the evaluator is clearly in a better position to evaluate whether the materials are appropriate in relation to the goals of a particular set of learners given the constraints and characteristics of the context.

Pre-use evaluation

Pre-use evaluation is more common than both whilst-use and post-use evaluation for two reasons: it is usually designed to inform the important decision as to which materials to adopt, and it is easier to carry out than whilst-use or post-use evaluation, which, as we shall see, may both require more time-consuming evaluation methods such as classroom observation or tests. As Tomlinson (2003b) laments, pre-use evaluation is often carried out impressionistically, though there are, as we shall also see, clear alternatives, e.g. a framework of evaluation criteria. Pre-use evaluations may cover largely the same ground as whilst-use criteria, but they will be worded differently, e.g.:

> *Pre-use:* How far are the materials likely to motivate the learners?   5 4 3 2 1
> *Whilst-use:* How far do the learners find the materials motivating?   5 4 3 2 1
> *Post-use:* How far did the learners find the materials motivating?   5 4 3 2 1

Alternative methods of pre-use evaluation are noted by McGrath (2002), who refers to the possibility of trialling/piloting the materials, consulting colleagues who have already used the materials (in other contexts), and observing classes where the materials are already in use.

Whilst-use evaluation

Tomlinson (2003b: 24) notes the usefulness of whilst-use evaluation and points to a number of potential foci which may lend themselves particularly to it:

- clarity of instructions, layout
- comprehensibility, credibility, achievability of tasks
- achievement of performance objectives
- potential for localisation
- practicality, teachability, flexibility

- appeal, motivating power, impact
- effectiveness in facilitating short-term learning

However, Tomlinson (2003b) also sounds a cautionary note about whilst-use evaluation: an evaluator can easily be deceived by activities which *appear* to work well. Lessons which generate 'student talking time', for example, are often rated highly, but we need also to evaluate the *quality* of the talk: we might be interested, for example, in whether the student talk constitutes 'pushed output', i.e. the speaking activity stretches learners beyond their 'comfort zone' (see Chapter 2). We could also add that, in considering the criteria suggested by Tomlinson (above) through observation, it would not always be straightforward to isolate the effect of the materials from other variables, most notably the teacher. How clear is, for example, the extent to which the 'motivating power' evident in the observation resides in the materials or the teacher? Most of the whilst-use evaluation aspects noted above, Tomlinson (2003b) argues, can be assessed impressionistically through observation, though he advises that it is preferable to focus on one aspect per observation. He also points to more objective (if rather time-consuming) methods of evaluation such as 'recording the incidence and duration of each student's oral contribution' (ibid.: 24). While Tomlinson's (2003b) discussion of whilst-use evaluation seems to imply that it will be carried out by an external evaluator, McGrath (2002: 120) focuses specifically on the role of the teacher in such evaluation, calling for the 'planned use of teachers' daily experience' in effecting both whilst-use and post-use evaluation. Teachers can, he argues, ask themselves questions of the following kind as prompts for whilst-use and post-use evaluation:

- What proportion of the materials was I able to use unchanged?
- Did the unchanged materials appear to work well? What evidence do I have for this?
- What spontaneous changes did I make as I taught with the materials? Did these improvisations work well? If not, what do I need to do differently?

Broad evaluative criteria such as these can then be used as a principled basis for adaptation of the materials.

McGrath (2002) also refers to the potential role of classroom observation in whilst-use evaluation (this could be carried out by peers) and to the possibility of teachers and learners keeping diaries recording their impressions of the materials.

Post-use evaluation

While pre-use evaluation has an important role in pre-empting poor selection of materials (or selection of poor materials), post-use evaluation is potentially the most informative type, as it can be informed by teachers' and learners' experience of the materials or, ideally, based on actual evidence of the effect of the materials on the learners. Tomlinson (2003b) notes that post-use evaluation can potentially 'measure the short-term effect [of the materials] as regards motivation, impact, achievability, instant learning etc.' He also points to the possibility of measuring the long-term effects of the materials through, for example, delayed tests. He acknowledges, however, the significant challenges to this kind of evaluation presented by intervening variables such as the degree of exposure outside class, and varying levels of parental support and individual motivation. McGrath (2013) refers to retrospective evaluation (by teachers), noting that this can lead to the identification of weaknesses in the materials, leading to constructive revision and adaptation.

HOW IS THE EVALUATION CARRIED OUT?

Evaluation criteria

In our discussion of different types of evaluation (pre-use, whilst-use, post-use), we have necessarily made passing reference to some of the evaluation instruments or methods used, e.g. observation or trialling. However, in principled materials evaluation the choice and design of the evaluation instrument are so crucial that we need to revisit this issue in more detail. The most important factor in the design of an evaluation instrument should be the criteria against which the materials are evaluated (Tomlinson 2003b). Criteria are often associated exclusively with the so-called 'checklist method': we consider the term 'checklist' unfortunate, as it can seem to imply an activity which is done quickly and superficially, like checking you have packed everything for a holiday. It can also imply, we would argue, that there is an obvious and generally agreed list of items to be checked, and that the process of checking these items is quick and easy (see McGrath 2013: 55 for an overview of such checklists). Constructing evaluation criteria, as we shall see below, can be a complex process, as can the application of these criteria.

Generating evaluation criteria

As McGrath remarks, one of the main challenges the evaluator has to meet is the specification of criteria. A number of commentators have suggested systematic ways of approaching this task: a basic division, for example, between general and specific criteria is suggested by Ur (1996), while an acronym (CATALYST) to facilitate the generation of criteria is suggested by Grant (1987: 119):

Communicative
Aims
Teachability
Available add-ons
Level
Your impression
Student interest
Tried and tested

Task 4.2

Use the CATALYST framework to generate some specific evaluation criteria to be applied to a set of materials of your choice. For example, from the 'Communicative' aspect of the framework, we might generate evaluation questions such as:

- To what extent do the materials provide meaningful speaking tasks?
- To what extent do the materials offer opportunities for personalisation?
- How useful did you find the framework in generating principled evaluation criteria?

The CATALYST framework is, perhaps, potentially useful as a point of departure for brainstorming criteria. The framework has, however, a number of limitations. It is worth considering these limitations to remind ourselves of what we are looking for in a set of evaluation criteria:

- Two of the categories – 'Level' and 'Available add-ons' – are analysis rather than evaluation questions in our terms.
- 'Your impression' is avowedly impressionistic.
- 'Tried and tested' is rather an empty criterion and is hardly likely to lead to principled innovation. It might be that the materials used have kept teachers and learners reasonably happy, but that does not mean that the materials are principled and maximally effective: they may just provide 'comfort food'.

In short, the framework seems to foreground impressionistic and practical issues as much as if not more than teaching and learning principles. Evaluation criteria, however, by definition, express values, so it is important that these values should be articulated as a basis for generating criteria (Tomlinson 2003b). As Tomlinson (p. 22) argues, 'Ultimately what matters is that an evaluation is principled, that the evaluator's principles are made overt and that they are referred to when determining and carrying out the procedures of the evaluation.'

Criteria frameworks which address theoretical concerns more directly have, however, been proposed by Tomlinson (2003b) and Rubdy (2003). Tomlinson (2003b), for example, suggests five *categories* of evaluation criteria, each of which can be used to develop a number of specific criteria:

- universal (driven by SLA theory): e.g. are the materials motivating?
- local (related to the context): e.g. are the materials culturally acceptable in the context?
- media-specific (e.g. audio or computer): e.g. is the sound quality of the audio materials good?
- content-specific (e.g. exam or English for specific purposes (ESP)): e.g. do the materials replicate the types of real-world tasks the target group will need to do?
- age-specific: e.g. are the visuals likely to appeal to children?

Rubdy (2003) argues that evaluation criteria can be generated from three key notions: psychological validity; pedagogic validity and process validity. These terms are described thus:

- psychological validity: learners' needs, goals and pedagogical requirements
- pedagogical validity: teachers' skills, abilities, theories and beliefs

- process and content validity: the thinking underlying the materials writer's presentation of the content and approach to teaching and learning respectively

Rubdy (2003) provides a further gloss to clarify these terms. Psychological validity encompasses such notions as independence and autonomy; self-development and creativity. Pedagogical validity refers to notions such as guidance; choice and reflection. A particularly interesting aspect of Rubdy's (2003) framework is the emphasis on teacher development: 'An important criterion for evaluating materials would . . . relate to the extent to which they engage the teacher's constantly evolving critical standpoint and facilitate the expanding and refining of the teacher's schemata in the process' (ibid.: 50). Process and content validity seems to be rather a broad-brush category covering aspects from methodology and content to layout and graphics. It is, however, a framework for generating criteria rather than a framework of set criteria.

It is evident from these three examples (Grant 1987; Rubdy 2003; Tomlinson 2003b) that criteria frameworks can vary both in focus and in scope, but McGrath (2002: 43) notes the following areas common to most of them:

- design: includes both layout of material on the page and overall clarity of organisation
- language content: coverage of linguistic items and language skills
- subject matter: topics
- practical considerations: e.g. availability, durability and price

Operationalising criteria
Whichever framework we design, adapt or adopt, we need to consider how we actually generate the specific criteria for each category and operationalise the framework. McGrath (2002: 40–1) suggests the following procedure:

1. Decide general categories
2. Decide specific criteria within each category
3. Decide ordering of general categories and specific criteria
4. Decide format of prompts and responses

Tomlinson (2003b), however, suggests a slightly different procedure: brainstorming criteria before dividing them into the categories of his framework, e.g. universal; local; age-specific. He then suggests a number of questions which evaluators could use to monitor and revise the criteria they have generated:

1. Does each question only ask one question?
2. Is each question answerable?
3. Is each question free of dogma?
4. Is each question reliable in the sense that other evaluators would interpret it in the same way?

The following are examples of questions that violate each of these monitoring criteria in turn:

1. Are the texts authentic and interesting?
2. Will the materials stand the test of time?
3. Is there extensive controlled practice of every grammar item?
4. Is there a good balance between the four skills?

Tomlinson (2003b: 27) also suggests a set of questions which could be used more generally to monitor evaluation criteria in any evaluation framework:

- Is the list based on a coherent set of principles of language learning?
- Are all the criteria actually evaluation criteria?
- Are the criteria sufficient to help the evaluator to reach useful conclusions?
- Are the criteria organised systematically (for example into categories and subcategories which facilitate discrete as well as global verdicts and decisions)?
- Are the criteria sufficiently neutral to allow evaluators with different ideologies to make use of them?
- Is the list sufficiently flexible to allow it to be made use of by different evaluators in different circumstances?

Even when a set of coherent criteria has been generated and categorised, however, there are further organisational tasks. What is the balance between open and closed questions? How should the categories and the questions within those categories be sequenced? It is interesting that McGrath (2013) cautions against a 'false uniformity', i.e. the idea that every section of the evaluation instrument should have the same number of questions and the same 'scoring value'. This points to a crucial, but often ignored question: how should criteria be 'weighted', i.e. how many points should be assigned to each criterion? It would, for example, be absurd to attach equal weight to the two questions below:

- Does the book have an attractive cover?
- Does the book address the aims of the syllabus?

We have seen, then, that by referring to theory, by making our own principles and values explicit, and by judicious exploitation of previous work in the field, it is possible to produce detailed, comprehensive and principled evaluation frameworks which can be operated with at least a degree of objectivity by one or more evaluators. We need to keep in mind, however, as Riazi (2003) notes, that evaluation criteria change over time as views on language teaching change.

WHO CARRIES OUT THE EVALUATION?

One potential problem with principled evaluations based on explicit criteria is that they can give the impression that evaluation is, or should be, the exclusive domain of the specialist. Published evaluations in the *ELT Journal* by Tomlinson et al. (2001), for example, contain well over a hundred criteria. It is important to realise, however, that an evaluation method has to suit the evaluators, the purpose of the evaluation and the audience. The evaluation by Tomlinson et al. (2001) *is* fit for purpose: it is written by academics and experienced practitioners for academics and experienced practitioners to comment on the commonalities between a range of coursebooks. A summary of the findings can be written in a form accessible to teachers, but it would probably not be possible for a group of busy teachers to apply such a framework. We need to consider the role in evaluation of stakeholders who are not specialists in this specific field: teachers, learners and publishers.

Teachers as evaluators
Masuhara (2011) has interesting proposals for how teachers can be involved in pre-use evaluation. She suggests, for example, that meetings could be held where new materials are presented and demonstrated to teachers, leading to discussions of which activities the teachers preferred and, crucially, why they preferred these activities to others. Masuhara also suggests that teachers could be presented with materials which exemplify different approaches, for example, to the use of the same text. What these activities have in common, we would argue, is structured and focused discussion to elicit what it is teachers are really looking for in materials. We have already noted that McGrath (2002: 120) proposes a number of questions teachers can ask themselves to systematise whilst-use evaluation. Teachers, McGrath (2013) suggests, might keep records of use, noting sections of the materials they had used or omitted, which sections went well and so on. These records can then inform adaptation and supplementation of the materials. Structured reflection along these lines is also suggested by Masuhara (2011), and is as applicable to post-use evaluation as it is to whilst-use evaluation. What is needed to underpin all these potential activities, Masuhara (2011) stresses, is recognition by the institution that materials evaluation is important and that teachers' role in this process is vital.

Learners as evaluators
Learners, as McGrath (2013: 151) argues, also have an important role to play in evaluation: 'learners are capable of evaluation. They do not always opt for the same point on a scale. They discriminate. Given the opportunity, they can make judgements which may sometimes surprise their teachers.' Among the methods he suggests learners might use are learner diaries, rating of tasks and pyramid discussions. An interesting, though perhaps indirect kind of evaluation can be gained through metaphor study. As we noted in the introduction, McGrath (2006) carried out such a study, which required the learners to produce a metaphor for the coursebook, and observed that the reactions were often colourful and mainly positive.

Publishers as evaluators
An interesting insight into publishers' perspectives on evaluation is offered by Amrani (2011), who notes that publishers can use either piloting or reviewing of

materials to determine their suitability. She points out, however, that reviewing (comments on materials made by stakeholders) is now more common than piloting as a reviewing practice by publishers, as they have to meet tight production deadlines. It is particularly interesting that Amrani (ibid.: 273) draws attention to a significant difference between publisher evaluation and other perspectives: 'instead of evaluating whether materials are ideal for a very specific audience, the publisher is often evaluating whether materials are suitable for the widest range of possible users, or at the very least versatile enough to be adapted easily'. Amrani (ibid.: 268) also underlines that publishers have limited scope to revise materials, as 'Course content, approach and task design is often already established by exam syllabuses, guidelines or standards such as the Common European Framework.' The CEFR is available at http://www.coe.int/t/dg4/linguistic/Source/Framework_EN.pdf

9.2   Thus far in this chapter, we have established that evaluation should be motivated by an explicit set of learning/teaching principles and, ideally, related to a specific context. We have also argued that, while the primary function of evaluation is to assess the suitability of materials for a given teaching and learning context, the process of evaluation can be a salutary experience for the evaluators in revealing, for example, their own methodological preferences and beliefs. Among the potential beneficiaries of the evaluation process are teachers themselves. As McGrath (2002: 4) remarks, 'If, as is often said, knowledge is power, then wider awareness of materials-evaluation procedures and an understanding of the concepts that typically underpin evaluation criteria might encourage those who have been silent to speak.' It is interesting that McGrath refers to 'an understanding of the concepts that typically underpin evaluation criteria': if teachers are to be empowered through taking part in evaluation, it is vital, we would argue, that evaluation procedures are made accessible to teachers. However, McGrath (2013) refers to a study carried out by Wang (2005) in which six teachers carried out predictive evaluation using a checklist. The teachers, she reports, did not feel equipped for the task and found it very time-consuming. If evaluation is to become a mainstream activity, there are, we would argue, two complementary ways forward: (1) teachers need training in evaluation (McGrath 2013), and (2) we need manageable and accessible evaluation instruments. An interesting step in this direction has been taken by Evans (2012), who produced an evaluation toolkit designed to help ELT managers develop evaluation instruments suitable for their context. It suggests, among other things, setting up a teachers' panel and a progression from impressionistic to criterion-referenced methods. Evans's (2012) framework, as we see in Figure 4.1, follows the main stages recommended in the literature, but what distinguishes it are the 'how to' tips which accompany each stage.

Task 4.3

How far do you agree that teachers need training in evaluation? (How) do you think this chapter on materials evaluation might benefit you?

Task 4.4

What are the weaknesses of the following criteria?

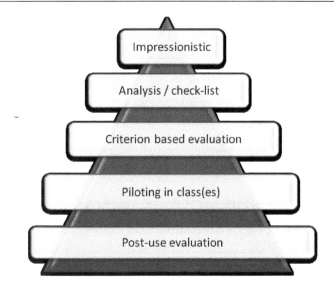

Figure 4.1   Evans's (2012) stages of selection

- Do the texts only expose learners to vocabulary they have already learned?
- Will the materials improve exam results?
- Are the materials motivating and exam-specific?
- Is the methodology up to date?

Task 4.5
- In groups, decide on six or eight universal criteria you would use in the evaluation of any materials.
- Compare your criteria with another group's criteria.

4.4 MATERIALS ADAPTATION

WHAT IS MATERIALS ADAPTATION?

At the beginning of this chapter we made a distinction between impressionistic materials evaluation and systematic, principled materials evaluation. It will be useful to make a parallel distinction in our discussion of materials adaptation: in this case between ad hoc adaptation and principled adaptation. *Ad hoc* adaptation is clearly a common activity: in many (well-resourced) ELT staffrooms, you will find, for example, teachers looking through resource books for a particular kind of activity, photocopying newspaper articles or asking questions such as, 'Does anyone know a good activity for . . . ?' While such adaptations may be successful, the danger is that they are driven by teachers' preferences, or even whims of the moment, as much as, if not more than, by learners' needs or wants. Tomlinson and Masuhara (2004) note that materials adaptation is rarely researched or taught on teacher education courses, so teachers often have to rely simply on experience or intuition. Ideally, principled adaptation will be informed by prior evaluation of the existing materials. Such evaluation need not be extensive or detailed, but it will help to provide a principled rationale for the adaptation (Tomlinson and Masuhara 2004). McGrath (2013) notes that adaptation can vary in timing, scale and focus: it can be carried out reactively in response to classroom events or proactively before a lesson or course. Adaptation can, McGrath points out, be at the level of activity, unit or course. Islam and Mares (2003: 86) also stress the scope of the term 'adaptation': 'Materials adaptation can span a range of procedures from adding carefully contextualised role plays with the objective of providing more opportunities to communicate to not finishing a pronunciation drill because of time constraints.'

REASONS FOR MATERIALS ADAPTATION

Potential reasons for adapting materials are listed by Cunningsworth (1995, cited in Islam and Mares 2003: 88):

- dynamics of the classroom
- personalities involved
- constraints imposed by syllabuses
- availability of resources
- expectations and motivations of the learners

Classroom dynamics and personalities involved might, for example, lead teachers to incorporate either more or less pair and group work than the materials propose. Syllabus constraints might lead to the omission of some language points and a heavier focus on others. Materials might call for the use of an IWB when the teacher doesn't have access to one. It can also happen that learners are presented with a general English coursebook when they are highly motivated to pass a specific exam. All these cases may require the teacher to adapt the materials to suit the learners, the learning context and the course aims. We can add to the kinds of constraints we need to consider the limitations imposed by the physical nature of the coursebook: teachers may, for example, want to use long texts, which are rarely found in the coursebook (Islam and Mares 2003). There are also serious restrictions on the kinds of topics which can be included in coursebooks as they are designed to cater for a wide range of cultural contexts (see Chapter 3). Freed from this kind of constraint, Saraceni (2013) argues, teachers may be able to adapt, using more provocative texts in the classroom than those typically provided by the coursebook.

Tomlinson and Masuhara (2004: 12) list the following factors to take into account when considering possible adaptations to materials:

- Teaching environment (national, regional, institutional, cultural)
- Learners (age, language level, prior learning experience, learning styles)
- Their [teachers'] own preferences (personality; teaching styles; beliefs about language learning and teaching)
- Course objectives

It is interesting that Tomlinson and Masuhara include teachers' preferences. It is certainly true that it is more difficult to teach with conviction if you yourself don't 'believe' in the materials, but at the same time we need to be careful of projecting our own preferences onto learners.

The list of potential reasons for adaptation produced by Islam and Mares (2003) focuses heavily on learner factors. Among the reasons for adaptation they list are:

- To add real choice
- To cater for all sensory learning styles
- To provide for more learner autonomy
- To encourage higher level cognitive skills
- To make language input more accessible
- To make language input more engaging.

It should perhaps be noted in relation to these aims that some are more easily achieved than others. Adding choice and catering for different sensory learning styles may not, for example, be easily achieved in large classes.

Although McGrath (2013: 66) refers to his list below as 'principles' of adaptation, it is equally valid, we would argue, to see them as reasons for adaptation. Materials should:

- Be perceived as relevant by learners (localisation)
- Be up-to-date (modernisation)
- Cater for differences in learning styles (individualisation)
- Encourage learners to speak/write about themselves and their own experiences (personalisation)
- Engage the whole person (humanising)
- Be appropriate to the learners' level/offer an appropriate level of challenge (simplification/complexification/differentiation)
- Be varied (variety)

Potential problems with applying some of these principles are noted by McGrath (2013) himself. In terms of localisation, for example, it can be difficult for teachers (and materials developers) to judge what will be regarded as relevant and interesting in a given context – localisation may be better done locally (see Chapter 3)! There may also be problems with simplification: Mishan (2005), for example, has argued that simplification is quite a difficult art and, in some cases, can even make a text more difficult to understand (see also Chapter 2).

WHAT SHOULD WE ADAPT?

McGrath (2013: 62–3) produces a very useful summary of the potential foci for adaptation:

- *language* (the language of instructions, explanations, examples, the language in exercises and texts and the language learners are expected to produce) [presumably the language they are expected to produce in controlled practice activities]
- *process* (forms of classroom management or interaction stated explicitly in the instructions for exercises, activities and tasks, but also the learning styles involved)
- *content* (topics, contexts, cultural references)
- *level* (linguistic and cognitive demands on the learner)

HOW SHOULD WE ADAPT MATERIALS?

To conclude this section, it is worth reminding ourselves of the purposes of adaptation: 'to make the material more suitable for the circumstances in which it is used; to compensate for any intrinsic deficiencies in the materials' (McGrath 2002: 62). The prototypical process of adaptation would involve the following stages (Tomlinson and Masuhara 2004: 15):

- Profile of teaching context
- Identifying reasons for adaptation
- Evaluating the materials (in relation to a specific group or context)
- Listing objectives (for a specific group)
- Adapting
- Teaching
- Revising

As Tomlinson and Masuhara (2004) acknowledge, it may not be necessary for teachers to go through all these stages every time they adapt materials, but it may be a salutary exercise from time to time.

The ability to adapt materials is a necessary part of any teacher's repertoire. It is not, however, as McGrath (2002) points out, a risk-free enterprise: learners may not react well to adaptation, either because they have invested in the coursebook or because a coursebook gives a certain *sense* of security and progression. There is also a risk that large-scale adaptation may lead to a loss of focus on the original aims of the course. It is not unknown for teachers to pick out what they consider to be the most interesting texts and activities from a variety of sources with the aim of producing lively and entertaining classes. This can, however, lead to a loss of coherence in the programme. For this reason, it is important that adaptation, like evaluation, is principled: it should focus on the goals of the learners.

We have seen in this chapter that evaluation and adaptation play an important part in context-sensitive, learner-centred teaching. Some of the skills required to carry out such activities are doubtless picked up through experience, but we can make these processes more efficient and effective by taking a principled approach and allying theory with practice.

Task 4.6

What do you think are the most important reasons for adapting materials, from those given in the chapter?

Task 4.7

Do you think it is right to adapt materials according to the teacher's own preferences? Discuss why/why not.

Task 4.8

- Decide on a teaching context.
- Develop some evaluation criteria for materials to be used in that context.
- Evaluate a unit of materials from a coursebook to be used in that context.
- Adapt the materials in relation to the evaluation.

4.5 FURTHER READING ONE

Johnson, K., Kim, M., Ya-Fang, L., Nava, A., Perkins, D., Smith, A., Soler-Canela, O. and Lu, W. (2008). A step forward: investigating expertise in materials evaluation. *ELT Journal,* **62(2): 157–63.**

Johnson et al. carried out an experiment in which three teachers of differing levels of experience were asked to evaluate the same materials in relation to their own teaching context. The least experienced evaluator (T1) had one year's teaching experience, T2 had five years' and T3 had twelve years'. The research was carried out using a 'think-aloud protocol', i.e. the teachers verbalised their thoughts while they were carrying out the evaluation task and were audio and video recorded during the process. The research team analysed the recordings and identified five categories to interpret the data: sequence of evaluation, teacher preferences, use of terminology, methodological concerns and flexibility in usage. Johnson et al. note that the three evaluators took quite different approaches, as the following excerpts from the article illustrate:

> T1 started at Unit 1, but did not find an activity that she considered to be suitable for a first lesson ('a warmer') and so jumped to Unit 5. This was one manifestation of her greater concern for classroom logistics than for the overall evaluation of the textbook.
>
> T2 took a more direct approach, though it was not necessarily more time-efficient. He quickly found all the components of the book, looked at the front and back covers of the books and then flicked through both the student's book and the teacher's book before returning to the contents pages. He then looked through every page of the student's book in turn, until he reached Unit 13 (of 14).
>
> T3, on the other hand, adopted a more selective approach. He decided early on to focus on Unit 4, explaining that he expected the textbook to have 'settled down' by then. He looked at all the activities in this unit while referring to the other components of the course. Then he turned to the teacher's book and

compared it to the student's book for Unit 4. He then looked at the methodology notes in the teacher's book in more detail, before briefly looking through Unit 8, comparing the student's book to the teaching notes. (pp. 159–60)

Johnson et al. note that a major difference between the evaluators was depth of evaluation: T3 evaluated a smaller sample in more detail. T3 also knew what he was looking for in evaluating a textbook, and he knew where to find it:

> The general impression is that the more teaching experience an evaluator has (which obviously also involves at least some experience in textbook evaluation) the more able he or she is to view a textbook with detachment, and take account of other users' needs as well as his or her own. (p. 161)

Johnson et al. summarise the distinctive approach of the most experienced teacher (T3) thus:

> T3 seemed to comment on a wider range of issues than the other evaluators. In particular, many of his evaluations concerned the book's linguistic rationale . . . T3 was also less categorical and more flexible in expressing what he liked and did not like about the book. That is, he weighed up pros and cons of different features of the book, activities, and methodological options, and took great pains in accommodating other people's (teachers' as well as students') needs and expectations. (p. 161)

By contrast, the least experienced teacher (T1) was most concerned with the textbook as a 'survival' resource for the teacher. T2 was able to look at the textbook from the learners' point of view, but was primarily concerned with one aspect: how far it prepared the learners to operate in an English-speaking environment.

Johnson et al. note that training in materials evaluation could be a useful component in teacher training courses. We hope that this chapter is a step towards this kind of training.

Task 4.9
- Try the experiment yourself. Record yourself evaluating a coursebook for use in a context of your choice.
- Listen to the recording you have made and note the criteria you actually applied.

4.6 FURTHER READING TWO

Maley, A. (2011). Squaring the circle: reconciling materials as constraint with materials as empowerment. In B. Tomlinson (ed.), *Materials Development in Language Teaching*, 2nd edn (pp. 379–403). Cambridge: Cambridge University Press.

Maley points to two common problems with published materials: (1) they cannot appeal to local interests as they are developed for a global market, and (2) they present a linear syllabus although SLA research shows clearly that language acquisition is not a linear process. He argues (p. 380) that there is a need for 'greater flexibility in decisions about content, order, pace and procedures'. Four ways of achieving this flexibility are discussed: (1) processes for adaptation; (2) a model where teachers can mix and match inputs, processes and outcomes; (3) using IT as a resource; and (4) content-based learning.

Maley lists a number of what he calls 'coping strategies' as processes for adaptation: omission; addition; reduction; extension; rewriting/modification; replacement; reordering; branching. Most of these terms are self-explanatory, but it is worth pointing out that 'branching' refers to providing additional options to the coursebook activity. Maley refers to Prabhu (2001) in relation to the inputs, processes and outcomes model. Inputs might include listening or reading texts, visuals, realia and reference materials (among other things). Processes might involve different techniques, e.g. information gap; different task types, e.g. problem-solving; and different modes, e.g. pair work or group work (among many other possibilities). Maley refers to the potential of the internet as a resource for texts, for reference works and for online communication. In relation to content-based learning, Maley claims that the advantages are 'plain to see' as it provides interesting content, and motivation to succeed in the specific subject can enhance motivation to learn English. Throughout the chapter, Maley emphasises the importance of choice and flexibility and the teachers' role in determining what is best for their students.

Task 4.10
Look at a unit from a coursebook and decide where you think it would be appropriate to add optional activities for a specific group.

Task 4.11
Can you think of two or three specific criteria you would use to evaluate internet materials?

Task 4.12
How far do you think it is possible to reconcile the kind of creative adaptation Maley (2011) suggests with coherence and progression?

Task 4.13
How far do you agree that the advantages of content-based learning are 'plain to see'? Discuss this question in groups.

4.7 CONCLUSION

In this chapter we have discussed the processes of evaluation and adaptation, arguing that both processes need to be carried out in a principled manner and based on criteria with a clear rationale. The framing of such criteria, we noted, can be an important teacher development activity in itself. Key points in this chapter are:

- the difference between the superficial flick test and systematic, principled evaluation
- the difference between analysis (what is in the materials) and evaluation (how suitable the materials are for a given group)
- the options for pre-use, whilst-use and post-use evaluation
- the options for generating evaluation criteria, e.g. universal, local, age-specific etc.
- the variety of potential reasons for adapting materials
- the link between evaluation and adaptation

4.8 ADDITIONAL READINGS

Littlejohn, A. P. (2011). The analysis of language teaching materials: inside the Trojan horse. In B. Tomlinson (ed.), *Materials Development in Language Teaching*, 2nd edn (pp. 179–212). Cambridge: Cambridge University Press.

Littlejohn describes a three-phase *analytical* framework. The first level of analysis is simply concerned with content: what do the materials include? At the second level, which Littlejohn considers to be the most important, analysts have to work out what teachers and learners will have to do when using the materials. At the third level of analysis, Littlejohn argues that the analyst can use the data from the first and second levels to infer the overall aims of the materials, the basis for selecting and sequencing content, and the proposed roles for teachers and learners.

Mukundan, J. (2009). *ESL Textbook Evaluation: A Composite Framework*. Cologne: Lambert Academic.

Mukundan describes a three-phase *evaluation* framework. The first phase is pre-use and involves an evaluation checklist. The second phase, however, is distinctive in that it calls for corpus analysis of the materials to calculate the range of vocabulary covered and the frequency of recycling. The third phase is whilst-use and/or post-use and calls for focused reflection on how successful different aspects of the materials were through, for example, reflective journals.

NOTE

1. McGrath (2002) uses the term 'in-use' rather than 'whilst-use'.

5

RECONCEPTUALISING MATERIALS FOR THE TECHNOLOGICAL ENVIRONMENT

5.1 INTRODUCTION

In the early boom years of computing, the mid-1990s, a cartoon made the rounds in business and educational circles with the caption 'Technology is the answer. What was the question?' After this sort of initial 'because-we-can' attitude (Meskill's term, 2007), the use of technology in language learning has been steadily situated within SLA theory and pedagogy. Technology is, as Blake stresses, 'theoretically and methodologically neutral. But how technology is used – its particular culture of practice – is not neutral; it responds to what the practitioners understand or believe to be true about SLA' (2008: 11). The prodigious amount of research in the area is testament to the diversity in this field.

The archive of one of the major journals in this field, *Language Learning & Technology,*[1] lists nearly 800 articles (1997–2013), the majority of them empirical studies. Meta-analyses also reveal the scope of research here. Another major journal on computer-assisted language learning (CALL) technology, *ReCALL,*[2] offers a number of these. The most recent at the time of writing, a meta-analysis of effectiveness studies (Grgurović, Chapelle and Shelley 2013), examined thirty-seven research studies between 1970 and 2006. An earlier one, Felix (2008), synthesised studies relating to the effectiveness of CALL between the years 1981 and 2005 and analysed what they revealed about 'the effectiveness of CALL'. These studies included thirteen meta-analyses which themselves covered several hundred research studies in total, with numbers of subjects exceeding 20,000. The study also included 114 other studies, selected on the basis of the breadth of their application and areas of focus, which were either (1) effect of CALL on learning processes or outcomes, or (2) the impact of technology on writing.

Today, in the second decade of the twenty-first century, the rate of normalisation of technology in society in general has arguably taken us past the point of no return as far as its use in education is concerned. Technology is, as Bax (2003) predicted, quite literally part of the classroom furniture in many parts of the world. Even if some educational institutions are still without resources such as wifi (wireless networking technology), IWBs or computer labs, few are without PCs at least for teacher use –

and fewer students are without that ubiquitous mobile networking device, the mobile phone. (See also Further Reading Two on digital technologies in low-resource ELT contexts). Indeed our students are ably equipped to 'lead the charge' in this environment, as we will illustrate further on. So while we by no means take an uncritical stance as regards the use of technology in the language learning environment, our standpoint is that as teachers and materials developers, we need to be accepting of the changes technology has wrought in the ways we interact and source information. We need to consider the impact this has had on how we learn and even on how we think (see, for example, Thomas 2011), and bear these in mind when seeking to integrate technology into language learning in pedagogically valuable ways. Indeed, Gruba and Hinkelman talk of a 'technological ecology' in which technology permeates the language learning environment (2012: 28), and this requires fresh thinking in the design of materials within it; 'the . . . medium cannot be used in the same way as a conventional classroom setting and both the design of tasks and their implementation need to reflect the affordances[3] of the environment' (Hampel 2006: 118). This chapter avoids a 'tool-centric' perspective (Gruba and Hinkelman 2012: 28) and seeks to illustrate the use of tools, resources and media within pedagogically sound materials design. Finally, we note that although treated separately in this chapter, the use of technology is diffused throughout the chapters of this book, in particular in the designing of tasks for language skills in Chapters 6 and 7. To set the context for the chapter we first look at the relationship with technology of the principal actors in the classroom: the learners.

Technology is renowned for its rapidly changing terminology. In language learning (and elsewhere), terms relating to the use of technology reflected the educational trends of the time. Terms that have endured or are current at the time of writing are:

- **CALL** (computer-assisted language learning): Used from the early 1980s, the 'C' of CALL highlighted the entry of the computer into the language classroom. It has remained the default acronym despite arguments over the years that it inaccurately represents interactions with technology. It is fast becoming obsolete as today we increasingly use digital technologies which run on laptops, tablets and other mobile devices rather than computers.
- **CMC** (computer-mediated communication): Used predominantly in the 1990s, this echoed the prevailing 'communicative' era in language teaching and related to the use of communications technologies (e.g. email and later on, video-conferencing and social networking) in collaborative communication projects (ranging from individual to inter-institutional).
- **ICT** (information and communications technologies): A more general and neutral term which remains in use today.
- **Blended Learning**: A concept current at the time of writing, blended learning refers to a more holistic integration of technology into learning environments: 'a *principled* mix of online and classroom-based activities' (Gruba

and Hinkelman 2012: 46), implemented ideally at institutional/curriculum level.

For more on terminology, see the ICT for Language Teachers (ICT4LT) portal: ict4lt.org

5.2 THE CONTEXT: NORMALISATION OF TECHNOLOGY

In 2012, an organisation called One Laptop per Child (OLPC) delivered several dozen boxed, solar-powered iPads to children aged four to 11 in two remote villages in Ethiopia. The villagers had no previous experience of technology, and were completely illiterate. The children were given the boxes to unpack, and researchers monitored what happened next via an installed wireless connection that the project called the 'Sneakernet'. Results came quickly. Within a few minutes the children had switched the devices on. Within a week they were using an average of 47 installed apps per day. And after a couple of months they had even worked out how to disable a block the researchers had installed to prevent them taking pictures of themselves. So the preliminary conclusion has to be that, yes, young children have innate technology-related learning abilities that most adults patently lack. (Stokes 2012: 2)

The idea that the present younger generation (those born around or after the millennium) are 'hard-wired' for technology is a controversial one: 'Given that the brain is now generally understood to be highly plastic, continually adapting to the input it receives, it is possible that the brains of those who interact with technology frequently will be restructured by that interaction' (Prensky 2009).

Prensky had coined the term 'digital native' in 2001 to describe the degree of comfort that the 'younger generation' have with technology (as opposed to their 'digital immigrant' parents' generation, who acquired these skills as adults), glossing the term as '"native speakers" of the digital language of computers, video games and the Internet'[4] (2001: 1). It has been pointed out that for this generation, digital devices are not perceived as 'technology' but as the ordinary set of tools used in their daily lives, just as telephones and televisions were to the generation before them (Oblinger 2003).

This has crucial implications in the context of language learning, to do with, firstly, students' expectations for the learning environment and, secondly, the skills set that they bring to it. Today's students expect facilities and points of reference within the educational environment that match the ones outside it, and successful learning requires such perceived relevance. Their 'digital literacy' refers to a broad set of skills which are continuously developing in line with technological innovation. These include the ability to retrieve, create and contribute resources, handle information systems and evaluate information, collaborate, network, multi-task, problem-solve, 'code-switch' on various communications (social) media and intuit the functionality of new applications. What is essential is that as teachers we both acknowledge and leverage these skills, in the same way that we do the sets of skills students possess for reading, writing and so on, as discussed in Chapters 6 and 7. Some teachers, as 'digital immigrants', may be aware that they are less comfortable and confident with technology than their students, and this can have an inhibiting effect on using it. However, technology-mediated learning does not involve massive shifts in the teacher's role. Since students, for the most part, will launch readily into the technology being used for the set task with little need for technical support (this is usually sought from peers in any case, if required), the teacher's chief roles remain those of scaffolding language learning and setting pedagogically valid tasks. The latter concern is the business of the rest of this chapter.

Task 5.1
- Draft some of the 'criteria' that you think characterise a 'digital native'. For example:
  - ☐ use of social media (such as Facebook) for socialising and contact
  - ☐ ability to multi-task
- Where would you place yourself on the 'digital native'–'digital immigrant' scale?
- Does this influence your current use of technology in the classroom?

Task 5.2
Language teaching coursebooks have failed to enter the digital age.

🖥 Conduct some online research looking at ELT publishers' web sites (some are given
5.1 below and on the web page) and decide whether you agree with this statement.

Oxford University Press Portal, for sites for *New Headway*, *New English File* and other Oxford University Press coursebooks:
http://elt.oup.com/?cc=globalandselLanguage=en
Cambridge University Press Portal, for sites for *face2face*, *Touchstone*, *English in Use* and other Cambridge University Press coursebooks:
http://www.cambridge.org/ie/elt/catalogue/subjects/item382365/Adult-courses/?site_locale=en_IE
Pearson ELT portal for *Speakout*, *Top Notch* and other Pearson coursebooks:
http://www.pearsonelt.com

Task 5.3
🖥 The organisation EUROCALL (the European Association for Computer-Assisted
5.2 Language Learning) provides a focus for research and practice relating to the use of technology for language learning: http://www.eurocall-languages.org
  It hosts a discussion list (among other social media) which can be joined by non-members and which is an extremely useful and vibrant forum for pooling ideas, research and information: http://www.eurocall-languages.org/about/discussion-list
  Consider joining it to open discussions about technology and language materials and/or other issues that you feel this chapter raises.

5.3 RECONCEPTUALISING MATERIALS FOR THE TECHNOLOGICAL ENVIRONMENT: MATERIALS AS *PRODUCTS* AND MATERIALS AS *PROCESSES*

The advent of technology complexified our conceptualisation of language learning materials. Pre-technology, materials were authored by materials writers or teachers, or were 'authentic', sourced from cultural products like newspapers or literature, and were classically printed texts, pictures or (from the 1970s) audio and audio-visual resources. With Web 2.0 came technologies that afforded online interaction and user-created materials, and these altered the authorship paradigm, as well as blurring the line between materials and the tools that produce them. In the literature on technology in materials development, we witnessed a transition from materials conceived as 'products' – such as courseware, the digital equivalent of a coursebook – to materials conceived as 'processes' – of socialising, networking and collaborating (using tools such as social networking sites (SNSs), wikis and so on). We saw a shift, in other words, 'from the concept of creation of "materials" (as in content created for learners' use), to harnessing and exploitation of "tools"' (Kiddle 2013: 192).

We thus arrive at a broadened definition of materials that embraces technology: 'CALL materials, that is, artefacts produced for language teaching . . . can be taken to include tasks, Web sites, software, courseware, online courses, and virtual learning environments' (Reinders and White 2010: 59). With this expanded definition, we see that in the technological environment, the concept of language learning materials is increasingly conflated with interactivity – and by extension with the *tasks* which so often act as the pedagogical framework for this.

The distinction between product and process referred to above is one also used in the teaching of language skills (see Chapters 6 and 7). In the context of technology, this has been usefully transferred to a distinction between *content* and *process*: '*content* materials as sources of information and data and *process* materials that act as frameworks within which learners can use their communicative abilities' (Reinders and White 2010: 59, italics in original).

MATERIALS AS PRODUCT/CONTENT

The product/content concept depends, critically, on the ability to separate the 'material as product' from the 'tool' that generates it. A useful perspective for this is to view 'materials' as factors of how they are presented rather than how they are generated or delivered (after Mayer 2005, cited in Gruba and Hinkelman 2012). To illustrate this, we can think of a piece of information generated from an interactive resource, a wiki. Once printed out and presented to learners, this becomes as much a 'product' as any handout or coursebook. Its presentation dictates how it is used for learning, unrelated to the technology that generated it.

Using this perspective, materials can be characterised according to where they fall on the spectrum from static through to dynamic (see Figure 5.1). At the static pole would be such materials as textbooks and printouts (newspaper articles,

Figure 5.1   The materials dimension, adapted from Mishan (2013: 217)

web-generated authored material such as quizzes, cartoons, word clouds and so on) ranging through more dynamic materials such as Powerpoint® and Prezi® presentations, then to audio and audio-visual recordings (sourced from YouTube®, for instance), and finally, at the 'dynamic' pole, to 'live' texts being produced synchronously and interactively; instant messaging, texting and so on (Mishan 2013).

Much of the 'static' material here, it should be pointed out, is produced by arguably the most useful and versatile technologies for language teachers: 'content-neutral' tools (Slaouti 2013: 85) such as online generators of web pages, quizzes, cartoons, comic strips and word clouds, not forgetting the humble word processor, which are all in effect 'authoring tools' (see box below). 'Static' material can also be generated from epistemological/information resources; search engines, knowledge databases (e.g. Google, Wikipedia) and corpora (as the following sections describe). All these offer possibilities for teacher-generated materials (as well as learner-generated ones, within interactive tasks; see below).

Edging away from the 'static' end of the materials spectrum, we will now, therefore, examine the case of the use of corpora in language learning.

We are very aware that websites date and change rapidly. Here we list some well-established ones offering authoring tools (software which allows users to design and generate their own materials):

5.3

Cartoon generator	www.goanimate.com
Comic-strip generator	www.makebeliefscomix.com
Mind maps	www.prezi.com (presentation tool)
News lessons creation	www.lingleonline.com
Quiz generator	puzzlemaker.school.discovery.com
WebQuests	www.webquest.org
Website creation	www.weebly.com
	www.google.com/sites
Wiki creation	www.wikispaces.com
Word cloud generator	www.wordle.net

From product to process: corpora and data-driven learning

A 'corpus' is a large collection or database of machine-readable texts involving natural discourse in diverse contexts (Bernardini 2000). Such discourses can be spoken, written, computer-mediated, spontaneous or scripted, and may represent a variety of genres (for example, everyday conversations, lectures, seminars, meetings, radio and television programmes, and essays) (Huang 2011: 481).

Alongside the development of computer corpora, there emerged a technology-based language learning technique known as DDL, most often associated with the work of Tim Johns (e.g. Johns 1991). DDL is defined by Hadley (2002: 99) thus: 'Data-driven learning studies vast databases of English text (corpora) with software programs called concordancers, which isolate common patterns in authentic language samples. It is essentially a new form of grammatical consciousness-raising.'

In DDL, then, a corpus provides the data from which learners discover patterns for themselves. In this sense, as DDL exploits the output of the corpus, we can see it as a product-based technique in the sense we defined it above.

It will be helpful to look at a brief example to clarify the basic nature of DDL. In this case the materials writer (Ivor Timmis) had compiled an 8,000–word corpus of music examiners' reports to use with a group of Spanish music teachers on an English language improvement course. He designed an exercise to help the teachers notice how the word *show*, a very frequent word in this corpus, is typically used in music reports. This involved first using a concordance program to select all the examples of the word *show* in the corpus. The materials writer then chose to edit the concordance printout to focus on examples of *show* + noun; see Figure 5.2.

This is quite a straightforward example of DDL, but it illustrates the fundamental DDL principle of giving learners data and asking them to notice linguistic features in the data, in this case collocations of *show* + noun. One would hope, for example, that the learners might, among other things, notice:

- *show an understanding of*
- *show evidence of*
- *show awareness of*

DDL, then, places responsibility on learners to discover patterns in the data presented. The learning theory behind DDL has much in common with CLT, as it emphasises the role of learners as active constructors rather than passive recipients of knowledge: they need to make inferences from the data. This clearly has implications for the role of teachers, who, in DDL, are seen as facilitators or guides, helping learners to formulate hypotheses and questions and providing support as they investigate corpus data. In our example, the materials writer specified quite closely what the learners had to look for, but it would be possible to leave the question more open. A lot of DDL work focuses on the border area between lexis and grammar. Our example with *show* focused on collocations with nouns and lexical chunks including the word *show*. However, similar data could be used to look at the tense(s) the verb appears in or at the clause structure *show* + adverb + *that*. It should be noted that a consequence of 'letting learners loose' on the data in this way is that conventional views on grammar can be challenged and the data can often show that coursebook descriptions of, for example, the rules for *some* and *any*, the rules of reported speech or 'the three conditionals' are a considerable (over-)simplification of the reality. Boulton (2009) argues that DDL can be useful for focusing on features

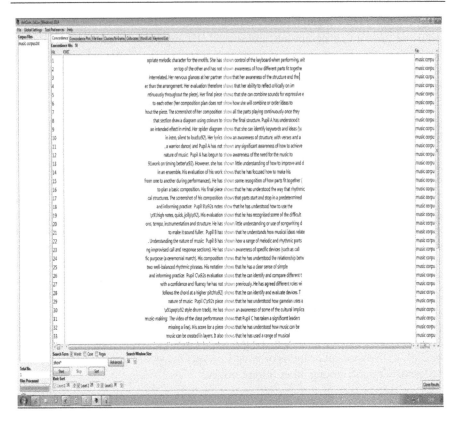

Figure 5.2   *Concordance of* show

Figure 5.3   *Concordance of* enjoy

such as linking adverbials which are often neglected or misrepresented in reference books or coursebooks, while Fox (1998) suggests that DDL can help learners acquire new meanings of words they are already familiar with. In the task in Figure 5.3, for example, we are assuming that the learners are already familiar with the basic meaning of *enjoy*.

The data for DDL can come from two types of corpora:

1. Open-access 'published' general corpora such as the British National Corpus (BNC), the Corpus of Contemporary American English (COCA) or the Michigan

Corpus of Academic Spoken English (MICASE). (See another book in this series, Cutting 2014: chapter 2, for further information on available corpora.)

2. Corpora specifically designed for learning purposes (pedagogic corpora) such as System Aided Compilation and Open Distribution of European Youth Language (SACODEYL), a corpus 'based on structured video interviews with pupils between 13 and 18 years of age . . . annotated and enriched for language learning purposes' (www.sacodeyl.um.es). There is also the BACKBONE corpus, which builds on the work of SACODEYL, and is available at http://projects.ael.uni-tuebingen.de/backbone/moodle

5.4

Pedagogic corpora can also be self-made, as was the case with the music examiners' corpus referred to above, so that language work can be geared closely to the needs of the learners. (See Cutting 2014: chapter 2 for advice on how to build your own corpus.)

The advantages claimed for DDL are that it provides authentic materials for language study, encourages autonomy, develops cognitive and analytical skills and opens learners' minds to the reality of language use. From the practical point of view, corpora and analytical (concordance) software are often freely available online. Open-access corpora such as the BNC and COCA, hosted at http://corpus.byu.edu, have built-in software, and freeware such as antconc at http://www.laurenceanthony.net/antconc_index.html is suitable for DDL purposes.

Unsurprisingly, we must also consider the potential drawbacks of using concordances for pedagogical purposes:

5.5

- Concordance lines may present materials from authentic texts, but they are not natural reading matter; they are often drawn from a variety of contexts which may be obscure to learners.
- The co-text (the text surrounding the target item) may contain infrequent vocabulary and opaque cultural references, and the concordance line itself is often not a complete sentence. DDL may therefore be useful only for more advanced learners.
- DDL may primarily suit analytical learners.

None of these potential weaknesses, however, need be an absolute impediment to DDL. The materials writer can edit the *selection* of concordance lines (rather than the concordance line itself) to omit those which might be culturally or linguistically inaccessible to the learners; and it is usually possible to switch from the concordance line to the wider context from which the line came with a single key stroke. There is also the possibility of using a corpus of graded language, e.g. a corpus made up of graded readers (Allan 2009) or, indeed, a corpus made from the coursebook (Römer 2004) to increase the chances of the learner being familiar with the co-text around the search word in the concordance line. In terms of the 'target market' for DDL, Boulton (2009) goes against the grain and argues that DDL *can* be used effectively with lower-level learners. In sum, we would argue that DDL is a technique which, if used *judiciously*, can be of significant value to *some* learners.

The role of materials in this case can be to introduce learners to DDL and to foster autonomous use of this technique. In the 'ultimate' version of DDL, learners interact directly with the corpus/concordancer, generating their own concordances, frequency lists and so on – pushing DDL towards the process end of the materials spectrum.

Material as product/content: conclusion

Referring back to our schema for 'the materials dimension' (Figure 5.1), therefore, as we move towards the dynamic pole, we transit from materials as content/product to materials as processes/tasks. Social networking, instant messaging or texting, for example, certainly generate a 'product', however ephemeral. However, in order to fulfil a pedagogical purpose, learner use of these technologies needs to be framed within the 'tasks' which have become part of our broadened, technology-inclusive definition of materials as noted above.

MATERIALS AS PROCESSES/TASKS

In this section we will look firstly at the concept of 'material as task' and then illustrate this with a selection of technologies.

The task concept has, of course, been channelled into language pedagogy as TBLT (see Chapter 3), an approach that, fortuitously, synergised with the use of technology for language learning: 'despite being conceived before the digital age, the characterisation of task as free-standing, goal-focused and learner-driven in nature is perfectly in tune with the work modes which have come to be associated with using the internet' (Mishan 2010a: 150).

The identification of the task with technology was reinforced with the rolling out of Web 2.0 in 2004. With its range of participatory media, such as SNSs, blogs, wikis etc., Web 2.0 was seen by some in the technology and language teaching community as an opportunity to explore the educational philosophy of social constructivism 'in action' (see, for example, Thomas 2009). Social constructivism (identified with Vygotsky and other philosophers writing in the early twentieth century) conceived knowledge as being 'socially constructed through interaction'. This could be literally 'played out' by using social collaboration tools – such as social networking, instant messaging or wikis – for learning. The pedagogical framework for this, was, of course, the task. This interplay between educational philosophy, technology and pedagogy emerges thus as a 'tripartite synergy' (see Figure 5.4), a sound basis for our 'materials as tasks' paradigm, which we will now illustrate further.

Materials as processes/tasks: web tools

The 'materials as task' paradigm operating within the digital environment offers infinite possibilities, limited only by our pedagogical imagination (a concept from Chapter 1). We have tried to 'future-proof' the selection of web resources we offer here, by suggesting well-established sites and tools which we anticipate will have a reasonable 'shelf-life'.

A classic technology task is the WebQuest, which is, as its name suggests, an inquiry-oriented research project in which the information is sourced from the web

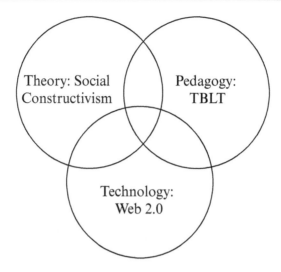

Figure 5.4   The 'tripartite synergy' between social constructivism, TBLT and Web 2.0

Introduction	Presents central challenge of the WebQuest
Task description	Describes task goal; transform information sources to solve a problem, design a product, write a journal article etc.
Task process	Step-by-step task procedure Includes suggested web resources to fulfil the task
Evaluation	Rubrics for students and teachers to use to assess performance and findings
Conclusion	Summary of task achievement

Figure 5.5   WebQuest structure drawn from webquest.org

and usually set to be carried out in groups. The WebQuest can be seen, therefore, to encapsulate TBLT in an online environment, and the portal webquest.org provides a task template (see Figure 5.5) reminiscent of that from TBLT. This template is for teachers (or learners) to construct a 'ready-to-go' WebQuest which is then saved on the database for public use.

The structural simplicity of the WebQuest makes it usable and flexible and argu-ably belies its theoretical complexity. For although as a concept it predates Web 2.0's collaborative tools (the WebQuest can be dated to the late 1990s), it is seen as a 'powerful means for supporting the principles of constructivism' (Zlatkovska 2010: 19), in the sense that group collaboration and 'knowledge-building' are central to its operation.

Turning to 'neutral' tools not designed with pedagogy in mind, these can be exploited in two ways: for their potential for interactivity or for user generation of content – or, frequently, both. Using a comic-strip generator, for example (such as makebeliefscomix.com), students can work together to create a comic for their peers,

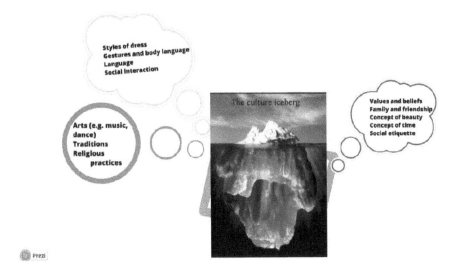

Figure 5.6   ESOL class brainstorming on 'culture', generated on Prezi

perhaps with speech bubbles to fill in, or a satirical cartoon to stimulate discussion; this can be uploaded to a virtual learning environment (VLE), wiki, blog or web page, or printed, and so be accessed by their companions. Thus we have material as an interactive task (creating a comic/cartoon) and material as a product. A similar task procedure can be followed for such things as:

- vocabulary quizzes (using, for instance, puzzlemaker.school.discovery.com)
- word clouds (wordle.net) used, for example, for genre analysis
- mind maps (e.g. prezi.com) for brainstorming language or concepts and so on

Figure 5.6 illustrates a mind map for the concept of 'culture' brainstormed by a group of trainee teachers of English for speakers of other languages (ESOL), and generated as a mind map on the presentation software Prezi.

From the TBLT theoretical standpoint (see Chapter 3), the learning gain from these types of tasks comes less from completing tasks set for each other per se than from the student interaction and engagement in devising and creating materials, and from the empowerment this authorship engenders. This is also the case, of course, in using social media, to which we now turn.

Materials as processes/tasks: social media – 'I share therefore I am'

Social media have radically altered the behaviour patterns of the generation who use them to network, socialise and, uniquely, share the everyday minutiae of their private lives in the public domain. Language educators were quick to spot the potential of tapping into these ready-made social spaces. As we noted above, from the perspective of educational philosophy, social media are an extraordinary arena for actualising social constructivist theory, which sees knowledge as 'collaboratively constructed'. For this to be 'activated', tasks and materials using social media need to cultivate interaction, cross-fertilisation of ideas and creativity, and finally, genuine sharing with the community, either at a restricted level (e.g. on a VLE) or on the web.

It is important not to be overly idealistic, however; practitioners also find themselves 'caught in a bind' with respect to the boundaries between private and educational spaces (see Schwartz 2009, for instance) (there are the same reservations about use of mobile devices: see below). The way out of this bind, using a separate SNS (a popular one for educational use is edmodo.com), can make for somewhat contrived or limited interactions.

This reservation apart, one valuable aspect of social media that can be exploited in language learning is that they are skewed towards the written mode. The unique affordances of communications media – email, blogging, Facebooking, instant messaging, online chat, texting and so on – mean that they capture that hitherto ephemeral mode, speech. Exchanges on these media are effectively 'written conversations' (although each medium tends to have some distinctive features) allowing us to 'see' (and write) words and expressions that are, or were, characteristically spoken. Layered on to this are paralinguistic features (emoticons such as the 'like' symbol/link on YouTube and Facebook and so on) which simulate the 'multi-modal' aspect of face-to-face communication. With the exception of online chat, however, communication on these media is asynchronous (and thus distinct from face-to-face conversation), slowing the pace of the interactions. Freedom from pressure for the instant response expected in face-to-face conversations allows more 'preparation time', a very useful aspect for learners. It also makes for conversational 'turns' that have more content than face-to-face ones, which tend to include more backchannels (supportive expressions such as 'oh!', 'really?' and 'right').[5]

While acknowledging that the language produced as a written trace of interactions does seem somewhat artificial when viewed in isolation from the circumstances of its production (this may be the impression from the Facebook dialogue in Figure 5.7), it can nevertheless be profitably used as content material (at the static end of the materials continuum; see Figure 5.1 above). We invite you to explore this in Task 5.4.

Task 5.4

Using Figure 5.7 as a sample, or your own Facebook page if you have one, think about the potential for using Facebook dialogues in the language classroom for materials for:

- **genre analysis**: e.g. identifying characteristics of online writing (e.g. spoken register *cheers mate*)
- **discourse analysis**: e.g. tracing turn-taking between participants, identifying how interactants indicate turns, identifying backchannelling
- **analysis of orthographical features**: paralinguistic use of punctuation, emoticons and capitalisation

---

June Parsons* Perhaps could be fun for a holiday with the gang and all our little people next summer?!....

[web link and photo]

Like · · Share
Patricia Stokes and **3 others** like this.

Tina Curtin   Ooh yes very nice. & it looks a bit like teletubby land too!

Sunday at 19:19 via mobile · Like

Jake Sands hello

Sunday at 20:13 via mobile · Like

June Parsons   That's what I meant by the little people Tina...
Sunday at 20:22 via mobile · Like

Patricia Stokes i thought you meant me.

Sunday at 20:45 · Like

June Parsons   No you're way less annoying than a teletubby
Sunday at 22:03 via mobile · Like

Patricia Stokes cheers mate.

Yesterday at 08:09 · Like

*Names have been changed

Figure 5.7   Sample postings on Facebook

Materials as processes/tasks: digital tools

Task-based formats can also frame use of the device that has been creating a lot of interest in language pedagogy since the mid-1990s: the mobile phone. Mobile learning, also termed m-learning, or mobile-assisted language learning (MALL), has become a subfield in its own right as the language teaching profession 'cashes in' on the almost blanket possession of the mobile phone. By 2011, 87 per cent of the world's population owned a mobile phone (statistics from MobiThinking n.d.), and significantly some of the most technology-deprived areas of the world have the highest rates of mobile phone growth (e.g. Africa and Bangladesh). While ELT publishers have started producing stand-alone or coursebook-related apps, the attraction of the device for many teachers is the potential offered by its core applications, e.g. messaging, phoning, visual and audio recording (particularly since smartphones or iPads are not the global norm yet). Such applications can be used at the most basic level for tasks conceived for other media. The text application can be used for that most traditional language exercise, dictation (Hockly 2013a: 82), for example, then given a TBLT 'twist' if the dictation contains an instruction or sets a task. Texting can also be used to circulate other classic task types: questionnaires or surveys. Similarly, the classic activity of bringing 'family' photographs to class as 'icebreakers' can be recast to use the student's phone photo gallery, the task being to observe specific criteria such as 'find a picture of . . . a pet . . . a family member . . . a celebration . . . someone doing a sport . . .', and share them with a partner (Hockly 2013b). But the capacities of today's mobile devices of course also allow for modifying and ultimately transforming what has been done before. Hockly (2013b) suggests a classic task type, a treasure hunt, using clues encoded in barcodes (QR, quick response codes) (read via a downloaded QR app) and/or using the global positioning system, GPS. The popular 'microblogging' service Twitter offers both social networking opportunities and linguistic challenges. A 'quick and dirty' task is to ask learners to create their own Twitter account and compete as to who can attract the most 'followers'. Expressing ideas concisely in 140 characters offers a sort of 'creativity through constraint' paradox (a similar principle to that of the haiku): doctoral students in University College Cork, Ireland, for example, were challenged to synthesise their theses in a 'tweet'.[6] Use of the mobile device for learning comes with a 'health warning', however. The veritable 'relationship' people have with their mobile phones (McNamara 2011; Godwin-Jones 2011) means that teachers might need to be wary of crossing the divide between the personal and the pedagogic.

Task 5.5
Discuss with a partner or consider this question yourself, completing the speech bubbles in Figure 5.8.

Figure 5.8   Discussion: technology and 'materials', generated on www.makebeliefscomix.com.

Task 5.6
It is difficult to define what is meant by the term 'materials' in the technological dimension, particularly with the Web 2.0 affordances of user interfaces such as wikis, SNSs and other social media forums, where it is hard to separate the 'material' from the 'tool' that generates it.

Consider/discuss this, if possible with references to 'technology-based' materials/ tasks you are familiar with.

5.4 A TEMPLATE FOR MATERIALS USING TECHNOLOGY

The unique interactional features of mobile devices and apps, Web 2.0 tools and social media all feed into the design of our extended definition of materials for the digital age. Extrapolating from the suggestions in this section and drawing, of course, on the basic task-based model which is part of the theoretical framework for this chapter, we arrive at the set of materials design parameters shown in Figure 5.9.

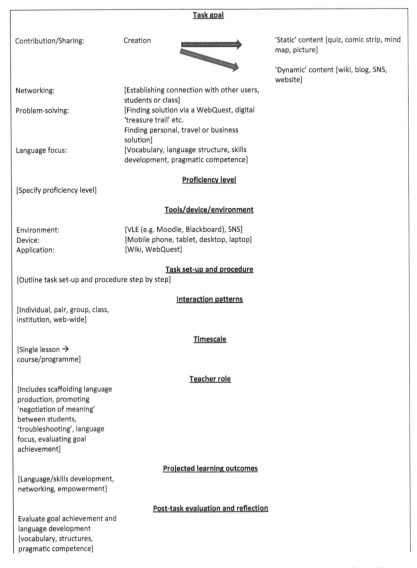

Task goal

| Contribution/Sharing: | Creation | 'Static' content [quiz, comic strip, mind map, picture] |
| | | 'Dynamic' content [wiki, blog, SNS, website] |

Networking:	[Establishing connection with other users, students or class]
Problem-solving:	[Finding solution via a WebQuest, digital 'treasure trail' etc. Finding personal, travel or business solution]
Language focus:	[Vocabulary, language structure, skills development, pragmatic competence]

Proficiency level

[Specify proficiency level]

Tools/device/environment

Environment:	[VLE (e.g. Moodle, Blackboard), SNS]
Device:	[Mobile phone, tablet, desktop, laptop]
Application:	[Wiki, WebQuest]

Task set-up and procedure

[Outline task set-up and procedure step by step]

Interaction patterns

[Individual, pair, group, class, institution, web-wide]

Timescale

[Single lesson → course/programme]

Teacher role

[Includes scaffolding language production, promoting 'negotiation of meaning' between students, 'troubleshooting', language focus, evaluating goal achievement]

Projected learning outcomes

[Language/skills development, networking, empowerment]

Post-task evaluation and reflection

Evaluate goal achievement and language development [vocabulary, structures, pragmatic competence]

Figure 5.9   Parameters for the design of materials using digital media
Examples and notes are given in brackets.

Task 5.7

Using these parameters, and bearing in mind the basic TBLT framework (see also web page activity 3.6 for Chapter 3), draft a piece of material using a web tool or digital app with which you are familiar. It might be useful to look at Chapter 9 where task frameworks are discussed in fuller detail. A worked example can be found in Figure 5.10 on the web page.

5.6

Task 5.8

An article by Doughty and Long (2003b) in the online journal *Language Learning & Technology* situates the use technologies for language teaching on a TBLT methodological basis, and can be accessed at http://llt.msu.edu/vol7num3/doughty/default. html

Consider the potential for following the authors' 'ten methodological principles' of TBLT' in digital materials which you design.

Task 5.9

Look back at the section 'From product to process: corpora and data-driven learning'. Produce a trial piece of DDL material either modelled on Figures 5.2 and 5.3 in that section, or using other ideas suggested there. Choose from the corpora available through the corpus portal http://corpus.byu.edu or any others suggested in the section.

5.5 FURTHER READING ONE

Kiddle, T. (2013). Developing digital language learning materials. In B. Tomlinson (ed.), *Developing Materials for Language Teaching* (pp. 189–206). London: Bloomsbury.

As we have pointed out in our chapter, the concept of language learning material has always been tricky to define in the technological environment. However, Kiddle confidently steers a course towards describing digital materials from the viewpoint of their being created by teachers (in the first section), by learners (in the second section) and lastly by publishers.

By positioning his chapter at the current leading edge of technology, Kiddle has endeavoured to 'future-proof' it (as far as this is possible in such a rapidly evolving industry), and he situates it at the 'border-crossing between the ages of Web 2.0 and Web 3.0' (p. 189) (which he explains is a more 'intelligent', user-responsive web). True to the digital mode indicated in his title, Kiddle provides QR codes (i.e. phone-readable barcodes) to enable instant access to websites and tools referenced.

We have already alluded to Kiddle's expanded 'definition' of materials in the digital environment as coinciding with ours:

> Another feature of the development of digital educational (and non-educational) approaches in recent years is a shift from the concept of creation of 'materials' (as in content created for learners' use) to harnessing and exploitation of 'tools', both those initially designed for language learning and teaching, and those

adopted and adapted from an alternative intended use. (p. 192)

He stresses that the focus of the chapter is on the innovative aspect of what digital tools have to offer, so he looks primarily at 'those tools or materials which can be said to truly exploit a digital mode or media in their design or delivery' (ibid.). He therefore selects tools in which the technology alters our conceptions of 'text' and working with it. These include the 'infinite canvas' concept underlying Prezi, the Swype keyboard (swype.com) where the user swipes across the keyboard instead of pressing individual keys, intelligent tools which personalise data collection and use (e.g. the dictionary lingro.com) and the IWB.

The IWB is only one among the number of tools discussed in the first, 'teacher-created digital materials' section. In terms of pedagogy, this section positions itself within a blended learning framework (the most recent 'approach' to frame the use of technology for language learning; see also above), which Kiddle usefully quantifies as involving '20 per cent to 79 per cent of course time spent online' (p. 195), and which is allied, as he indicates, to the VLE.

A popular model for the stages of adoption of technology is given in this section too; we cite it here as it encapsulates this progression and offers a recognisable (if aspirational!) picture for most technology-adopters;

> – Infusion – the spread of the use of technology into existing pedagogical practice, with learners as passive observers of the tool.
> – Integration – the technology embedded in the curriculum and attention paid to how it can enhance learning goals. Learners are more active participants.
> – Transformation – the technology adds value to the learning process. Learners are centrally involved in an enquiry-based construction of knowledge. (Burden 2002, cited in Kiddle 2013: 197)

Of the three sections of Kiddle's chapter, the second, 'student-created digital materials', has the most to do with creation of content. Here, the author suggests the advantages of exploiting Web 2.0's potential for user-generated content in terms of cultivating autonomy and self-expression and of participation in social frameworks/communities of practice. As we do in this chapter, he stresses the need for pedagogical parameters:

> Central to the effective implementation of such resources in a language teaching programme are the establishment of parameters – of task, content, nature of collaboration, timeframes etc. – as well as principled provision of feedback which respects the learners' ownership of content and rights over its creation, while focussing usefully and efficiently on the language learning aims.
> (p. 199)

It is interesting that Kiddle seems constrained (by space?) from developing much on the use of mobile devices, which we have suggested may well be 'the way forward' in this area (see also Further Reading Two), although he acknowledges that 'the importance of mobile learning opportunities as an increasingly inclusive form of access to digital materials has been highlighted' (p. 200).

In the final section, on publisher/professionally created digital materials, Kiddle gives us the plight of the ELT publisher twenty-first-century style, once again caught out by publishing time delays:

> There is a sense in which one can feel sympathy for large ELT publishers as we move through the second decade of the twenty-first century, for they face a perhaps unprecedented challenge in the history of production of language teaching materials. They are faced with the demands of the consumer marketplace for digital content, yet by the time the required investment has been put in place . . . the game has changed. (p. 201)

At the end of a litany of the ELT industry's digital woes, Kiddle puts his concerns for technological materials into the context of global materials production, and we recognise a familiar refrain:

> A final challenge . . . is the need to balance global approaches to English and its varieties, and content for a global market, with the strengths of material designed and developed for local contexts, cultures, needs and plurilingual influences. (p. 201)

Finally, in his conclusion, Kiddle 'future-proofs' the chapter by pointing to some of the technological innovations which he predicts will make inroads into language learning. The first is Web 3.0, which is fairly imminent at the time of writing. Two aspects of the new platform are seen as being keenly relevant to language learning. The first is its capacity for 'learning analytics' (p. 202), that is, for collating data about the individual user and thus for personalising content (we already see this in its infancy on sites such as Amazon, which pulls up books, DVDs and so on tailored to your tastes based on previous viewings and purchases). Web 3.0's 'geospatial' capacity is the second aspect, in which:

> Location is a determining factor in content selection . . . this may mean that topic areas, text content and language type are selected according to learner location . . . It may also allow for cultural differences in learner attitudes to digital learning. (p. 202)

This feature of Web 3.0 may thus help us bridge the digital divide so often alluded to that separates the first and third worlds. The platform also offers augmented reality or AR, which layers digital content over real-world content via a smartphone or tablet; the author gives the example of a bringing a textbook to life by viewing it through a digital device. Other features of Web 3.0 with potential for language learning are increased access to voice recognition software and software that responds to gestures, movement, facial expression and sound: 'TPR for the digital age, anyone?' quips Kiddle. (TPR refers to the methodology of total physical response, in which learners learn language through connecting it with physical action; see, for example, Spiro 2013.)

Kiddle grounds his chapter in one of the classic concerns about the use of technology in pedagogy, a reservation that 'technological innovation can often outpace pedagogical consolidation' (p. 203), and he also alludes to more fundamental warnings about the effect of technology on a generation of digital natives in terms of their 'attention span, writing and face-to-face communication' (ibid.). However, his main thrust is towards technology as an innovative force for language pedagogy: 'Developers and users of digital materials need to be conscious of these concerns as they strive for technology use which adds something different, and is equally or more effective, to the learning process' (ibid.).

Task 5.10
Consider these three concerns expressed in Kiddle's chapter (2013: 203):

Technological innovation can often outpace pedagogical consolidation.

Students [have] issues with their attention span, writing and face-to-face communication.

Developers and users of digital materials need to be conscious of these concerns as they strive for technology use which adds something different, and is equally or more effective, to the learning process.

Task 5.11
Conduct some of your own research to find journal articles or books that deal with these issues. Two recommended online journals and a relevant project on designing materials for IWBs can be found at:

5.7

- *Language Learning & Technology*: llt.msu.edu
- *ReCALL*: www.eurocall-languages.org/publications/recall
- The ITILT (Interactive Technologies in Language Teaching) project: https://www. academia.edu/2983386/Designing_IWB_Resources_for_Language_Teaching_ The_ITILT_Project

5.6 FURTHER READING TWO

Hockly, N. (2014). Digital technologies in low-resource ELT contexts. *ELT Journal,* 68(1): 79–84.
This article has been selected for a number of reasons, not least because it is from one of the main names publishing on digital technology in language teaching today. It was also selected because it illustrates 'technology for all', as its title suggests, describing possibilities for and experiences of technology use in low-resource contexts. Thirdly, there is a lot on mobile phone use, which is seen as 'obviating the need for expensive hardware and infrastructure' (p. 81) and which we consider at the leading

edge, in terms of hardware, for the language pedagogy of the future. Finally, it serves as a launching point for readers to consider initiatives in their own contexts, either existing or future ones.

It is notable that the core concerns for the effective deployment of technologies in diverse global contexts remain consistent with those stressed with regard to language learning materials throughout this book: 'the cultural appropriacy of materials and approaches' and correspondingly, 'using appropriate technologies' (p. 80).

In this article, Hockly identifies and describes three different levels of digital initiatives within low-resource contexts: national projects, institution-led projects and projects carried out by individual teachers.

Among the national projects, we have the OLPC initiative (already mentioned in this chapter) being implemented in many countries, from Uruguay, Argentina and Afghanistan to Venezuela, Nepal and Rwanda. Other projects are funded by diverse stakeholders, such as non-governmental organisations, ministries of education, hardware and/or software providers, mobile telephone companies, and educational institutions such as the British Council or universities (p. 80). The agendas of such projects include 'social justice' (p. 81), children's literacy (the MILLEE project in India) and providing technology access for disadvantaged women (the BBC Janala project). All of these projects use mobile devices for reasons given above. However, Hockly notes that the older technologies of television and radio still have significant impact in the third world, especially in Africa, and that British Council radio programmes are still listened to by millions of English language learners (p. 81).

At the institutional level, technology is often introduced within a blended format and delivered by an existing VLE, but the impulse for this can be pragmatic (e.g. in Egypt, political tension dissuading students from attending classes, or based on sheer class numbers, as in a Nigerian project) as well as pedagogic.

As for individual-level projects, Hockly refers to an assortment of case studies based variously in the Middle East, Sudan, Nigeria and Brazil, and refers the reader to other compilations of case studies in Egbert (2010) and Motteram (2013) and on the Oxford University Press website.

Significantly, Hockly expresses concerns in her conclusions that chime with those in Kiddle's chapter – and with the ethos of this book:

> Whatever their scale, a number of issues need to be borne in mind if the deployment of digital technologies in low-resource contexts is to be effective . . . the choice of not just hardware and software but the teaching and learning approach and the instructional design of materials must be aligned to the reality of the local cultural and educational contexts. Clearly there is no single technology that 'works best' in low-resource contexts. As in any context, myriad factors such as (lack of) teacher training, student motivation, class size, limited class time, educational beliefs, access to resources, culturally appropriate materials, culturally sensitive approaches, and even political realities will determine how to work most effectively with digital technologies. (p. 83)

Task 5.12

- Share with others any technology initiatives in your own contexts which work at national, institutional or individual level.
- Using the article as a starting point, sketch out an idea for an initiative at any of the above levels.

Task 5.13

5.8

Look through the table of contents of the special issue of *Language Teaching & Technology* on MALL for one or more ideas that you consider would be doable/ adaptable for your own teaching context: http://llt.msu.edu/issues/october2013/index.html

5.7 CONCLUSION

This chapter has sought to address the conceptual, pedagogical and practical issues involved in reconciling technology (ephemeral, interactive, unmediated and with freedom of authorship) with our traditional concept of language learning materials (tangible and centrally authored/mediated). We have done this by:

- extending the notion of materials to embrace the digital environment
- appropriating the distinction between product and process used elsewhere in pedagogy and extending it to apply to materials, now conceived as ranging from traditional physical products to interactions
- adopting the construct of 'task' as the basis of materials, marrying this (by now) traditional pedagogical concept to the affordances of technology
- suggesting Web 2.0 applications for use on the spectrum from authored materials to tasks and interactions
- providing a template with parameters for the design of materials using digital media

5.8 ADDITIONAL READINGS

Chapelle, C. (2010). The spread of computer-assisted language learning. *Language Teaching*, 43(1): 66–74.

The starting point for this seminal theoretical paper on CALL is the difficulty that we have put at the centre of our chapter: that of drawing a 'clear distinction between CALL and other language materials'. Chapelle attributes this to the 'vertical' spread of CALL (through the language curriculum). Part of the interest of the paper for us in the field of materials design is that Chapelle draws together strands which we have also threaded through this book: 'The three lessons prompted by work in CALL suggest directions for expanding perspectives from applied linguistics to the practice of materials development and evaluation.'

Dudeney, G., Hockly, N. and Pegrum, M. (2013). *Digital Literacies*. Harlow: Pearson Education.

Starting from the premise that 'Reading is an unnatural act; we are no more evolved to read books than we are to use computers' (Shirky 2010, cited in Dudeney et al. 2013: 3), Dudeney et al. build on our learners' digital literacy (defined as 'the individual and social skills needed to effectively interpret, manage, share and create meaning in the growing range of digital communication channels' (p. 2)) to bring us a valuable 'handbook' for the teacher integrating technology into the classroom. The book combines a strong theoretical background with a large set of clearly described and intriguingly titled activities ('Footprints in the wire', 'Envisioning the facts') which use the full range of Web 2.0 tools as well as mobile devices.

Farr, F. and Murray, L. (forthcoming). *The Routledge Handbook of Language Learning and Technology*. London: Routledge.
This is an admirably well-rounded and comprehensive volume, offering both theoretical and practical perspectives on the use of technology in language learning. In its forty-odd chapters it covers collaborative technologies for language learning, corpora and DDL, digital gaming and CALL tools while also including chapters setting the historical and conceptual underpinnings of the use of technology in language learning.

Hampel, R. (2006). Rethinking task design for the digital age: a framework for language teaching and learning in a synchronous online environment. *ReCALL*, 18(1): 105–21.
This article combines well-argued theory with pedagogy and practical models for task design, providing a very useful and usable introduction to the principles of designing digital materials/tasks.

Thomas, M. and Reinders, H. (eds) (2010). *Task-Based Language Learning and Teaching with Technology*. London: Continuum.
Following quickly on the heels of Thomas's previous volume, *Handbook of Research on Web 2.0 and Second Language Learning* (2009), this one focuses on the potential of using Web 2.0 tools in task-based formats, thus consolidating the association of technology with this methodology. It gives us both theoretical and empirical perspectives on the technology-mediated task, with contributions from many familiar names in the field such as Ellis, Hampel, Hauck, Hegelheimer and Motteram.

NOTES

1. *Language Learning & Technology* is a refereed online journal, available at llt.msu. edu
2. *ReCALL* is a refereed online journal published by Cambridge University Press: www.eurocall-languages.org/publications/recall
3. The term 'affordances' is commonly used in the context of technology to refer to the characteristics (of an app or other piece of software) which allow or enable the performance of an action.

4. In later writings (2009), Prensky argued that with time, we will all be digital natives, evolving into what he termed 'Homo sapiens digital'.

5. Although backchannels play an essential role in conversation; see McCarthy (2003).

6. The doctoral showcase website set this challenge to its doctoral students: 'We are looking for [University College Cork's] best **Tweesis**. This one is simple – just describe your thesis work in 140 characters maximum in such a way that anyone can understand what you are doing' (www.ucc.ie/en/graduatestudies/current/showcase, retrieved 14 June 2013).

6

MATERIALS TO DEVELOP READING AND LISTENING SKILLS

6.1 INTRODUCTION

The integration and 'blending' of resources, media and approaches has been a thread running through this book as being fundamental to effective language learning materials. This is especially true of language skills, traditionally categorised broadly as the 'macro-skills' of reading, writing, speaking and listening, which in learning tasks, as in other aspects of our daily lives, are rarely used in isolation. Frameworks for combining skills within materials/tasks will be discussed in Chapter 9. This chapter and the next lay the groundwork for that, by focusing on the individual aspects of each skill in turn. We emphasise immediately that this separate treatment is not something that should or can be transferred to teaching or task design (other than in materials for dedicated skills training, such as academic writing programmes). This is in line with contemporary approaches to teaching language skills, operating within prevailing pedagogies (communicative, task-based) all tending towards integrated and multi-skilled instructional models (Hinkel 2006: 113); and this is corroborated in the more integrated skills approaches taken in many of the coursebooks since the early 2000s.

It is useful to begin by defining our core terms, starting with language 'skills' and 'strategies'. We might distinguish the two (often, confusingly, used interchangeably) by defining skills as 'automatic actions that . . . usually occur without awareness of the components or control involved' (Afflerbach, Pearson and Scott 2008: 348). A skill automatically used when reading, for example, is use of one's 'world knowledge' to help make sense of the text. So while we cannot 'teach' skills exactly, we can design materials which provide opportunities for skills to be practised and eventually automated. We can, in other words, teach *strategies*: conscious procedures which are oriented towards the goal of making learning more efficient and effective (Oxford and Crookall 1989). For example, when listening, we might suggest to learners that they try to ignore any redundancy they notice (repetition, paraphrasing) to gain extra 'processing time'. Some terminological inconsistency in the use of the two words might be attributed to the fact that there is an effective overlap between them, since with practice, consciously used strategies can become automated as skills (Learned, Stockdill and Moje 2011).

Another important distinction with implications for materials design is that between the skills being practised and the resource providing the context for this practice. The resource might be in any medium: written, audio or audio-visual input and so on. What should be borne in mind is that this resource does not need to be in a medium corresponding to the skill(s) practised: so a written text, for example, may not necessarily be used to 'practise' reading skills, but perhaps to practise those associated with speaking or writing. This is frequently the case in coursebooks; 'writing' activities, for instance, are often supported by a written model (which has to be read). Varied combinations of resources and skills can make for imaginative materials. This notwithstanding, there can be a tendency in coursebooks (and teacher-produced materials emulating them) to extend this principle to 'disguising' other foci, notably grammar work, as skills practice. Sections headed 'reading' and 'listening', for example, often require learners to use their skills with the rather narrow focus of spotting or practising grammar forms.

This raises the broader question as to whether 'skills' work in materials and coursebooks is actually designed to help students hone skills, or to accumulate lexical and grammatical knowledge. Are 'skills', in other words, often no more than 'flags of convenience' for teachers and materials writers? The breakdown into four macroskills would seem somewhat over-simplistic and over-exclusive in any case. Why did it exclude culture, for example, famously proclaimed by Kramsch as a 'fifth skill' (1993)?[1] All this provides some 'food for thought' while reading this and the following chapter.

6.2 MATERIALS TO DEVELOP READING SKILLS

Task 6.1

- Look at this extract from a coursebook (Oxenden and Latham-Koenig 2008: 15) which has the rubric 'Reading'.
- Match the various learning objectives (inferred from the activities in the extract) to the activities set. The first one has been done as an example:
  - ☐ *To engage cognitive skills, e.g. evaluating* – activity (b)
  - ☐ *To practise reading skills (scanning, reading for main ideas)* –
  - ☐ *As a 'vehicle' for introducing new vocabulary items* –
  - ☐ *To prompt another skill (speaking, discussion)* –
- Add any other learning objectives you perceive, and match these to the activities.

You may notice that the inferred objectives are quite varied in these 'reading' materials, not all of them having strictly to do with practising reading skills or strategies.

The variation in the list in Task 6.1 highlights the principle that in developing materials, and in forming our learning objectives, we need to be aware of the resource/skill distinction made above. Our 'input' material may be in the written mode as in this case (i.e. a reading passage) but this does not limit our learning objectives to developing reading skills only, or to achieving outcomes that depend specifically on them. To look at it from the opposite perspective, 'using a text does not necessarily equal teaching reading' (Williams 1986: 45).

In Figure 6.2, we have schematised the various learning objectives we can build

6 READING

a What symptoms do people have when they feel stressed?

b Which *three* of these things do you think are the most stressful? Number them 1–3 (1 = the most stressful) and compare with a partner.

☐ Packing for a trip at the last minute.
☐ Being stuck in a traffic jam when you have an appointment.
☐ Writing a report for your boss when you don't have much time to finish it.
☐ Running for a bus or train.
☐ Looking after a family member who has a chronic illness.
☐ Shopping in your lunch break.
☐ Programming a DVD player using the instruction manual.

c Read the article once quite quickly and then tick (✔) the activities that are bad for your health. What does the article say about the others?

d Read the article again more slowly. Circle the correct *main idea* for each paragraph.
1 a Being in traffic jams is bad for our health.
  b Some people think that not all kinds of stress are bad for us.
  c Doctors don't agree how we can reduce our levels of stress.
2 a Young people suffer more from stress than older people.
  b Alzheimer's is one of the illnesses many old people suffer from.
  c Good stress stops us from getting ill.
3 a Situations which produce good stress are always short term.
  b Some stress can make our cells stronger.
  c Too much protein can make us ill.
4 a We need some stress to exercise our cells' self-repair mechanism.
  b Doing physical exercise makes us feel less stressed.
  c Packing your suitcase in a hurry is an example of good stress.

e Complete the sentences using words from the article.
1 When we try to do less of something, we try to c_____ d_____ (paragraph 1).
2 An illness that you have for a very long time is called a c_____ illness (1).
3 Something which is good for us is b_____ (2).
4 The verb to make something stronger is s_____ (2).
5 Our body is made up of millions of c_____ (2).
6 When we treat our body badly we d_____ it (3).
7 Another word for illness is d_____ (3).
8 Something which is bad for us is h_____ (3).
9 Doing exercise helps to make our m_____ bigger and stronger (4).

f Use your dictionary to check the pronunciation of the words in e.

g Discuss these questions with a partner.
1 Do you agree with what you have read in this article? Why (not)?
2 What kinds of 'good stress' do you have in your life?
3 What other health stories have you heard about recently? Do you pay much attention to them? Do you believe them?

○ p.157 *Phrasal verbs in context File 1.*

Get stressed, stay young

1 For decades doctors have warned us about the dangers of stress and have given us advice about how to cut down our stress levels. Everyone agrees that long-term stress, for example having to look after someone who has a chronic illness, or stressful situations where there is nothing we can do, for example being stuck in a traffic jam, is bad for our health and should be avoided whenever possible. However, some medical experts now believe that certain kinds of stress may actually be good for us.

2 Dr Marios Kyriazis, an anti-ageing expert, claims that what he calls 'good stress' is beneficial to our health and may, in fact, help us stay young and attractive and even live longer. Dr Kyriazis says that 'good stress' can strengthen our natural defences which protect us from illnesses common among older people, such as Alzheimer's, arthritis, and heart problems. He believes that 'good stress' can increase the production of the proteins that help to repair the body's cells, including brain cells.

3 According to Dr Kyriazis, running for a bus or having to work to a deadline are examples of 'good stress', that is situations with short-term, low or moderate stress. The stress usually makes us react quickly and efficiently, and gives us a sense of achievement – we did it! However, in both these situations, the stress damages the cells in our body or brain and they start to break down. But then the cells' own repair mechanism 'switches on' and it produces proteins which repair the damaged cells and remove harmful chemicals that can gradually cause disease. In fact, the body's response is greater than is needed to repair the damage, so it actually makes the cells stronger than they were before.

4 'As the body gets older, this self-repair mechanism of the cells starts to slow down,' says Dr Kyriazis. 'The best way to keep the process working efficiently is to 'exercise' it, in the same way you would exercise your muscles to keep them strong. This means having a certain amount of stress in our lives.' Other stressful activities that Kyriazis recommends as being good stress include redecorating a room in your house over a weekend, packing your suitcase in a hurry to reach the airport on time, shopping for a dinner party during your lunch break or programming your DVD or video recorder by following the instruction manual.

So next time your boss tells you that she wants to see that report finished and on her desk in 45 minutes, don't panic; just think of it as 'good stress' which will have benefits for your long-term health!

From *The Times*

1C 15

Figure 6.1   Extract from New English File: Upper Intermediate Student's Book *(Oxenden and Latham-Koenig 2008b: 15)*

RESOURCE: READING PASSAGE Objectives			
To practise reading skills and strategies	To promote skills and strategies involved in *extensive* reading	To prompt use of other skill(s), e.g. *writing* and/or *speaking*, and/or to prompt interaction	To present vocabulary or grammatical structures
	Chapter 6	Chapters 8 and 9	

Figure 6.2   Reading: objectives

into use of a reading passage and highlighted those that we will deal with in this chapter (the shaded areas) and those that are left to later ones.

Figure 6.2 will provide the baseline for the rest of this section on developing materials for reading skills (with some cross-references to listening skills as well). As indicated above, we will keep our focus on reading skills development and approaches/ issues surrounding these, leaving the other two objectives noted in Figure 6.2, in which a reading passage is used for multi-skills/tasks, vocabulary building or form-focused work, to where they are treated in detail, in Chapter 8 and Chapter 9.

The skill of reading is more important than ever in a digital age in which written text is the predominant mode of communication. Whether the source is digital or print, reading, as Maley and Prowse remind us, 'involves the most incredibly complex, interrelated set of brain processes humans ever have to engage in', involving;

> decoding visual squiggles on paper, making connections between these and sounds, understanding the literal meanings of the words, then interpreting the writer's intentions, situating the text in a linguistic and social context, relating what we read to what we have read earlier in the text, and to our previous world knowledge, visualising and engaging in inner dialogue with ourselves, asking questions – and all more or less simultaneously. (Maley and Prowse 2013: 165)

Having acquired these skills and strategies in reading in their L1, the degree to which learners can transfer them to reading in the L2 is a topic hotly debated in reading research. Is reading comprehension, in other words, a reading problem or a language problem (Alderson 1984)? According to Maley and Prowse, 'if students have acquired efficient reading in their L1, they can do so in their L2 as well', with the proviso that they need to 'reshape their mental processes' (2013: 165) and adapt to different writing systems if applicable. Other researchers warn against the assumption of L1–L2 skills transfer. Walter (2007) demonstrates that particularly at lower levels, students have problems 'accessing' the 'structure building skill that they deploy well in identical circumstances in their L1' (Walter 2007: 29) but that this access increases with proficiency. Ediger (2001) likewise maintains that L1 reading skills do not readily transfer to L2 reading: he argues that this manifests at the stages of word recognition and even sound–letter relationship. We will see this discussion continue with regard to 'top-down' and 'bottom-up' processing models of reading, further on.

This debate is just one in a long and varied history of approaches to teaching reading, many of these grounded in research into L1 reading (see, for example, Koda 2004 for a 'cross-linguistic' perspective on reading). The move in contemporary research is towards a *process-oriented* approach in which the focus is on fostering the development of the strategies and skills, including cognitive ones, required for effective reading. This can be contrasted with a *product-oriented* approach concerned with outcomes and learner performance (checked, for example, by comprehension questions, more of which later), rather than with the skills required to achieve these. Like all other views on pedagogy, the process-oriented approach did not go unchallenged. Its critics contend, for example, that with its emphasis on metacognitive strategies (conscious strategy development and use) the approach 'needlessly draw[s] readers' attention away from text content and meaning' (Learned et al. 2011: 163), or even risks 'cognitive overload' as learners are asked to process language, construct meaning and monitor their own strategy use all at the same time (Masuhara 2003: 349). The two approaches are not, of course, mutually exclusive in practice, and it would be fair to say that many teaching and published materials for reading use elements of both.

A major influence on contemporary reading skills pedagogy has been the conception of reading as the operating of two sets of processes, one working from the *bottom up*, the other from the *top down*. The first involves learners using 'micro-skills' to 'decode', depending on how much new language they encounter, at the level of morphemes, single words ('word recognition'), expressions, syntax and discourse, and interpreting meaning on this basis. Top-down processes involve using prior knowledge – situational, cultural etc., as well as 'schemata' (mental 'scenarios' of common experiences; see below) – to contextualise bottom-up interpretations and thus make sense of the whole. Key top-down micro-skills include deducing the meaning of unfamiliar lexis from context and deducing the 'gist' of the whole text via strategies such as skimming and scanning. Operating in these ways (top-down, bottom-up) involves different levels of cognitive processing, and we will look at this later on.

The exercise of 'bottom-up' skills has at times had a bad press over the years, with changing approaches to reading. It is true that used exclusively they remain limiting strategies for text decoding which can lead to the 'word-bound' condition identified with poor readers – and that they need to be teamed with top-down processes. On the other hand, it has come to be recognised that these cannot operate either unless and until the learner has achieved the understanding of the text which bottom-up processing provides (see a discussion of the evolution of reading approaches in Hinkel 2006). This has made for an 'interactive model' of reading (e.g. Grabe 2009), in which reading is conceived as an interplay between top-down and bottom-up processes. This interactive approach underlies the way in which reading is treated in most language teaching coursebooks and materials today.

Task 6.2

- Look back at the extract from the coursebook *New English File: Upper-Intermediate – Student's Book* in Figure 6.1. Think about which activities would tend to involve learners in using predominantly 'bottom-up' skills and where they will using 'top-down' ones, and identify the micro-skills that will be called upon in both cases.
- Analyse the 'balance' of these in this piece of reading material and think about ways to achieve balanced coordination of reading skills in your own materials.

Before we move on we will look in a little more depth into what is involved in top-down processes. The key to understanding a text (written or spoken) is the ability to use our knowledge of the world to place it within a context that makes sense of it – commonly expressed as the psychological concept of 'schemata'. Schemata can be defined as an individual's mental 'script' of the way common life scenarios – shopping, school, eating in a restaurant – play out. This prior knowledge that we bring to the comprehension process thus actually 'shapes' our comprehension; a sort of 'virtuous circle' (Duke, Pearson, Strachan and Billman 2011: 53). Schemata are keenly culture-specific or even unique to one culture (an example might be the Jewish tradition of the Bar Mitzvah, heralding a boy's entry into manhood at the age of 13). (See more on schemata on the web page for Chapter 3, activity 3.3.) Normal strategies such as guessing the meaning of an unknown word or expression from the context do not work if there is a schematic 'gap' – they can only operate if the context (via the schemata) is recognisable enough to render clues.

The implications of this are that the schemata triggered by a reading (or listening) text need to be a consideration from the initial stages of selection (this can be related to discussions on ensuring familiarity by localising language materials; see Chapter 3). In fact, the influence of the concept can be seen in materials design and classroom procedures in general, where it is realised as the popular pre-reading/pre-listening activities of brainstorming and semantic mapping, which are in effect techniques for 'activating' the relevant schemata. These can be as simple as asking learners to look at photographs or at key terms relating to the reading/listening and to discuss them. For example, preceding a pair of readings on culture and society in the EAP course-book *Cambridge Academic English: Student's Book* (Hewings and Thaine 2012), students are asked to discuss what they think these terms mean: *cultural heritage, cultural industries* and *cultural tourism* (p. 70).

What we have referred to as the top-down processes learners deploy when reading are, of course, cognitive processes. To guide the development of reading materials we can turn again to work done on stratifying the cognitive domain (originally by Bloom et al. 1956) discussed in Chapter 2. It will be recalled that in Bloom's work and revisions of it (e.g. Anderson and Krathwohl 2001), cognitive skills were conceived as a pyramid, working at the most basic levels of remembering and understanding information, then upwards through applying, analysing or evaluating it, and finally to the 'peak' of building onto it to create something new. As was emphasised in Chapter 2, language acquisition is particularly associated with the operation of 'higher-order' thinking skills. For the purposes of designing materials around written texts, then, it is useful to consider activities that can be expected to invoke these.

Figure 2.3 in Chapter 2 has already offered samples of general tasks to deploy each 'level' of cognitive skills. In Figure 6.3, with an eye to the design of reading (and listening) materials, we have adapted Figure 2.3, adding a list of question prompts along with sample questions for the tale of Little Red Riding Hood. (Read the story online at http://www.eastoftheweb.com/short-stories/UBooks/LittRed.shtml)

6.1

Task 6.3

In the reading material from the coursebook *Innovations* (Dellar and Walkley 2008: 26) in Figure 6.4, the start of the first reading exercise, '2 Before you read', has been deconstructed in terms of the cognitive skills it stimulates. Continue this analysis of Figure 6.4, using Figure 6.3 as a model.

Task 6.4

Analyse a selection of reading materials and accompanying activities from a coursebook identifying the cognitive levels at which the questions operate by applying the descriptors and prompts in Figure 6.3.

- Look out for *wh-* questions (*where. . .? who. . .?* etc.) and *how* + quantifiers (*how many. . .?* etc.) and consider the cognitive level(s) at which these would work.

You may like to use this cognitive-skills-check technique when developing your own materials.

None of this is to deny that fact- and meaning-checking and recall have their place in examination and ESP courses (in business, science, law, engineering etc.), where the reading genres or activities involved are likely to require 'precision' understanding, and where extracting and remembering factual detail is an essential skill to hone. The more analytic learning styles of some students (such as some of those choosing these disciplines) may also be consistent with such activities, and ill-suited to the imaginative and creative tasks classed as 'higher-order' thinking skills. We have, however, tried to locate our suggestions for reading (and listening) skills development materials in the more neutral ground of students learning in non-specialised contexts using texts ranging from fiction to leisure reading (e.g. newspapers, magazines), which tend to be the resources used in general coursebooks.

General coursebooks currently on the market measure up fairly poorly in terms of 'likelihood' to engage learners cognitively, according to three overview studies (Tomlinson et al. 2001; Masuhara et al. 2008; Tomlinson and Masuhara 2013; also discussed in Chapter 2). This can be seen to correlate with findings in Freeman (2014) that the frequency of 'explicit' reading comprehension questions (where the answers can be found stated in the text, thus calling on 'lower-order' cognitive skills) increased in the coursebooks/editions covered by the research (published between 1998 and 2009) in three of the four series examined. Alongside this, Freeman's

Cognitive skill level	Processes	Prompts	Sample activities	Sample questions for the story of Little Red Riding Hood
Creating	Based on given information; reformulating, extending, building, planning, hypothesising, generating new patterns/structures	*create, compose, predict, design, devise, formulate, imagine, hypothesise*	Devise/perform role plays, advertisements, games or mazes using the input as a launching point Compose a sequel or prequel to the input –genre/media-switch e.g. written input transferred to aural/graphic output or newspaper article transferred to dialogue, poem, blog	*Compose a sequel or prequel to the story of Little Red Riding Hood choose to use a different medium/genre, e.g. social networking site, news media report, poem or dialogue, and/or a different cultural context*
Evaluating	Making/defending judgements and arguments based on evaluation of criteria Linking to own values/ideas Critiquing/reviewing	*judge, debate, justify, critique, review, argue*	Write a set of rules or conventions relating to conduct in a particular situation or context e.g. school rules, hospitality conventions in a specific culture Conduct a debate Write a critique or review	*What can you infer from the story of Little Red Riding Hood about conventions of behaviour in the culture in which the story is set?(For instance, it is not acceptable for animals to eat people – although the other way around is acceptable, as in some versions of the story Little Red Riding Hood's basket contained sausages.)*
Analysing	Separating information into its component parts to identify how the parts relate to each other and the overall structure Inferencing (and distinguishing between facts and inferences) Differentiating Organising Deconstructing	*compare, contrast, categorise, deconstruct*	Conduct a mini research project (design a survey, gather and analyse data)	*Design and conduct a survey, and analyse your findings from it, to investigate how your classmates/friends would react to each event in the story of Little Red Riding Hood (e.g. what would they do if confronted by a wolf?)*
Applying	Abstracting and reapplying to a different situation. Selecting and/or connecting information/ideas Implementing, changing	*illustrate, interpret, transfer, infer, change, complete*	Recast input as a different genre/medium, e.g. rewrite a newspaper article as a dialogue, or write a description of a photograph	*Tell the story of Little Red Riding Hood via a different medium/genre, e.g. social networking site, news media report, poem, dialogue.*
Understanding	Determining the meaning of written/audio/graphic communication, i.e. interpreting the message	*explain, paraphrase, summarise, exemplify, categorise, predict*	Re-tell or summarise input (in written, oral or graphic form)	*Summarise the story of Little Red Riding Hood.*
Remembering	Recalling data or information.	*tell, list, draw, locate, recite*	Make a list, timeline or fact chart Answer list of factual questions	*List what Little Red Riding Hood carried in her basket.*

Figure 6.3   Sample prompts/questions matched to descriptors of Bloom's taxonomy as revised by Anderson and Krathwohl (2001)

4 The law

Reading

1 | Speaking

Which three jobs or professions do you most respect? Why?

Work with a partner. Compare your ideas and decide on the three jobs most respected by both of you.

Now work with another pair. Can you all agree on the three jobs you respect the most?

2 | Before you read   *Explain, compare, contrast, evaluate, create*

You are going to read an article about a job voted as one of the *least* respected in Britain. First, read the introduction. Are you surprised by this news or not? Why?

MONEY CAN'T BUY YOU LOVE!

EVEN MORE hated than tax inspectors! Disliked even more than traffic wardens! The targets of even as much venom as estate agents! It can't be much fun being a lawyer! Not that you're likely to feel much sympathy for them, of course, for in a recent survey of the least respected professions, lawyers came fourth! There are also countless websites containing anti-lawyer jokes. So why is it that they attracted so much hatred when they seek justice and defend people's rights?

With a partner, list five reasons why you think lawyers tend to be so disliked.

1. ....
2. ....
3. ....
4. ....
5. ....

3 | While you read

Now read the rest of the article. As you read, think about these questions.

1. How many of your ideas does it mention?
2. Are there any reasons you totally agree with? Why?
3. Are there any reasons you strongly disagree with? Why?
4. Are there any reasons you simply don't understand?

When you finish reading, discuss your ideas with a partner.

■ Well, first and foremost, it seems that many of us perceive lawyers as being money-grabbing. Lawyers have such a reputation for being greedy that people accept as fact the many urban myths about ridiculously high legal fees and clients being billed for coffee, waiting time and small talk, whether they are true or not. The fact that so much money can be made out of other people's misery doesn't exactly help them either. Part of the problem for lawyers is the fact that we tend not to seek their services when life is going well. Rather, we turn to them when our lives are completely falling apart. We bring them our divorce cases, our custody battles and our paternity suits. They are often associated with the very worst points in our lives – and whilst we may be grateful to our own lawyers for their work and dedication at such times, we rarely feel the same way about the lawyers of our opponents!

■ To make matters worse, the law has, in many cases, become more of a business than a profession, leading to some lawyers acquiring a reputation for dodgy financial practices. The stereotype of many lawyers as 'ambulance chasers' – keenly pursuing those recently involved in an accident in the hope of picking up a case – has done their image real harm. The more lawyers work on a no-win, no-fees basis, the more endless litigation is actively encouraged. As a result, 'compensation culture' seems to be becoming a more and more accepted part of our society.

■ Furthermore, not only will certain lawyers scramble over one another in an attempt to land the best jobs, but they will often use underhand means in a bid to win their cases. Lawyers often seem quite happy to engage in character assassination if it will get results. It is this kind of behaviour that has contributed to the idea of lawyers as being at best, amoral, and at worst, totally unethical. Added to that is the fact that many lawyers sell themselves to whoever offers the most money. That these clients may be the bosses of organised crime mobs, the CEOs of companies that have polluted the environment or wealthy superstars who have committed awful crimes does not seem to bother them at all. On the contrary, they seem perfectly happy to explore legal loopholes and think up clever plea bargains before trials begin. Nevertheless, whenever it is suggested that perhaps the legal profession should be subject to external watchdogs, lawyers frequently react with horror!

■ To add insult to injury, we then have to listen to lawyers claiming that they are the defenders of justice and free speech. To many of us, this is total hypocrisy. One final annoyance is the incomprehensible jargon that lawyers always seem to use. Most of us can't tell our *herewiths* from our *hereinafters* and have never quite understood why none of this business could be conducted in plain English! One thing that is plain, however, is that when it comes to jobs we just can't stand, lawyers remain in a class of their own!

26

Figure 6.4   Extract from Innovations Advanced *(Dellar and Walkley 2008: 26)*

research showed that numbers of 'inferential' comprehension question types (in which the reader has to combine background knowledge with information in the text), while more prevalent in three of the four series, fell progressively edition by edition (see Further Reading One below).

All this should alert us to the need for a critical look at the convention of comprehension questioning in reading activities (and again, in listening ones). Perhaps the main culprits as regards comprehension questioning (as we hinted in Task 6.4) are the teachers' classic repertoire of *wh-* and *how* + quantifier questions, or more fundamentally maybe, the teacher training convention that requires us to engage in this type of 'checking as classroom management' behaviour. (Michael Long (1991: 45) famously asks whether comprehension checking is 'merely a classroom artifice to justify the teacher's presence'.) As may have emerged when doing Task 6.4, these question words tend to prefix 'detail' questions that require quite superficial involvement at the level of both linguistic skill and cognitive processing ('Where did James and Monica go on their honeymoon?', 'How many books has J. K. Rowling written?'). This would seem unlikely to promote the cognitive and affective engagement with the material which, it is argued in Chapter 2, is essential to language acquisition. It has even been suggested (Krashen 2009) that the degree of detail involved in comprehension checking is inversely proportional to its value for language acquisition. Similarly, Maley and Prowse question the need for any comprehension checking at all, maintaining that 'there is little or no evidence to suggest that activities and questions make any difference to the quality of the reading experience or to the learning that derives from it' (2013: 172).

It should be noted that these three authors represent the 'extensive reading' (ER) school, which makes the case for a central place for ER in both L2 and L1 education. There is indubitable evidence of the affective, cognitive and linguistic benefits of reading, reflected in educational policies such as the USA's 'No Child Left Behind' act of 2001, which embedded early reading proficiency in the primary curriculum. Using the simple premise that we learn to read by reading, the main job of the teacher would seem to be, as Eskey points out, 'to get students reading and keep them reading, that is, to find a way to motivate them to read and facilitate their reading' (2005: 574). Maley and Prowse suggest that the sorts of activities which might usefully support the reading experience are 'relatively unstructured and open-ended activities such as keeping a reading journal or giving short book talks to other students or broad-ranging discussion questions . . . or creative post-reading activities' (2013: 172).

These suggestions involve the cognitive skills whose importance we have emphasised in this section. They likewise use the integrated skills model which underlies our approach to skills work in this chapter and the book as a whole. This brings this section 'full circle' in a way – and to a logical transition point to look at the other (so-called) 'receptive' skill: listening. First, however, look at Figures 6.5 and 6.6, and think about the reading/cognitive skills each of the three types of tasks described there require of the learner.

The tasks below were set for an EFL class at C1 level, studying for a semester in Ireland as part of the Erasmus (European University Exchange) programme. The class were asked to read a novel over this period, *Paddy Clarke Ha Ha Ha* by Irish author Roddy Doyle (1993) as an exercise in extensive reading. Sample tasks carried out in class included:

Familiarisation

Genre analysis and identification: students examined samples of different types of writing to identify key features of genres.

Interpretation

Brainstorming activity: students worked in groups interpreting a single passage (a conversation between the young protagonist, Paddy, and his father) from different viewpoints. The outcome of the activity is schematised in Figure 6.6.

Figure 6.6   Brainstorming activity (Mishan forthcoming)

Summative task

Look at this blog about Roddy Doyle: www.guardian.co.uk/books/booksblog/2010/may/30/falling-roddy-doyle
The blogger, Sarah Crown of *The Guardian* newspaper, ends by asking the question: 'which is the best Roddy Doyle novel to start with?' Write an essay making an argument for why she should read *Paddy Clarke Ha Ha Ha*.   (word limit: approximately 1,500 words)

Figure 6.5   Extensive reading: sample tasks

Familiarisation and summative tasks devised by Dr Elaine Vaughan, co-tutor on the module, and reproduced here with her permission.

Task 6.5

Berardo sees reading as having three main purposes: 'for survival, for learning or for pleasure' (2006: 61).

- Match some 'purposes' to written genres. (For example, the 'purpose' of reading a menu might be considered 'for survival', while the 'purpose' of reading a short story is 'for pleasure'.)

- Think about how this can be 'translated' into the purposes we build into our reading materials.

6.3 MATERIALS TO DEVELOP LISTENING SKILLS

Task 6.6

We have regularly cross-referenced to listening in the section on materials for reading skills. Have a look over the section again, extracting the aspects of designing reading materials that relate to listening ones as well; for instance:

- the use of brainstorming techniques to activate schemata as a pre-listening activity
- the need for 'comprehension' questions which involve higher-level thinking skills

You will have inferred from Task 6.6 that the issues in listening pedagogy have a lot in common with those of reading. We see the same practice, for instance, of using listening input to serve other language learning objectives such as introducing or practising new grammar and lexis (see Chapter 8). Reading and listening are, furthermore, frequently 'teamed up' in coursebooks, presumably on the basis that they have traditionally been bracketed together as 'receptive' skills. This is something of a misnomer, we would argue, as it implies a passivity that is belied by our knowledge of the intense and interactive nature of the skills involved in each. Commonalities of pedagogical treatment also underplay what makes listening so distinctive – and critical – for language learning, and we will look at this first.

Hearing is the skill that has the largest impact on the learning of our L1. It is the most 'natural' or innate of the language skills, the only one that does not have to be 'learned' in the L1; yet paradoxically, listening is the most challenging to master in an L2. It is surprising, therefore, that relatively little attention has been paid to listening skills in L2 pedagogy until fairly recently (see, for example, Field 2008). The cause may be that historically, language pedagogy grew out of the classical tradition of reading; and it was only with the invention of portable audio devices in the 1960s that 'listening' work as we know it today could be brought into the L2 classroom. We might note here that modern-day classroom access to resources that offer audio-visual materials, while naturally adding visual clues to meaning, still carries the same sort of issues as the audio-only listening that we discuss in this section.

The tendency in early listening pedagogy was to treat listening material as if it were a 'text' just like reading material. But as soon as we look at what is involved within 'decoding' each, we see that the parallels are few; unlike written text, audio is transient and invisible, with no visible trace to decode ('the voice is nothing but beaten air' (Seneca, quoted in Field 2008: 140)). This means that there are 'perceptual' challenges. Audio input is connected speech, which means that boundaries between words (or 'chunks' functioning as one unit, such as *you know* and *I mean*) have to be identified before meaning processing can commence. There are a number of characteristic phonological features of connected speech which affect word recognition. These include:

- blurred word boundaries (in common 'minimal pairs' such as *this guy* and *the sky*)
- contracted forms (*he'd gone, he'd go*)
- elision (*gimme, wanna*)
- weak forms (e.g. *must* realised as /məs/)
- varied intonation patterns
- speaker accent

Added to this are discourse features, including discourse markers (*anyway, like, right*), repetition and paraphrasing, pauses and self-correction (see more on discourse features in Chapter 8; see also Cutting 2014). All this has to be done, of course, 'in real time'. Furthermore, listeners need to retain appropriate chunks of the input in their short-term memory in order to make sense of it – and if involved in conversation, formulate and utter a response.

What has recently come to the fore in listening research is that decoding at a micro-level, and devising strategies to do this, are fundamental to developing effective listening skills (see, for example, Field 2008). This has given rise to a move in research in listening pedagogy, similar to that in reading, towards an approach which focuses on the *process* of listening, and so on the training of listening skills. This signals a move away from a *product* approach, which focuses on learner *understanding* of the material (checked by comprehension questions and the like), rather than the processes by which this is achieved.

The product-to-process transition in research has been slow to trickle down into pedagogy, however. Most coursebooks are still heavily weighted towards the 'product' ethos (we see a lot of permutations of comprehension check exercises, as we noted above), with little attention paid to learner training in listening skills. Materials still predominantly *test* listening, in other words, rather than concentrating on *teaching* it (Paran 2012: 456) – although some of the newer coursebooks are beginning to redress the balance (see below). Balance is in fact key here, with the approaches being seen as interdependent; skills training would seem pointless if the skills are not put to the test, and skills testing without training seems hardly pedagogically sound (see Field 2008: 80). In this section we will look at what each approach means for the design of listening materials, while stressing the need for a combined or 'integrated' process–product approach to listening overall.

LISTENING MATERIALS: A PROCESS APPROACH

As with reading, the process approach brings with it a focus on the micro-skills involved in processing input and the strategies learners can employ for this. Listening research and pedagogy have likewise arrived at the same sort of 'interactive model', an accommodation between 'top-down' and 'bottom-up' skills. While the basic top-down skills for listening have similar descriptors to those for reading – 'listening for gist', 'deducing meaning from context', 'activating schemata' – it is at the level of the bottom-up micro-skills that the difficulties specific to listening surface, as we have seen above. Indeed, it is the difficulty of accessing and impacting on these 'internalised processes' that has always been a challenge in pedagogy, and probably accounts for why coursebook materials have tended to steer clear of micro-level listening skills work.

Where coursebooks do take a process approach to listening, one technique is to tackle the difficulties head on, giving learners controlled practice in word-for-word decoding and/or raising awareness of features of connected speech. This is done routinely in the *face2face* series (Redston and Cunningham) in the 'help with listening' sections, as in this example from the *Intermediate – Student's Book*:

> Listen to the questions . . .
> Notice how we say *do you* /dəjə/, *have you* /həvjə/, *are you* /əjə/, and *did you* /dɪdʒə/. (Redston and Cunningham 2013a: 7)

Task 6.7
The following exercise is likewise intended as bottom-up processing work. (It is based on the second part of an authentic interview with the American actor Liza Minelli.)

> Listen to part two. Complete the interviewer's questions.
> 1. Did it _____ to you?
> 2. I think yours _____ , though, wasn't it?
> 3. How _____ all of that?
> 4. So you haven't _____ over it?
> (Soars and Soars 2003b: 45)

The complete sentences in part two (taken from the transcript of the audio) are as follows:

> 1. Did it *manage to still feel like a personal affair* to you?
> 2. I think yours *was a bit more glamorous*, though, wasn't it?
> 3. How *did you cope with* all of that?
> 4. So you haven't *fallen out with him* over it?
> (Soars and Soars 2003b: 136)

Evaluate the activity, looking at factors such as:

- The exercise rubric (is the rationale for the activity clear?)
- The procedure (are students asked to do this at first or subsequent listenings?)
- The lengths of the sections to be transcribed (is this a decoding exercise or a memory test?)
- The selection of language focused on (e.g. idiomatic expressions, common collocates or chunks?)
- The layout (is there enough space for words to be written in?)

What are the implications for the design of 'bottom-up' listening materials?

Another aspect of the process approach to developing listening skills is to address them from the opposite perspective: strategy training. Representative of this, in fact, is Redston and Cunningham's above-mentioned technique in *face2face*: awareness-raising of features of speech, which is effectively early-stage strategy training. Cultivating this type of 'metacognitive knowledge', which includes awareness of their own individual listening practices, can help learners develop conscious strategies for dealing with listening. Techniques for doing this might include, for example, the learner analysing what makes a particular listening situation (such as a lecture, conversation or phone call) difficult for him or her and then consider strategies she or he might use to deal with these (see, for example, Goh 2010). However, this sort of training appears to be confined to listening skills books without much overspill onto general coursebooks (with the notable exception of *face2face*) – perhaps reflecting the feeling that 'the jury is still out' with regard to its effectiveness (Renandya and Farrell 2011).

Other common coursebook techniques, such as pre-listening work on context and language familiarisation, can also be seen as broadly process-based, in that they give learners the means for decoding from the top-down perspective (what Field (2008: 133) calls 'large to small' processing). The key factors for designing pre-listening tasks are that they provide context, motivation and any (and only) language crucial to the understanding of the listening passage. Field suggests that for the first of these, the criterion should be 'authentic' and limited thus: 'what would the listener already know in real life before the speech event began?' (2008: 18). The balance between the other two – motivation and language familiarisation – however, is a fine one. One pre-listening convention is to 'feed in' key language, sometimes for manipulation by the learners, as in the extract in Task 6.8, or by providing a short written text on the same topic as, or a summary of, the listening passage. Alternatively, the key language can be generated by the learners themselves using the sorts of schemata-raising techniques described in the reading section. It should be noted that if over-extended, though, these types of activities can dull rather than pique interest and/or can spoil any 'suspense'.

Task 6.8
Evaluate this pre-listening task on the basis of the discussion above.

> You are going to listen to an interview with two pilots. Before you listen, discuss questions 1–6 with a partner and guess how the pilots will answer them.
> 1. What weather conditions are the most dangerous when flying a plane?
> 2. Which is more dangerous, taking off or landing?
> 3. Is it really worth passengers wearing seat belts?
> 4. Is it worth listening to the safety instructions?
> 5. Are some airports more dangerous than others?
> 6. How important is it for pilots to speak English well?
> (Oxenden and Latham-Koenig 2008: 27)

LISTENING MATERIALS: FROM PROCESS TO PRODUCT

The product and process approaches are not mutually exclusive in designing listening materials, as we stressed above. In fact, the classic 'product' technique of comprehension checking can be used as a sort of 'way stage' to a process approach if we refocus it as a diagnostic activity in which the teacher seeks to establish not *whether* the 'correct' or 'incorrect' answers were arrived at, but *how* (Field 2008), through raising learners' awareness of techniques they use; thus transitioning towards skill building – rather than skill testing (see also Further Reading Two). It is useful, therefore, to look at traditional techniques of the product approach, principally comprehension work, to see how they can be given a 'process gloss', whereby understanding is checked in more indirect and communicative ways.

One 'indirect' way of checking comprehension involves providing genuine 'reasons for listening' (the title, in fact, of an early but forward-looking resource book, Scarborough 1984). The three basic principles it used remain essential ones for the design of listening materials. The first was to give learners a 'reason for listening' – one that is more motivating than simply 'because it features in the coursebook'. The second is that in 'real life', we listen 'for a reason' – and consequently, we listen to different genres in different ways. We do not concentrate on the entire weather forecast, for example: we only attend to what is said about the weather in the area that will affect us. On the other hand, we might try to listen in detail to a radio phone-in programme on a topic that interests us. The third principle is that in 'real life' we listen 'interactively' – and we react or respond to different genres in different ways. On hearing the weather forecast, we might make (or cancel!) plans for an outdoor trip. The radio phone-in might prompt a comment to, or discussion with, a companion – or indeed, a call to the radio station. These reactions and responses can be stimulated by appropriate task design (see also Chapter 9). This sort of genre-led approach is also flexible in that it allows the teacher/materials developer to tailor listening to the interests and needs of their learners.

The importance of stimulating cognitive involvement in any interactive or comprehension-checking work was discussed in the reading section and this remains as valid for listening material – with the added caution, though, that with audio (and particularly audio-visual) material, we are far more likely to touch on the affective domain, and this has implications for sensitivity in prompts and questions.

Task 6.9

Evaluate these questions extracted from a coursebook listening task on journalist Fergal Keane's broadcast 'letter to a new-born son' (aired on BBC radio in 1996; audio accessible at http://news.bbc.co.uk/2/hi/programmes/from_our_own_correspondent/4278450.stm) with reference to their attention to the cognitive and affective domains. The questions below relate to the middle section of the letter.

Are these statements true or false? Correct the false ones.
1. His Chinese friends say that his son has to be given a Chinese name.
2. He might call him 'Son of the Eastern Star' after the beautiful sunrise.

3. He used to be very ambitious in his work.
4. These children he mentions were all hurt in floods.
   - Andi Mikail from Eritrea
   - Sharja from Afghanistan
   - Domingo and Juste from southern Angola
   - Three young children from Rwanda

(Soars and Soars 2003b: 64)

In concluding this section, we return to the parallels between reading and listening. Echoing the extensive reading movement comes *extensive listening*, in which learners listen to longer stretches of audio(-visual) material without the intrusion of comprehension checks and memory tests, or the anxiety that these can create (see Renandya and Farrell 2011 for research on this). The benefits of listening for pleasure, like reading for pleasure, would seem to be self-evident considering what we know about the importance of affect for learning. This will no doubt have struck any teacher who opts to listen to a popular song, watch (a scene from) a film or indeed read aloud with his or her class. More extensive materials are ideal candidates for what Ableeva and Stranks call 'task-less listening' (2013: 209) where learners simply listen without the distraction of a task. Although these might be 'a methodological leap too far for most editors and publishing houses' (ibid.), with possible face validity problems for some students, this does not prevent us, as materials writers and teachers, from using an approach like this which gives learners a 'relaxed space' in which to hone their listening skills and strategies at their own pace.

6.4 FURTHER READING ONE

Freeman, D. (2014). Reading comprehension questions: the distribution of different types in global EFL textbooks. In N. Harwood (ed.), *English Language Teaching Textbooks: Content, Consumption, Production* **(pp. 72–110). Basingstoke: Palgrave Macmillan.**

The idea for Freeman's research, on which this recommended chapter is based, is in many ways a very obvious one: how far has Bloom's taxonomy (which we discussed in this chapter and in Chapter 2) influenced the design of 'comprehension' questions in language learning coursebooks? All the more surprising, therefore, that (as far as we are aware) this research study is the first to address this. Freeman creates her own taxonomy of question types, drawing on that of Bloom and others and on her initial analysis of coursebook question types, and analyses the post-reading question and activity types within a number of editions of four intermediate-level global coursebooks. (Her doctoral research, on which this chapter is based, additionally covers pre-reading questions.) Freeman's taxonomy consists of three categories of these 'comp-qs' (comprehension questions), 'content' questions, 'language' questions and 'affect' questions.

She subdivides these, to give her full taxonomy as shown in Figure 6.7.

Freeman notes that her three content and two affect question types span lower- to higher-order thinking: in textually explicit questions, for example, the answer can be found in the text, working up to inferential questions where learners have to detect allusion and employ background knowledge in order to answer the question.

The types of questions that:	Label:	Description:
Require the learner to understand content	*'Content' questions*	*Textually explicit*
		Textually implicit
		Inferential
Require the learner to carry out language-related tasks	*'Language' questions*	*Reorganisation*
		Lexical
		Form
Address learner affect regarding the text	*'Affect' questions*	*Personal response*
		Evaluation

Figure 6.7   Taxonomy of question types, based on Freeman (2014: 83–4, figure 3)

Similarly, Freeman grades the 'evaluation' question type as being more demanding on the cognitive scale than 'personal response' (the language questions are not graded hierarchically).

This is thus the framework for Freeman's analysis of the comp-qs in a total of ten coursebooks, namely *Cutting Edge* (Cunningham and Moor, 1998, 2005), *English File* (Oxenden and Latham-Koenig 1999, 2008a), *Headway* (Soars and Soars 1986, 1996, 2003a, 2009) and *Inside out* (Kay and Jones 2000, 2009).

Freeman considered the distribution of these question types in post-reading activities in the books in terms of *frequency, occurrence* and *range*. The results section of the chapter is peppered with diagrams which comprehensively cross-match the findings. Unsurprisingly, the most frequent category of comp-qs was 'content' – of which *Headway* contained 'significantly more' than the other series (p. 88). Less predictable perhaps was that in three of the four series, the most frequently asked type of content question was the *inferential* one calling on the 'highest-order' thinking skill. Nevertheless, this number steadily falls over each revised edition, and this movement is consolidated by a steady rise in explicit-type questions (the lowest-order skill) in three of the four series over the years, again most significantly in *Headway*.

Turning to language questions, the most favoured is 'lexical', with an interesting trend from 'form' questions to a lexical focus over time and with only one series, *Headway*, bucking the trend by generally offering a balance between lexical and form-type questions. The general trend, however, could be said to reflect the increased interest in lexis in the 2000s, prompted in part by the contribution of CL to ELT, and the influence of approaches such as 'the lexical approach', which was based on the findings of CL.

Finally, in the affect category, numbers of questions requiring 'evaluation' are far outweighed by the lower-order personal response questions:

> the more superficial and certainly the more subjective of the two [which] requires the reader to express a purely personal point of view when reacting to a text, such as preference or surprise, or amusement, to which there can be no 'correct' answer. The second category, evaluation, requires a deeper, more

considered response to the text, with some kind of judgment or assessment, and involves the reader applying criteria to support or justify their answer. (pp. 93–4)

Task 6.10
- Do you agree that personal response questions require 'lower-order' thinking?
- What, in your opinion, is the function of prompting personal response questions to reading (or listening) input?

What we hear from the materials writers/editors themselves via Freeman's interviews gives a different perspective. It suggests that the picture she has revealed actually results from an organic, unplanned process rather than systematic implementation of principles:

writers rely on their . . . experience of teaching and materials writing (p. 101)

generally it's the text that suggests [the] type of question (ibid.)

the process tends to be unscientific [i.e.] organic (pp. 101, 102)

All this confirms a lot of other reports in the literature (e.g. Prowse 2011) (see also Chapter 9) of the materials design process as being guided by teaching and writing experience, intuition and personal beliefs.

This being so, we can hope that Freeman's thorough research study is a step towards a more systematic approach to the development of materials for reading and listening in particular, and materials for language learning in general.

Task 6.11
Consult the taxonomy in Figure 6.7 of this report (or in the full chapter if possible).

- Analysis: Analyse the post-reading questions/activities in a coursebook, generating a breakdown of the questions according to question type.
- Production: 'Perhaps the greatest value of the taxonomy is the support it can provide teachers in their own materials writing' (Freeman 2014: 107). Design a pilot piece of reading material using the question types in Freeman's taxonomy.

6.5 FURTHER READING TWO

Siegel, J. (2014). Exploring L2 listening instruction: examinations of practice. *ELT Journal*, 68(1): 22–30.
This paper provides a useful, accessible reference and starting point for the design of listening materials. The empirical study of practices in L2 listening provides a revealing 'snapshot' of contemporary practice, models for listening materials design and a methodological template for further (much-needed) research in this area (see below).

In its introductory sections, the paper synthesises the main approaches in listening pedagogy which we have looked at above, and notes the move away from a 'comprehension approach' towards developing metacognitive strategies, working on bottom-up as well as top-down interpretative strategies, and so on.

Siegel notes that there is little empirical research in the area of listening instruction (and, we would add, that there is even less on the *design* of materials for listening). He justifies the imperative for work in this area via this gloomy picture of current listening instruction practice:

> Teachers lacking in pedagogic knowledge about L2 listening may rely on the same 'listen, answer, check' pattern for all of their listening lessons. Other techniques for listening instruction may not be incorporated into their teaching repertoires. As such, teachers may have limited pedagogic resources when it comes to developmental progression for their learners' listening abilities. In other words, students may do essentially the same thing in each listening lesson: listen to a text, respond to questions, and check their answers. If used over and over again, this approach would seem more like a continuous test of present listening ability than scaffolded guidance meant to improve that ability. In addition, learners may not be exposed to a flexible array of listening activities. Instead, the same comprehension based approach may be used regardless of student proficiency level, age, or background. Such circumstances are less than ideal because students would not have adequate opportunities to expand their listening skills and strategies. (p. 23)

The empirical study reported in this paper confirms the prominence of the 'comprehension approach', with comprehension questions heavily predominating in listening instruction; they were used four times as frequently as the next activity type, bottom-up activities. There was, nevertheless, an encouraging presence of attention to what Siegel calls 'newcomers to listening methodology' (p. 28), such as metacognitive strategies (in almost half the lessons). These were not, however, Siegel noted, well enough generalised by the teachers, thus missing the opportunity of pointing learners towards transferring listening skills and strategies to future listening situations within and beyond the classroom.

As we noted at the start, this paper offers some useful models for listening materials that push the boundaries of the 'comprehension approach'. One technique for fostering the development of metacognitive strategies (although notably rare in Siegel's empirical data) is known as 'teacher modelling':

> This technique involves teachers performing think-aloud procedures in which they explain their cognitive processes while listening. The teacher sets a mental model for students to emulate by describing how they prepare for and monitor input during listening. Teachers also identify those parts of the aural text on which they focus their attention. (p. 25)

The other technique is to extend comprehension checking (which, after all, offers a familiar comfort zone for learners and teachers) by using responses to comprehension questions 'for diagnostic purposes, which ideally leads to targeted practice on problematic areas' (p. 29).

Task 6.12
Accessing the full paper if possible, use and build on the method of listening instruction analysis it offers to reflect on your own teaching materials (as Siegel invites the reader to do, p. 30) and/or design and conduct a mini-research study to investigate those of others.

Task 6.13
Conduct some research, via journal/database searches, into studies that have been done on materials that focus on helping learners develop metacognitive strategies for listening. Some suggested journals are:

6.2

- *The International Journal of Listening*: http://www.tandfonline.com/toc/hijl20/ current#.VCVmwpBwaM8
- *ELT Journal*: http://eltj.oxfordjournals.org

6.6 CONCLUSION

In this chapter we have looked to contemporary approaches to skills teaching for the design of reading and listening skills materials. *Integration* is the byword here. We have argued for materials in which skills are 'integrated' rather than 'segregated', in that skills are necessarily practised in tandem with others; 'integration' also in the sense that the resource itself does not dictate the skills used (a reading text can be used to promote speaking skills and so on). In the chapter, the key points made with respect to materials for reading and listening were as follows:

- Learner processes of dealing with reading and listening materials involve an interplay of bottom-up and top-down processing.
- Contemporary pedagogical approaches vary from a product to a process orientation; we have tended towards a process approach (which focuses on skills and strategies development) though integrating elements of both.
  □ We also consider integrating elements of ER and extensive listening approaches.
- The role of skills materials cannot be purely to develop skills and strategies but should exploit the language acquisition potential of the content of the reading or listening resources as well.
  □ Cognitive and affective engagement needs to be built into reading and listening materials in line with the language acquisition principles we put forward in Chapter 2.

It will be useful to bear these points in mind and consider their application to materials for speaking and writing skills as you read the following chapter.

6.7 ADDITIONAL READINGS

Field, J. (2008). *Listening in the Language Classroom.* Cambridge: Cambridge University Press.
This book was always going to be controversial, challenging the prevailing orthodoxy of the time, a 'comprehension approach' to teaching L2 listening, advocating instead a focus on the *process* of listening. This slant accepted, it is a practical and accessible book, with a welcome section on the treatment of authentic listening material.

Goh, C. (2010). Listening as process: learning activities for self-appraisal and self-regulation. In N. Harwood (ed.), *English Language Teaching Materials: Theory and Practice* (pp. 179–206). Cambridge: Cambridge University Press.
This chapter makes the case for the 'metacognitive' approach to listening, i.e. training learners '*how* to listen, not just what to listen for' (p. 180). The practical sections of the chapter give us blueprints for materials that help develop metacognitive strategies. These are of two types: *integrated experiential listening tasks*, where metacognitive activities are integrated into other listening activities, and *guided reflections on listening*. The chapter will be of interest to those who want to put the product-oriented tradition of listening behind them, and embrace the process approach.

NOTE

1. Today, though, we tend to talk of cultural or intercultural *competence*, recognising the knowledge and awareness involved in cultural learning, as discussed in Chapter 3. Likewise, 'language awareness' encompasses more than just abilities or skills, and is covered in Chapter 8.

7

MATERIALS TO DEVELOP SPEAKING AND WRITING SKILLS

7.1 INTRODUCTION

This chapter and the next continue with the approach adopted in Chapter 6 in that they concentrate on materials for individual skills and foci, while asking you to bear in mind that language learning materials should ideally be conceived with more holistic aims and an integrated skills aspiration. We look firstly here at the skill of speaking, arguably the primary skill in language learning for reasons which we explain below. We look at the difficulties involved with acquiring the skill (some of which, of course, match those for listening skills, including the speed at which the language user has to process the language) and we take a critical look at the materials designed to facilitate it. Finally, we argue that materials included in the speaking 'syllabus' should range from features of spoken language to those of different discourse types. We then turn in Section 7.3 to look at materials designed specifically for the skill of writing, to find this has been a relatively neglected area, until quite recently at least. Furthermore, the variety of genres and registers required for use in the ever-growing numbers of digital media has complexified the learning of writing. In discussing writing materials, we look at both process and genre approaches as well as considering the role of writing materials in providing both a *stimulus* and *scaffolding* (Hyland 2013) to learners' writing.

7.2 MATERIALS TO DEVELOP SPEAKING SKILLS

The importance of the speaking skill as part of language proficiency can hardly be overstated: it is, after all, far more common to be asked 'Do you speak English?' than 'Do you read/write English?' Nevertheless, treatment of the speaking skill in ELT materials has remained curiously ill-defined and unsystematic: Basturkmen (2001), for example, noted that coursebooks frequently have mini-syllabuses for reading, writing and listening which are described in terms of the sub-skills developed; speaking syllabuses, however, tend to be simple lists of activities. The situation is all the more curious when one considers that communicative approaches tend to prioritise the speaking skill. It is interesting in this respect that Bygate (2001: 14) argues that speaking has only recently 'begun to emerge as a branch of teaching, learning and testing in its own right'. Bygate (2001) suggests three reasons why a focus on speaking as a skill has taken so long to emerge. Firstly, the grammar translation method which held sway for so long (and still does in some parts of the world) prioritised reading and writing. Secondly, it is only recently that technological developments have facilitated the close study of spoken language, especially through spoken corpora (see Chapter 5). Thirdly, oral production was central to methodologies such as the audiolingual and the direct method, and a confusion has arisen between *intensive oral practice* of discrete language points and speaking as a *skill* in its own right. There is, we would argue, the world of difference between an oral repetition drill focusing on a single structure, where the focus is entirely on accuracy, and a class debate about gender equality, where the focus is entirely on fluency. That is not to say that accuracy and fluency work can never be combined, but we need to be absolutely clear about our aims.

Contemporary materials developers now have a rich knowledge base on which to draw for the design of speaking materials. They can draw on work in fields such as psycholinguistics (the mental processes by which talk is produced), conversational analysis (the way conversation is structured between speakers) and discourse analysis (the way stretches of connected talk are produced) to understand how talk is produced and structured. They can also draw on the lexical and grammatical findings of spoken corpus research to understand how (and why) speech differs from writing. In short, much is known about the process and product of speaking which is of potential value to materials developers.

THE NATURE OF THE SPEAKING SKILL

The nature of the speaking skill: process

Speaking is a demanding enough skill even in an L1. As Burns and Hill (2013: 232) note: 'Speaking is a complex mental process combining various cognitive skills, virtually simultaneously, and drawing on working memory of words and concepts, while self-monitoring.'

Levelt (1989) identifies four separate sub-processes in the speaking skill: conceptualisation, formulation, articulation and self-monitoring. Conceptualisation involves generating the content the speaker wishes to express; formulation entails selecting the language to express the content generated and organise it according to the norms of a particular genre; and articulation is the physical production of the sounds required to encode the message. These processes are self-monitored so that the speaker can ensure that all is going to plan, a process which will include attention to affective factors such as the relationship with the interlocutors. Managing these processes presents a formidable challenge, particularly since, as Bygate (2001: 16) notes: 'All this happens very fast and, to be successful, depends on automation: to some degree in conceptualisation, to a considerable extent in formulation and almost entirely in articulation.' For the learner operating in a second language, of course, automation in formulation and articulation present particular challenges. It is not surprising, then, given the circumstances of production, that spoken and written language tend to differ. As Bygate (ibid.) observes:

These conditions and processes affect the language that is typically produced. For instance, speech more often than writing refers to the interlocutors and the physical time and place of the communication. In addition, speech typically expresses politeness so as to protect the face of the interlocutors.

The nature of the speaking skill: product

Spoken corpus research in recent years has shed much light on the nature of spoken language (see O'Keeffe, McCarthy and Carter 2007 for an excellent summary of research findings with potential relevance for ELT). Illustrative examples of this kind of research are provided by Timmis (2013):

- the high frequency of discourse markers such as *well, just* and *right* in conversation (O'Keeffe et al. 2007)
- the frequent use of collocation in conversation, e.g *you know, a bit, come on* (Shin and Nation 2008)
- the frequent use of non-canonical grammatical features such as 'tails' or 'right dislocation' (McCarthy and Carter 1995; Timmis 2012a), e.g. *They're changeable, these moors.*

In addition to spoken grammar and lexis, a case has also been made for a focus on conversation strategies (e.g. Dat 2013; Goh 2007): 'Various communication strategies using the target language have been identified for instructional purposes. These include adjusting your message according to competence, paraphrasing, appealing for help, asking for clarification and repetition and comprehension checks' (Goh 2007: 7).

A further potential focus in teaching speaking is the structure of certain spoken genres, e.g. presentations, speeches or anecdotes.

Task 7.1

What criteria for the design of speaking activities are suggested by the section above?

- Materials for speaking should . . .

THE SYLLABUS QUESTION

Evaluations of speaking materials

We began this chapter by referring to the rather nebulous nature of speaking skill syllabuses in coursebooks. We noted that in many cases, a speaking syllabus consisted only of a list of activities, though lists of functions, also known as speech acts (see Chapter 3), began to appear with the advent of CLT (Basturkmen 2001). Such functions typically appeared under headings such as 'giving advice', 'making invitations', 'giving directions' etc. The inclusion of useful words, phrases and structures alongside speaking activities is noted by Hughes (2002), but it is often not clear on what basis such language was chosen, and it is also open to question whether learners can integrate such language into a speaking activity if it is simply presented as a list to consult. Cullen and Kuo (2007) carried out a survey of a number of popular EFL coursebooks to investigate how they dealt with spoken language. Coverage of spoken language, they concluded, was generally unsystematic:

> coverage of features of spoken grammar is at best patchy. Where it is dealt with at all, there tends to be an emphasis on lexicogrammatical features, and common syntactic structures peculiar to conversation are either ignored or confined to advanced levels as interesting extras. (Cullen and Kuo 2007: 361)

We should note, however, that their survey did not include the *Touchstone* series (McCarthy, McCarten and Sandiford 2006), which draws on the North America data in the Cambridge English Corpus and which advertises among its features a focus on conversation strategies and 'Conversation Panels which present interesting facts about how vocabulary and grammar are used in conversation'. The 'overt' nature of the influence of CL on *Touchstone* is noted by Norton (2009) in an evaluation of three coursebooks which also included *Advanced Innovations* and *Real Listening and Speaking*. Summarising her evaluation of these three, Norton (2009) writes:

> The course book evaluation reveals that some features of spoken grammar, such as vague language, hedges, and modifiers, appear in the above texts . . . There are, however, few explicit references to other features of spoken grammar, such as heads and tails, and there is the tendency to focus more upon lexicogrammatical items or formulaic expressions in I [*Innovations*] and T [*Touchstone*], and to a lesser degree in R [*Real Listening and Speaking*].

The general impression, then, is of greater attention being given to spoken language in contemporary materials, but in rather an ad hoc manner. There are, however, as we shall see below, proposals for more systematic oral syllabuses based on features of spoken language and/or on discourse types.

An itemised speaking syllabus

A syllabus based on features of spoken language might focus on one or more of the following aspects(spoken lexis, spoken grammar, functions and communication strategies.)In relation to features of spoken language, McCarthy (2004) speaks of the need for 'a carefully crafted syllabus' informed (but not driven) by corpus evidence, particularly frequency information. By contrast, Dellar (2004) insists that materials writers have enough knowledge of the nature of conversation to make sound intuitive judgements about which spoken features should be the focus of attention.

A third way of selecting spoken language items, which seeks to combine both systematic and intuitive approaches, is suggested by Timmis (2013), who argues that decisions may be best left to teachers in their own contexts making ad hoc decisions to focus on spoken language when opportunities arise during the natural course of classroom work. Timmis refers to the need for teachers to become *systematic opportunists*:

by acquainting them with spoken language research findings and equipping them with the methodological tools to exploit opportunities to focus on spoken language which are presented, for example, by the listening texts used in class or by conversations which take place in class. (Timmis 2013: 89)

Such an approach may only be applicable for unmediated materials (see Chapter 1), but Timmis (2013) acknowledges a role for published materials in providing examples of potentially useful spoken language features and sample activities.

A syllabus of discourse types

An alternative approach to an itemised syllabus is to arrange the syllabus around discourse types: e.g. informal conversations, service encounters, interviews, presentations and so on. Such a syllabus focuses on highlighting the link between language choice and genre, speaker and situation (Hughes 2002). It is important, we would argue, to ensure exposure to a range of discourse types: one criticism of task-based syllabuses, for example, has been that they over-emphasise transactional exchanges at the expense of interpersonal exchanges (Carter 2004; Thornbury and Slade 2006). It is interesting in this respect that Hughes (2002) argues that scant attention is given in materials to how language choice is influenced by genre, speaker or situation. Hughes (2002: 54–5) is particularly critical of pair work books where 'the notion of what is polite or appropriate is wholly divorced from any social, or indeed any realistic conversational context'.

A framework for developing a speaking syllabus

In terms of an overall framework for developing a speaking syllabus, Dat (2013: 413–16) proposes the following steps:

1) Conceptualising learner needs
2) Translating needs to subject matter and communication situations
3) Identifying verbal communication strategies
4) Utilising verbal sources from real life
5) Designing skill-acquiring activities.

Dat stresses that we need to consider both objective and subjective needs (i.e. needs and wants) and that needs analysis should be an ongoing process. As he acknowledges (2013), it is crucial that learners are aware of their needs if this kind of framework is to be of value: the more specifically learners state their needs, the more appropriately the subject matter can be established toward appropriate sets of topics, situations, functions, strategies, registers and key structures, as can the sources to build all these components with. An orientation towards needs is clearly desirable, but it is open to question, we would argue, how clearly these can be established either subjectively or objectively, as it is not always easy to predict in what circumstances learners will need or want to use English.

Task 7.2
Evaluate the speaking component of a coursebook.

- Is there a specific speaking syllabus in the map of the book?
- Can you see any rationale for the kinds of speaking activity included in the book?
- How would you improve the speaking component of the materials for your context?

METHODOLOGY FOR TEACHING SPEAKING

Process or product?
Once we have established the features and skills we need to teach, we need to decide on a methodology. Bygate (2001: 17) suggests that we may need a different kind of methodology for teaching the speaking skill:

> Oral skills and oral language should be practised and assessed under different conditions from written skills, and . . . unlike the various traditional approaches to providing oral practice, a distinct methodology and syllabus may be needed.

It is interesting that, by contrast, McCarthy (2004: 15) suggests that a switch in focus to an innovative, corpus-informed spoken language may need to be counterbalanced by a 'conservative' methodology: the traditional PPP paradigm.

> Teachers and learners should expect that, in most ways, corpus-informed materials will look like traditionally prepared materials. The presentation of new language and activity types will be familiar. Certainly, teachers do not need any additional knowledge to use them.

To judge by the quotations above, Bygate (2001) and McCarthy (2004) may appear to hold contradictory views on the most appropriate methodology to adopt. Here again, however, we need to keep in mind the distinction we made in Chapter 6, in relation to the speaking skill, between *process* and *product*: whereas Bygate's (2001) suggestion that a distinct methodology may be needed refers to *process* – the speaking skill – McCarthy's (2004) observation refers to *product* – spoken grammar and lexis. There is no *necessary* contradiction between the two views, though, as we shall see, some have argued that PPP is not the most appropriate paradigm for teaching spoken language.

Evaluations of methodology for teaching speaking
In their review of three coursebooks, *Inside Out* (Kay and Jones 2000); *face2face* (Redston and Cunningham 2006) and *Outcomes* (Dellar and Walkley 2010), Burns and Hill (2013) argue that the dominant methodology, even for spoken language, remains 'behaviourist' PPP. They lament in particular that the speaking activities are add-ons after reading, writing and vocabulary work, and that the role of the listener or conversation partner is given insufficient attention. As we noted above, a detailed

evaluation of three coursebooks in terms of the speaking skill was also carried out by Norton, who focused on the following books: *Advanced Innovations* (Dellar 2007), *Real Listening and Speaking* (Craven 2008) and *Touchstone 2* (McCarthy et al. 2006). Unlike Burns and Hill (2013), Norton does note in these coursebooks some shift in methodological emphasis towards a 'noticing approach'. Similarly, Cullen and Kuo (2007) in their extensive survey of twenty-four general EFL coursebooks note a shift away from PPP, or at least from the 'behaviourist' model of PPP identified by Burns and Hill (2013). Cullen and Kuo (2007) identified an approach to teaching spoken language which generally included some or all of the following components:

- exposure to the feature through a semi-scripted listening text
- global comprehension task on the listening text
- focus on the target feature (through repeated listening or use of the transcript)
- brief explanation of the feature and questions
- short controlled practice activity

Proposals for methodologies to teach speaking

Text-based proposals
Alternative methodological frameworks for teaching spoken language have indeed been proposed by McCarthy and Carter (1995) and Timmis (2005). McCarthy and Carter proposed an i-i-i paradigm consisting of illustration, induction and interaction, whereas Timmis (2005) proposed a framework incorporating cultural access tasks, listening tasks, noticing tasks and language discussion tasks. Both of these frameworks take spoken *texts* as a starting point and focus on noticing and awareness-raising rather than production. It is worth noting, however, that Jones (2007) argues there is a case that practice itself can be a form of noticing, as learners, through experimenting with new forms, gain a closer understanding of how and when to use them. It is worth noting here that 'practice' can cover a wide range of activities and is sometimes deprecated because it is wrongly associated only with activities at the controlled and repetitive end of the spectrum. Kuo (2006) also argues for a production stage, emphasising the potential value of active control of conversational language features for all learners. An alternative noticing approach is suggested by Jones (2001), who proposes comparison tasks to encourage learners to focus on discourse features typical of native speaker oral narrative. In his example, learners are presented with two versions of an anecdote: one which is a simple narration of events and one which includes authentic discourse features. The learners are then given questions which facilitate a comparison between the texts and draw attention to the discourse features of anecdotes. In Tomlinson's (2013b) framework for materials development, speaking activities are suggested as one option for the text-based development activities proposed in the framework.

Task-based proposals
While task-based approaches (see Chapters 3 and 5) are not dedicated solely to the development of the speaking skill (at least in theory), it has been argued that specific

aspects of task-based frameworks offer rich opportunities for work on speaking skills (e.g. Foster and Skehan 1996; Skehan and Foster 1997; Bygate 2001). There is evidence, for example, that allowing learners planning time before tasks can pay dividends in terms of fluency and/or accuracy and/or complexity of language produced (Skehan 1998, cited in Goh 2007). Among the potential benefits of pre-task planning are:

- more experimentation with complex or new forms to express complex ideas
- better monitoring during task performance
- greater fluency
- improved accuracy in certain tasks

Pre-task work may involve gathering ideas, planning the discourse structure or deciding on what lexis or grammar to use.

Task type is also likely to have an effect on both accuracy and fluency. In general, for example, linguistic complexity seems to be affected by the cognitive complexity of the task (Goh 2007): the more cognitively complex the task, the less complex the language. Willis and Willis (1996) suggest that a focus on accuracy and complexity might come at a post-task reporting phase, though they do not specify that the report should be spoken.

Research also suggests that learners can benefit from repeating tasks (e.g. Bygate 2001). Goh (2007: 36) summarises the potential benefits of task repetition:

- greater fluency
- more idiomatic speech and lexical accuracy
- better framing of narratives
- greater grammatical accuracy in some tasks
- greater language complexity

An interesting proposal for gradual and systematic development of the speaking skill is provided by Burns and Hill (2013), who suggest taking L1 conversation as a starting point (given a monolingual class). They suggest that learners might first analyse both their own and others' L1 conversation to get a feel for the nature of spoken language. Learners are then exposed to short, authentic L2 conversations which they can follow with the transcript. The next step is to focus on the language needed to discuss the topic of the recorded conversation and to practise both pronunciation of specific words and phrase intonation. Finally learners carry out and record their conversations, which they can analyse later.

In conclusion, we have stressed the importance of the skill of speaking. Indeed, it has arguably become more important as 'educational policymakers internationally have placed greater focus on spoken language skills' (Burns and Hill 2013: 231). We should also note that speaking, as well as being a skill in its own right, can play an important role in language acquisition. Swain (1995), for example, develops a 'comprehensible output hypothesis' (see Chapter 2) which stresses the value of 'pushed output' where learners are stretched just beyond their comfort zone and seek resources, perhaps from an interlocutor, to express what they want to say.

Corpus research, we observed, has provided a wealth of information about the nature of spoken language. This wealth of information, however, presents considerable challenges in terms of specifying an itemised syllabus. We should note here that the increasing international use of English throws into question the relevance of findings about *native speaker* spoken English (see Chapter 3 of this volume and Timmis 2012a for further discussion of this issue).

There is also a considerable methodological challenge: are traditional output-focused paradigms such as PPP appropriate for aspects of language which are particularly context-sensitive? We have stressed the importance of task design for optimal development of the speaking skill, arguing, for instance, that pre-task planning, task reporting and task repetition may add value to such activities. While we discussed product-oriented and process-oriented approaches separately, we need to emphasise that they are not mutually exclusive. Indeed, as Bygate (2001: 19) argues:

> A basic issue concerns whether or not tasks can involve learners in working with particular kinds of language feature, or whether the use of tasks is a kind of 'blind' pedagogy, allowing learners to express themselves in whatever way they wish. Generating 'Student Talking Time', sometimes seen as the benchmark of a good lesson, is not enough. Materials developers need to consider speaking activities in relation to fluency, accuracy, complexity and appropriacy, and to ensure, when designing a given activity, that it addresses at least one of these aspects of the speaking skill in a principled and systematic manner.

Task 7.3
Evaluate three speaking activities from a coursebook.

- What is the topic of the speaking tasks?
- (How) are the learners prepared for the task, e.g. through a listening or reading text, through pre-teaching specific language, through pair or group preparation?
- Is there any follow-up to the speaking task?

Task 7.4
Adapt one of the speaking activities you analysed to make it suitable for a specific group of your choice.

7.3 MATERIALS TO DEVELOP WRITING SKILLS

Task 7.5
Teaching writing skills can never simply involve giving students a topic and asking them to write about it. (Hyland 2013: 404)

What else should teaching writing skills involve other than 'giving students a topic and asking them to write about it'?

INTRODUCTION

It is only relatively recently that writing has been treated in materials as a skill in its own right. As Reid (2001: 28) observes, 'even as late as the 1970s, L2 writing was not viewed as a language skill to be taught to learners. Instead, it was used as a support skill in language learning to, for example, practise handwriting, write answers to grammar and reading exercises, and write dictation.' The unspoken assumption behind this treatment of writing as a support skill in materials seemed to be that writing involved no more than the transfer of accurate grammar and vocabulary to paper. However, the advent of CLT has led to a greater emphasis on the planned development of 'the four skills' based on detailed analysis of the knowledge, sub-skills and strategies which underpin each skill. The focus on writing as a skill is reflected in the writing syllabuses we currently find in many coursebooks.

We need to note at the outset that the nature of writing has changed somewhat in recent years thanks to the increasing use of electronic media and the emergence of hybrid spoken/written styles such as text messaging, chat room talk and blogs (see also Chapter 5). However, while electronic communication has led to the development of these genres, there is still a need to compose essays and reports, and to write job applications, invitations, complaints and so on, whether on paper or electronically. Indeed, much of the literature on writing in ELT deals with the rather traditional domain of EAP.

THE NATURE OF THE WRITING SKILL

Though our concern is with *materials* for teaching writing, it is useful to begin with an analysis of the writing skill itself so that we can consider how materials can be designed to work on each aspect of the skill. Drawing on Raimes (1983) and Byrne (1988), we can identify the following principal components of the skill:

- **Mechanical aspects**: Mechanical aspects of the writing skill include the ability to form letters (graphology), to spell and to punctuate. It is easy to underestimate the challenge of graphology unless you have learned to use a different script yourself. While we don't write by hand as often as we used to, word processing brings its own challenge: the need for keyboard skills (see also Chapter 5 on digital literacy).
- **Language resources**: Learners need to have good enough control of grammar and lexis to communicate clearly and a wide enough repertoire to be able to adopt the appropriate style for a given text. Hedge (2005) refers to the need for 'a careful choice of vocabulary, grammatical patterns, and sentence structures to create a style which is appropriate to the subject matter and the eventual readers' (p. 7). You will probably not, for example, adopt the same style in an email to a friend complaining about your tutor as you would in a letter of complaint to the university authorities.
- **Organisational skills**:
    - □ **Coherence**: Writing generally involves the production of a text, whether it is a two-line email or a 10,000–word essay, and we generally expect a text to be

coherent, i.e. to have a logical flow of ideas, clearly expressed and all relevant to the topic of the text. There will often be an expectation that texts of a particular type (genre) will be organised in a particular way. Argumentative essays, research reports and job applications, for example, all have their own typical structure, though that structure may be culture-specific.

☐ **Cohesion**: Learners need to have not only a logical flow of ideas, but also the ability to link clauses and sentences locally through the use, for example, of discourse markers, pronouns and synonyms to ensure that they have a *cohesive* text.

- **Genre knowledge**: Writers need to know the audience they are writing for, the expectations of that audience and the linguistic and structural norms of the genre they are writing in. This chapter, for example, needs to be written for an informed audience, in an academic style (though not necessarily a heavy academic style); it also needs to be divided into clearly marked sections with subheadings and to be appropriately referenced. That, at least, is what we are aiming to achieve.

- **Process knowledge**: Learners need to be aware of strategies for generating ideas, writing drafts, editing and revising. This chapter, for example, involved taking notes from a range of sources, organising the notes to form the sections of the chapter, composing a number of drafts and making revisions in response to comments by a co-author and editors.

Though our focus is on materials, we need to consider the main lines of the methodological debate concerning product and process approaches to teaching writing (see Chapter 6 for the process/product distinction in relation to reading and listening). Product approaches typically involve the study of a model text, for example a job application letter. Learners then focus on one or more structural or linguistic features of the model text. In our example, learners might focus on how particular paragraphs deal with topics such as previous experience and future ambitions. Reorganising jumbled paragraphs would be a typical way of doing this. Learners might also focus on specific linguistic features, such as the use of the present perfect to describe relevant experience or the use of specific formulae such as 'I look forward to hearing from you.' There will often be specific exercises to practise these linguistic features. Finally, learners will compose their own text, based on the model text but adapting the content, perhaps by including their own personal information. As Myskow and Gordon (2010: 284) note, texts in a product approach 'are largely seen as autonomous objects that can be analyzed or described independently of particular contexts, writers, or readers'. The strength of the product approach is that it gives learners a clear template to work from and plenty of scaffolding to support their writing. The weakness of the approach, it has been argued, is that it focuses only on surface features of texts and can lead to a rather uncritical emulation of the model text.

Badger and White (2000: 154) give a useful summary of process approaches: 'Writing in process approaches is seen as predominantly to do with linguistic skills, such as planning and drafting, and there is much less emphasis on linguistic knowledge, such as knowledge about grammar and text structure.' The emphasis in process approaches, then, is on generating and organising ideas and will often involve group work and peer editing of drafts. Typical stages in such an approach will be 'prewriting; composing/drafting; revising; and editing' (ibid.), though progression through these stages may be cyclical rather than linear. Badger and White (2000) go on to argue that a weakness of the process approach is its one-size-fits-all nature, which ignores the fact that different kinds of text place different demands on learners. It also fails to take into account that learners will differ in their previous experience of writing particular kinds of text and, therefore, in the amount of support they need. From our point of view as materials writers, it has to be noted that, while materials can provide suggestions about process, they can (and perhaps should) exert little control over the processes learners actually choose to follow, which, in the final analysis, are a question of personal preference.

We need also to consider the advantages of a genre approach, which combines elements of process and product approaches. As Kay and Dudley-Evans remark (1998: 308), most discussions of genre draw on the definitions given by Swales (1990) or Martin (1984). For Martin (1984: 25), a genre is 'a staged, goal-oriented, purposeful activity in which speakers engage as members of our culture'. For Swales (1990: 58), a genre 'comprises a class of communicative events, the members of which share some set of communicative purposes'.

Myskow and Gordon (2010) argue that the chief distinguishing feature of genre approaches is that they focus on the 'social dimension' of writing: texts are written for particular audiences to achieve particular purposes. These authors (2010: 284) acknowledge that a genre approach has something in common with product approaches in that it may involve familiarising learners with the typical discourse patterns of a given text, i.e. how the text is organised to create a particular effect; but a significant difference, Myskow and Gordon argue, is that 'genre-based pedagogies aim to develop a more flexible understanding of generic structures and the ways in which genres interact'. Genre approaches may include elements of a process approach in discussion of how to cater for specific audiences and how to create particular effects in the text. The particular influence of the genre approach on EAP has been noted by Hyland (2003: 175):

> While the focus in the process approach is on the writer, in recent years, the genre approach in EAP has shifted the focus back on the reader with the goal of having learners enter their own academic discourse community.

FROM METHODOLOGY TO MATERIALS

As mentioned above, Hyland (2013) argues that two important roles for materials in teaching writing are to provide a stimulus and to provide scaffolding. In this section, we will consider materials as stimulus, materials as scaffolding, and technological resources.

Stimulus materials

Hyland (2013: 393–4) argues that the main aim of stimulus materials is to 'provide content schemata and a reason to communicate, stimulating creativity, planning and engagement with others'. We need to stress firstly that texts can be a stimulus for writing whether or not they actually serve as 'models', i.e. they can serve as a stimulus for ideas and as a basis for discussion of a topic at the pre-writing stage. Indeed, we noted more generally in Chapter 2 the dual role of input as language data and as a stimulus for other activities. One obvious way to provide such a stimulus is to integrate writing with one or more of the other skills (see Chapter 6). This too reflects a more general argument, in this case that integrating skills is beneficial. If, for example, your aim is to get your learners to write an argumentative essay for or against the idea of compulsory military service, you might prepare your learners for this task in one or more of the following ways:

- provide a recording of a radio or TV debate about this issue
- provide material from an online discussion about the issue
- include a preliminary speaking activity, e.g. a formal debate or an activity where learners interview each other about the issue

The principal idea of these activities is to generate ideas about the topic, but, of course, they may also generate relevant language for the written task at the same time. We should also note that the stimulus for writing may come from visuals instead of or in addition to listening/reading texts and discussion. After all, the picture story has been a staple of the writing class for as long as anyone can remember. The visual may, however, be a single picture, e.g. a photo of an environmental disaster used to stimulate an argumentative essay about pollution. Diagrams, charts and graphs can be useful visual stimuli too – they are particularly (though not exclusively) useful for EAP and ESP classes (and often used in the IELTS writing examination), where the ability to analyse data and write up the analysis is important. The internet provides a rich source of audio-visual materials, texts and data which can be used to stimulate writing, though when writing materials you clearly need to be confident that the link will remain 'live' for their life-span.

Scaffolding tasks

Hyland (2013: 392) notes that scaffolding tasks provide opportunities for discussion, guided writing, analysis and manipulation of salient structures and vocabulary. A battery of tasks which have become popular through CLT can be turned to the service of scaffolding writing:

- reordering, e.g. jumbled sentences in a paragraph or jumbled paragraphs from a text
- matching, e.g. subheadings with text sections
- completion, e.g. completing gaps where discourse markers have been removed 'grammaring' (see chapter 8), where grammar has to be added to the lexical words from a section of the text

- deletion, e.g. removing a sentence or a paragraph which doesn't fit into the text
- substitution/addition, e.g. adding a conclusion to a text (from which the conclusion has been removed)
- transformation, e.g. rewriting a text in a more formal or less formal style, or rewriting a text in a more or less academic style

Hyland (2013: 394) comments on the general aims of such scaffolding tasks: 'the most effective language exercises focus on the features of the genre under consideration to help students create meanings for particular readers and contexts'.

Harnessing technology

While the use of technology in teaching writing does not constitute a unique methodology – technology, as we established in Chapter 5, is a resource not a methodology – it does offer some specific options which are worth considering separately. As long ago as 2001, Reid argued that the 'use of technology in English L2 writing courses may be the foremost curricular change today' (2001: 32). At the most basic level, the internet offers access to a massive supply of texts (Hyland 2013). Stapleton and Radia (2010) refer to a number of potential uses of technology to develop the writing skill:

- Learners, especially ESP learners, can use concordancers (see Chapter 5) to investigate the use of specific vocabulary and phrases.
- Learners can use a thesaurus to investigate synonyms, and access other online reference resources such as dictionaries and encyclopaedias.
- If learners are in doubt about the use of a particular word or phrase, they can enter it into Google: a low level of hits will probably indicate that they are not using the word or phrase conventionally.
- Using a programme called Check My Words (http://mws.ust.hk/cmw/index.php), learners can quickly investigate both concordances and collocations of a particular word or phrase.
- Learners can use online text analysis tools (e.g. on the Using English site: http://www.usingenglish.com/resources/text-statistics.php) to examine the lexical density of their texts (i.e. the number of different words relative to the total number of words), the frequency of the words they have used, the average length of sentences and so on.

7.1

We may have to wait for the widespread use of electronic coursebooks before these tools can be fully exploited, but in the meantime, materials can at least introduce learners to the potential of these tools by providing guidance on how to use them and sample tasks which illustrate this potential.

Task 7.6

7.2

- Visit the Check my Words site: http://mws.ust.hk/cmw/index.php
- Open the tutorial handout. Which of the functions do you think would be most useful for you and/or your learners?

- Visit the Using English site: http://www.usingenglish.com/resources/text-statistics.php
- Enter a short text in the text box. How useful do you think this resource would be for learners?

THE WRITING SYLLABUS

Thus far we have confined our discussion to methodology and resources, but we need also to consider the principles on which a writing syllabus might be designed. It should be noted that although the notion of a writing syllabus may seem to conflict with our notion of integrating skills, they are not in fact incompatible: the syllabus may stipulate a particular genre or writing sub-skill, but the preparatory or follow-up activities can still involve other skills. Hedge (2005: 10) states three (self-proclaimed) assumptions about the writing syllabus which are relevant here:

- Classroom writing activities should reflect the ultimate goal of enabling students to write whole texts which form connected, contextualised, and appropriate pieces of communication.
- Students need opportunities to practise various forms and functions of writing and within these to develop the different skills involved in producing written texts
- When setting writing activities, teachers need to vary the audience, identify who the readers are to be, and try to make every piece of writing fulfil some kind of communicative purpose, either real or simulated. When students understand the context, they are much more likely to write effectively and appropriately.

Chen and Su (2012: 185) refer to Sidaway's (2006) seven genre categories (listed below with examples), suggesting that these might form the basis of a syllabus:

1. recount, e.g. a witness statement
2. narrative, e.g. an anecdote
3. explanation, e.g. why volcanoes erupt
4. information report, e.g. a weather report
5. procedure, e.g. how to apply for a visa
6. discussion, e.g. the pros and cons of private education
7. exposition, e.g. a political manifesto

Each genre, Chen and Su (2012: 185) note, may be found in various text types: for example, 'a narrative may be found in email messages, newspaper articles, novels, and so forth'. Two further organisational possibilities for a writing syllabus are noted by Hedge (2005):

1. The syllabus could be organised around broad styles of writing, e.g. personal writing (e.g. personal experiences); study writing (e.g. academic essays); public

writing (e.g. complaints, inquiries); creative writing (e.g. stories and poetry); social writing (e.g. letters and emails); and institutional writing (e.g. minutes; agendas).
2. The syllabus could be organised according to functions, e.g. description, narration, argument, review and summary.

It is worth drawing attention to the mention of creative writing in (1) above. When discussion turns to writing, people in ELT who are normally relaxed and cheerful suddenly put on serious expressions and sensible suits and talk in earnest tones about discourse markers as if writing can never be an enjoyable activity per se. Among the possibilities for creative writing, Hedge (2005) notes poems, stories, rhymes and drama.

In conclusion, we have argued that writing is a complex skill and that materials have an important role to play in developing this skill, as emphasised by Hyland (2013: 404–5): 'Essentially, materials should contribute towards students' understanding of a target genre (its purpose, context, structure and main features) or provide opportunities to practise one or more aspects of the writing process (pre-writing, drafting, revising and editing).' We have considered what is involved in product, process and genre approaches, but argued that, as we argue in relation to other skills, we need not wed ourselves to one approach and, indeed, that these approaches can be combined. As Badger and White (2000: 157) note, an 'effective methodology for writing needs to incorporate the insights of product, process, and genre approaches. One way of doing this is to start with one approach and adapt it'. Key factors in choice of approach are the nature of the text to be composed and the likely familiarity of the learners with the kind of text in question. Let us end this section on an upbeat note with Hyland's (2013: 400) positive view of designing materials to teach writing: 'Designing new writing materials can be an extremely satisfying activity. It not only offers students a more tailored learning experience but also demonstrates a professional competence and perhaps fulfils a creative need in teachers.'

Task 7.7
Below is a list of common problems with published writing materials noted by Hyland (2013: 396). Begin by converting these observations into evaluation criteria for writing materials and then add other criteria of your own.

- Cultural and social bias in the readings (used as models or as a stimulus for writing);
- Ad hoc grammar not genre-specific;
- Vagueness about target users' backgrounds and proficiency;
- Lack of specificity about target needs;
- Over-reliance on writing themes addressing personal experiences;
- Obsession with a single composing process (e.g. simple product model);
- Invented and misleading text models.

Task 7.8

Compare the list of criteria you made in Task 7.7 with Hyland's (2003: 97) list of criteria below.

Do the writing materials:

1. represent a coherent view of the writing skill and how it is learned?
2. include interesting and appropriate readings that provide relevant content schemata?
3. cover topics that are culturally appropriate and are included in the syllabus?
4. present clear models of the genres we want our learners to recognise and reproduce?
5. stimulate learning and writing by engaging students' interest, building their confidence, and encouraging them to use their existing knowledge and skills?
6. contain varied, interesting, and relevant activities to help students develop appropriate pre-writing, composing and editing skills?
7. include helpful explanations and clear examples of relevant language use?
8. provide strategies, suggestions, and supplementary materials for presenting and practising writing?

Task 7.9

Design writing materials using ideas from this chapter tailored to learners in your own teaching context. Choose as your prompt an authentic visual/audio-visual or text from the internet.

7.4 FURTHER READING ONE

Thornbury, S. (2005). *How to Teach Speaking.* **Harlow: Longman.**
Thornbury provides a number of criteria for speaking activities (2005: 90–1). These criteria are presented below with excerpts from his explanation of each one.

1. '**Productivity**: a speaking activity needs to be maximally language productive in order to provide the best conditions for autonomous language use.'
2. '**Purposefulness**: often language productivity can be increased by making sure that the speaking activity has a clear outcome, especially one which requires the learners to work together to achieve a common purpose.'
3. '**Interactivity**: activities should require learners to take into account the effect they are having on their audience. If not, they can hardly be said to be good preparation for real-life language use.'
4. '**Challenge**: the task should stretch the learners so that they are forced ⟨ ⟩ their available communicative resources to achieve the outcome.'
5. '**Safety**: while learners should be challenged, they also need to fee⟩ when meeting these challenges and attempting autonomous ⟩ can do so without too much risk.'
6. '**Authenticity**: speaking tasks should have some relation t⟨ If not, they are poor preparation for autonomy.'

Task 7.10
- Evaluate a coursebook speaking activity according to Thornbury's criteria.
- Adapt the activity so that it meets all the criteria effectively.

Task 7.11
Conduct some research to assess how far criterion (6) above, authenticity, is a factor in coursebook speaking materials:

- Look at a selection of speaking materials in a range of coursebooks, assessing whether the materials relate to 'real-life' language use with respect to your own teaching context.
- If, in your opinion, they do not, consider:
    - □ why this is (for example, lack of relevance to the target group of learners on grounds of age, proficiency level, cultural context and so on)
    - □ how they might be adapted to be more authentic (see Chapter 4, Section 4.4, on materials adaptation)

7.5 FURTHER READING TWO

Kay, H. and Dudley-Evans, T. (1998). Genre: what teachers think. *ELT Journal*, 52(4): 308–14.
Kay and Dudley-Evans ran a workshop for teachers during which they consulted the participants about their views on the genre approach to teaching writing. There were fifty-eight participants from ten different countries. Among the views expressed were that teachers should do the following:

- ensure that generic structures are not considered prescriptive, but allow for variations due to cultural and ideological factors
- contextualise a text before its presentation by discussion of purpose, audience, institutional beliefs, values etc., and subsequently ensure that all discussion of linguistic features takes place in the context of their function in the text
- immerse students 'in a wide variety of texts within a particular genre' (p. 312)
- ensure that the genre examples selected for teaching/learning purposes are authentic and suitable for learners
- adopt a lesson procedure which facilitates, rather than inhibits, interaction, since this is a powerful aid to learning
- use a genre approach in conjunction with other methods – specifically mentioned was the desirability of combining genre and process approaches

Task 7.12
How far do you think the ideas expressed above are:

- desirable?
- practical?

Task 7.13

Access the site below to find an online (pdf) version of the following paper:

Hyland, K. (2007). Genre pedagogy: language, literacy and L2 writing instruction, *Journal of Second Language Writing*, 16: 148–64. http://www2.caes.hku.
hk/kenhyland/files/2012/08/Genre-pedagogy_language-literacy-and-L2–writing-
instruction1.pdf

Compare Hyland's ideas for a genre approach to teaching writing to those in Kay
and Dudley-Evans's paper summarised above. For example, Hyland maintains that
'writing is a social activity' (2007: 152) as do Kay and Dudley-Evans, who maintain
that lesson procedures should facilitate interaction.

As with other recommended online resources, we suggest that its in-depth coverage of genre pedagogy for writing makes this paper worth reading in its entirety.

7.6 CONCLUSION

We close this chapter by synthesising the main points we have made in each of the
two main sections. In Section 7.2, we argued that materials for **speaking skills** need
to respond to the complexity and demanding nature of the skill:

- While speaking has long been a priority in ELT, the focus on speaking has often
  been unsystematic due to a failure to distinguish between speaking as grammar/
  vocabulary practice and speaking as skill development.
- The real-time pressure and the interactive and interpersonal concerns which typically accompany speaking have an effect on the nature of spoken language, so that
  it differs from written language in important ways, e.g. grammatical and lexical
  choice and syntactic complexity.
- There are two types of speaking syllabus, though they are not mutually exclusive:
  a syllabus of spoken language features (e.g. ellipsis, discourse markers) and a syllabus of discourse types (e.g. conversations, service encounters, presentations).
- Materials writers need to do more than just provide activities which get learners
  talking. They need to provide activities which develop language and sub-skills
  specific to speaking.

With regard to Section 7.3 on designing materials to develop **writing skills**, the
main points we made can be synthesised as follows:

- As was the case with speaking, it is relatively recently that materials have begun to
  be based on an analysis of what the (writing) skill involves.
- Writing is a complex skill which involves mechanical aspects, language resources,
  organisational skills, genre knowledge and process knowledge.
- Product approaches (based on a model text) and process approaches (focusing on
  the act of writing) have traditionally been contrasted, but they are not incompatible. A genre approach involves elements of both.
- Materials can address writing by providing a stimulus to write and by providing

scaffolding, e.g. help with the structure of the text and/or the grammar and lexis required for the text type.

- Learners can exploit a number of online resources such as concordancers or word frequency highlighters to support their writing.
- A writing syllabus can be based on genres and/or text functions and/or specific grammar and lexis useful for writing particular kinds of texts.

7.7 ADDITIONAL READINGS

Hughes, R. (2010). Materials to develop the speaking skill. In N. Harwood (ed.), *English Language Teaching Materials: Theory and Practice* (pp. 207–24). Cambridge: Cambridge University Press.

This chapter stresses the need to base speaking activities on a clear understanding of what the speaking skill entails. It raises the question as to whether many speaking activities actually develop or teach the skill at all as opposed to just practising it. The chapter finishes with three very useful sample speaking activities which illustrate points made in the preceding discussion.

Tribble, C. (2010. A genre-based approach to teaching writing. In N. Harwood (ed.), *English Language Teaching Materials: Theory and Practice* (pp. 157–79). Cambridge: Cambridge University Press.

This chapter outlines the case for a genre-based approach to teaching writing and, importantly for our purposes, exemplifies the approach through a case study of preparing learners for the discursive essay in the Cambridge First Certificate exam. A further positive feature of this chapter is that Tribble underlines the implications for materials writers of the approach he recommends.

8

MATERIALS FOR VOCABULARY AND GRAMMAR

8.1 INTRODUCTION

This chapter follows the two-part structure of the preceding two chapters and focuses first on materials for teaching vocabulary (Section 8.2) and then on grammar teaching materials (Section 8.3). As with materials for the teaching of the four skills, there is a rich heritage of materials for teaching vocabulary and grammar, but this needs to be examined critically. Vocabulary teaching, for example, cannot be reduced to the level of simply 'learning words', and the availability of corpora in recent years has provided a means to avoid this. We offer a series of examples in this section illustrating how corpus material can be used in vocabulary materials. As for materials for grammar teaching, the preoccupation with these within coursebooks has been strongly criticised (see, for instance, Chapter 2). The concomitant proliferation of grammar materials on offer as models means that the materials developer has to be all the more critical in the selection of which to use. Thus we revisit the debate over PPP, probably the most common procedure used as a model for grammar materials and for grammar teaching, and conclude by recommending principled eclecticism in our selection of these.

8.2 MATERIALS FOR VOCABULARY

INTRODUCTION

It is generally acknowledged that vocabulary is a vital aspect of language learning. It is, after all, difficult to argue with Wilkins's (1972: 111) remark on the relative importance of vocabulary and grammar: 'Without grammar very little can be conveyed; without vocabulary nothing can be conveyed'. While this seems self-evident, it is only recently that vocabulary has assumed a prominent role in materials, with vocabulary syllabuses becoming common in coursebooks from the 1980s onwards (O'Dell 1997). One reason for this increased focus on vocabulary is that the nature of the vocabulary learning task facing learners has been more fully appreciated since the advent of large corpora such as the Collins Birmingham University International Language Database (CoBuild), COCA and the BNC. Thanks to corpus research, we now know far more, for example, about word frequency, vocabulary size, collocation and the relationship between lexis and grammar. Despite such research, it remains difficult to measure the size of the vocabulary learning challenge learners face *precisely*, as McCarten (2007: 1) explains:

> Counting words is a complicated business. For a start, what do we mean by a word? Look at these members of the word family RUN: *run, runs, running, ran, runner, and runners*. Should we count these as one 'word' or six? How do we count different uses of the same word? For example, is the verb *run* the same in *run a marathon* as in *run a company*? Is it the same as the noun *a run*? How do we deal with idiomatic uses like *run out of gas, feel run down*, or *a run of bad luck*?

In addition to *word* frequency, we need also to consider collocations and lexical phrases, for which separate frequency lists have been published (see Shin and Nation 2008 for collocations, and Martinez and Schmitt 2012 for lexical phrases). Despite the difficulties in calculating frequency, an expert estimate is useful in giving some idea of the challenge: Schmitt (2010) gives the following figures for words:

- Native speakers typically know 16,000–20,000 word families.
- Learners need a vocabulary of 8,000 words to read unsimplified material.
- Learners need to know between 2,000 and 3,500 words for reasonable understanding and use.

Considerable progress has clearly been made in defining how much vocabulary needs to be learned, but such research does not tell us exactly what vocabulary should be learned, nor how it should be learned. If, for example, we could assume that learners would make sufficient vocabulary gains through exposure to texts, using processes such as inferring meaning from context, then we might limit ourselves as materials writers to providing a rich variety of motivating texts to promote incidental vocabulary learning. Folse (2011: 363), however, argues forthrightly that explicit teaching (see Chapter 2) is needed in addition to such incidental approaches, particularly if learners need to learn a lot of vocabulary in a short time:

> Though lexical learning can take place through natural exposure (e.g. Pigada and Schmitt, 2006), many more studies have shown ELLs [English language learners] learn and retain vocabulary more effectively when it is explicitly taught (e.g. Laufer and Shmueli, 1997; Min, 2008; Zimmerman, 1997).

Given the size and nature of the task, it appears safe to conclude that *some* explicit focus on vocabulary is required in materials.

VOCABULARY SELECTION AND VOCABULARY KNOWLEDGE

Frequency as a criterion

A commonsense criterion for vocabulary selection is frequency, and the contemporary materials writer, as we have noted, is well served in this respect, as word frequency lists from large corpora such as COCA and the BNC are available, along with collocation and lexical phrase lists. It is also possible for the materials writer to access frequency lists for specific fields of teaching such as academic English (Coxhead 2000). An important question for us as materials writers, if we accept that frequency is a useful criterion, is, 'How can we ensure that frequent words are incorporated in the materials?' There would seem to be three possibilities: (1) lists of topic-related vocabulary for each unit; (2) constructing texts to incorporate the target vocabulary; and (3) selecting vocabulary from texts which have been included in the materials for other purposes (e.g. reading or listening work). It is important to note that these options are not mutually exclusive and it may be both necessary and desirable to combine them to ensure that learners get adequate exposure to high-frequency activity.

While frequency has a role to play, there are clear reasons why it should not be the sole criterion in vocabulary selection, as McCarten (2007: 8) observes:

> It may not be possible to use all the items in the list[1] for a number of reasons. Some may be culturally inappropriate, not suitable for class, or just difficult to use until students have more English. Also, the communication needs of students may be different from those of the people whose conversations are recorded in the Corpus. For example, a word like *homework*, a frequent word in any classroom, comes toward the end of the top 2,000 words, whereas words like *supposed, true, and already*, which are in the top 400, might be challenging for elementary learners.

Another clear reason why frequency cannot be the only criterion is pedagogic convenience: it would be absurd, for example, to separate days of the week in the vocabulary syllabus because some days are more frequently mentioned than others in the corpus.

Beyond frequency

We obviously need to consider criteria other than frequency in our vocabulary selection, and White (1988: 48–50) goes beyond frequency to consider a number of other interesting and useful selection criteria:

- Frequency of use
- Coverage: e.g. 'go' can be used in a wider range of contexts than 'walk' (O'Dell 1997)
- Range: words which can be used in a wider range of texts should be prioritised, e.g. 'acquire a language' may be common in language teaching texts, but 'learn a language' can be used in a variety of texts
- Availability: e.g. certain words seem to go together naturally, though their individual frequencies may be different– for instance (as noted above), days of the week
- Learnability: while adult learners may feel a need for abstract vocabulary, it will typically be easier to teach concrete vocabulary in the early stages, and probably

easier to teach vocabulary for concepts and phenomena which learners are familiar with in their own culture (Gairns and Redman 1986)

- Opportunism: we need to be alert to possibilities for teaching vocabulary as they
  arise, e.g. a topical event or an incident in the classroom may provide a suitable
  opportunity to teach a particular word or set of vocabulary
- Centres of interest: as O'Dell (1997) argues, the learners' own interests and needs
  will come into play the further learners progress through levels of proficiency.

It will clearly be easier to apply opportunism and centres of interest if we are writing
materials for our own classes or our own teaching context.

Selection criteria for collocations and lexical phrases

While the selection criteria we have noted are relatively well established for words,
and are to some extent transferable to collocations and lexical phrases, we need to
consider whether specific criteria are required for these items. The following criteria
for the selection of collocations are suggested by Timmis (2008):

- frequency
- difficulty
- semantic predictability
- strength of collocation
- pedagogic convenience

Two of these criteria are specific to collocations and require explanation: semantic
predictability and strength of collocation. Firstly, 'semantic predictability' refers to
how easy it is to infer the meaning of a lexical chunk from its component parts, e.g.
the meaning of the chunk *small talk* is not easily predictable from its constituent
parts, whereas the meaning of *strong coffee* is. There is an argument, then, for focusing on the former rather than the latter, as the latter is self-evident. Secondly, Conzett
(2000: 74) gives a useful definition of strong collocations: 'the presence of one word
means that you strongly expect the other'. In this sense *dulcet tones* is a very strong
collocation, as it is very difficult to think of any word but tones that could follow
dulcet; i.e. as soon as you hear the word *dulcet*, you strongly expect to hear *tones*.
High prices, however, would be regarded as a weak collocation, as *high* can collocate
with numerous other words. Hill (2000) suggests we focus our attention on medium-
strength collocations, where a word has a limited set of common collocates. The verb
achieve, for example, collocates obviously with the following words (among others):
goal, *target*, *aim* and *objective*. If the collocates themselves share a sense, as is the case
with the collocates of *achieve* above, so much the better.

Word knowledge

As well as considering what vocabulary needs to be learned, we also need to consider
what should be learned about a given lexical item, as illustrated in Task 8.1.

Task 8.1

What aspects of word knowledge have caused problems in the examples below? Match the types of word knowledge (listed as bullet points below) with the examples (1–10) that follow. You can use the word knowledge terms more than once.

Types of word knowledge:

- style/register
- pronunciation (stress)
- word grammar (morphology)
- word grammar (countable/uncountable)
- collocation
- lexical chunk
- word grammar (dependent preposition)

Examples:

1. I got big progress in English last year.
2. She commended the learners' courageous trials.
3. Are you married or are you a spinster?
4. I am not responsible of this problem.
5. I reckon TPR is a daft methodology but it might be OK for kids [written in an academic essay].
6. I have problems learning voca**bu**lary. [**Bold** marks the stressed syllable]
7. I am doing a research about learners' pronunciation.
8. Vocabulary is a large theme in my thesis.
9. It's just a figment of your thinking.
10. I admire your seriosity.

Task 8.2

Drawing on the examples you worked with in Task 8.1, consider the implications of the complexity of word knowledge for vocabulary teaching materials.

VOCABULARY LEARNING IN MATERIALS

Bring back 'old-fashioned techniques'

We must now turn our attention to practical ways of incorporating vocabulary work into materials. In this respect, it is interesting to note that certain traditional activities have enjoyed something of a renaissance recently: learning vocabulary from lists and bilingual dictionary work. While these activities may go against the grain for those brought up on the communicative approach, it is important to consider the research evidence so that we can appraise them more objectively. The case for using lists is made, for example, by Folse (2011: 363):

At first glance, using lists may seem counterproductive. In the rush toward natural language learning, word lists were downplayed, but there is no empirical research showing learning words from a list to be unproductive . . . In fact, research comparing studying words in a list versus various kinds of context has shown that lists yielded better results than extended context (Laufer and Shmueli, 1997; Prince, 1996).

Materials, then, might specify lists of key vocabulary to be learnt in each unit, however old-fashioned this practice may seem. Folse (2004) is equally emphatic about the value of dictionary work, arguing that the research evidence shows diction-ary work to be more effective than guessing from context, and the use of bilingual dictionaries to be more effective than the use of monolingual ones. This suggests that there is a role for materials in training learners to use dictionaries efficiently. Indeed, some coursebooks include mini-dictionaries in the materials package.

Semantic and thematic sets

In addition to the rehabilitation of 'old-fashioned' techniques and activities, recent years have also seen challenges to current orthodoxy. In particular, the very common practice in both materials and general teaching of presenting words in semantic sets has been questioned. The semantic set approach involves teaching words in meaning-related groups, e.g. fruits, transport, furniture, family members etc. If we take the semantic-set approach to teaching words for family members, for example, we might use a family tree diagram to teach a number of these words. Folse (2004), however, claims that it is more effective to present vocabulary in 'thematic sets' rather than semantic ones, and suggests that family vocabulary could be presented in a thematic set through a story about a trip to the beach which involves a number of family members. In similar vein, Papathanasiou (2009: 318) points to research which suggests that the semantic set approach to teaching vocabulary may not be the most effective:

> The result above [i.e. that the semantic set approach to teaching vocabulary may not be the most effective] is compatible with the results of previous research (Tinkham 1997; Waring 1997; Schneider, Healy, and Bourne 1998; Finkbeiner and Nicol 2003) illustrating that presenting L2 students (beginners) with their new vocabulary grouped together in sets of syntactically and semantically similar words impedes rather than facilitates the learning of those words.

There are, of course, other ways of grouping vocabulary than by semantic sets. Gairns and Redman (1986: 31), for example, suggest that 'grouping items together by synonymy, hyponymy, antonymy [i.e. opposites] and other types of relations [cause and effect, situation, narrative] will help to give coherence to the lesson'. However, they do not refer to any research evidence to support this assertion. The question which arises here is whether what is pedagogically convenient is in tune with learn-ing processes.

Depth of processing

Despite the sometimes conflicting views about how vocabulary should be taught, there does seem to be consensus around three areas: 'depth of processing' (Craik and Lockhart 1972), learner strategies and recycling are all vital for effective vocabulary learning. The sequence below, based on Cameron (2001), illustrates depth of processing used to present vocabulary for leisure activities to young learners:

1. The teacher mimes the leisure activities (e.g. swimming, cycling) and says the words at the same time.
2. The teacher says the words and the pupils mime the activity.
3. The pupils draw three of the activities. The teacher reads out the words, and the first pupil to hear three of the words he has drawn is the winner (i.e. bingo).
4. The pupils divide the activities into two groups: ones which are very dangerous and ones which are not so dangerous.
5. Pupils choose the activities they would like to try.
6. Pupils look at pictures and say the words.

In this case, we can see that the words are processed visually (1, 6), aurally (2, 3), kinaesthetically (2, 3), cognitively (4), affectively (5) and orally (6). There is no need, of course, for all these processes to be used in one lesson. The role of materials here could be to explain and exemplify depth of processing so that teachers incorporate this kind of 'routine' into their teaching repertoire. As Folse (2011: 364) notes: 'The single most important aspect of any vocabulary practice activity is not so much what [learners] do with the word but rather the number of times [they] interact with the word.'

Vocabulary learning strategies

O'Dell (1997), Folse (2011) and Nation (2012, 2013) all emphasise the value of vocabulary learning strategies. For Nation (2012: 100), teaching vocabulary learning strategies is the second most important task of the teacher (after vocabulary planning), and he goes on to prioritise the different strategies thus: 'guessing from context, learning using word cards, using word parts, and using a dictionary'. He also notes that such strategies need training and development over a period of time. Folse (2011) does not prioritise particular strategies but argues that the key factor is that learners have an individualised set of strategies which they apply consistently. We can see a role for materials, then, in presenting and modelling different vocabulary learning strategies which learners can experiment with and then choose those which they find most effective.

Recycling vocabulary

The case for consistent and systematic recycling of vocabulary is now well established, and one well-known approach to this is 'graduated interval recall' (Sokmen 1997) or 'expanding rehearsal' (Schmitt and Schmitt 1995). The guiding principle of this procedure is that words are recycled frequently, but with longer intervals between each instance of recycling: a set of words could be recycled, for example, a day after presentation, then a week after, then a month after and so on. The role of personalisation in retention is stressed by both Sokmen (1997) and McCarten (2007). Sokmen (1997) stresses the value of learners relating words to their own experiences, while McCarten (2007: 23) argues that 'materials should provide opportunities for students to use the vocabulary meaningfully, to say and write true things about themselves and their lives'. Sokmen also points to the value of learners imaging (i.e. visualising) words for vocabulary retention. Both these proposals suggest a role for production in vocabulary retention, an area which Nation (2012: 96) suggests is under-researched, though he proposes that 'meaning-focused output' does have a role to play in vocabulary retention. Materials can recycle vocabulary through games and tests and also by ensuring that learners meet key vocabulary on several occasions in the materials.

Text-based vocabulary work
When designing vocabulary activities to include in materials, some options for vocabulary teaching are easier to adopt than others: materials, for example, cannot include realia or perform mime (though a teacher's book can advise the teacher to do so). However, a variety of processes which are common practice in CLT can be turned to the service of vocabulary materials (Timmis 2008), e.g. identifying, categorising, matching, gap-filling and guessing from context. These processes offer opportunities for text-based vocabulary work and are illustrated in the example activities below.

Task 8.3
Look through the six example activities below and consider the following questions:

- What processes are used in the activities (e.g. matching, categorising etc.)?
- What stages would you add to each activity (e.g. pronunciation, activation)?

NB For all these activities the assumption is that the learners have already read and understood a text or texts which contain(s) the target words.

Example Activity 1

Accuse; sue; libel; trial; evidence; case; award; damages; an alibi; arrest; charge; perjury; defence; find guilty; sentence; investigation.

The words in the box above are all taken from the text you have just read. Match the words with the clues below.

(a) 2 things the police do
(b) 1 thing the police carry out
(c) 1 thing the jury does
(d) 1 thing the police try to find

(e) 2 things the judge does
(f) 2 crimes or offences
(g) 2 things which anyone can do
(h) the opposite of the prosecution
(i) something which should help the defendant
(j) something which can last for hours or days or weeks or even months
(k) something you can win or lose

Example Activity 2
The words in the box are all taken from the text you have just read. Divide the words in the box into two groups: those that describe how a person thinks and those that describe someone's personality.

Logical; emotional; creative; sequential; random; funny; sensible; rational; sensitive; intuitive; nice; holistic; mature; synthesising; considerate; analytical; dumb; objective; subjective; hare-brained.

Way of thinking	Personality
Logical	Emotional

Example Activity 3
Musical collocations

1. Complete the spaces in the sentences with one word from Box A and one word from Box B to make a collocation from the text you have just read.
2. Put the right collocation into the gaps in the sentences.

Box A	Box B
Record	Clubbing
Huge	Talent
Concert	Crown
Western	Hit
Sign	Deal
Theme	Market
Solo	Single
Release	Award
Go	Attendance
Win	Company
Raw	on

1. 'Billie Jean' was a .... for Michael Jackson all over the world.
2. Until recently, no Asian singers had made an impact in the ....
3. Elton John wrote the .... for the film 'The Lion King'.
4. After The Spice Girls had split up, some of them made ....
5. The promoters were disappointed because the .... was lower than expected.

6. There is no denying that he has the ...., but he will need training to make it to the top.

7. Many groups and artists try to .... a new single just before Christmas.

8. I wonder who will .... the Emmy .... this year.

9. The record company was so impressed by her performance that they .... her ....

10. Many young people like to .... until the early hours of the morning
·   at weekends.

Example Activity 4

Humanity; proud; poverty; deprivation; liberate; discrimination; freedom; justice; indignity; oppression; achievement; equality

---

1. The words in the box are all taken from the texts you have read in this unit. Divide the words into two categories: those which have positive meanings and those which have negative meanings:

Positive	Negative

2. Use the correct *form* of the words above to complete the sentences below:
Example: I think that this will be a difficult goal to _____.
Answer: I think that this will be a very difficult goal to achieve.

(a) This university does not _____ against people on the grounds of gender, religion or race.

(b) In a _____ society there is no discrimination.

(c) Rousseau said: 'Man is born _____ but is everywhere in chains.'

(d) Despite his _____ childhood, he achieved great things.

(e) In some countries, the gap between rich and _____ is getting wider.

(f) King wanted to _____ his people from oppression.

(g) Some people believe it is _____ to perform experiments on animals.

(h) The achievement of nationhood is a source of national _____ for Singaporeans.

(i) You can't guarantee that everyone will achieve the same, but you can make sure that people have _____ opportunities.

Example Activity 5

1. Explain in your own words what the expressions in bold mean which are all taken from the text you have just read.

• Dublin's alternative scene **has taken off** in the last few years.
• We wear what we like after school **without getting much hassle**

- Siobhan (17) is **watching the world go by** with her friends Brian (17) and Emma (16)
- we're going to **work like mad** to get the right points in our exams next June', says Siobhan.

Example Activity 6
Which word in the group does **not** collocate with the word in bold?

1. **Absorb**	information	water	concrete	details
2. **Take in**	facts	information	details	studies
3. **Avert**	your gaze	a person	a disaster	
4. **Perform**	a role	a task	a match	a play
5. **Carry out**	a task	research	studies	a career
6. **A demanding**	research	role	job	task
7. **To process**	information	job applications	data	facts

EVALUATING VOCABULARY WORK IN MATERIALS

As materials developers, we need to be able to generate sound and practical design principles for vocabulary work from the theoretical discussion above. A set of evaluation criteria for vocabulary work in coursebooks devised by Gairns and Redman (1986) provides, with a little adaptation and updating, a very useful basis for the generation of design principles:

- Is there a lexical syllabus? And a rationale for vocabulary selection?
- How are vocabulary items grouped?
- How many items are introduced at once?
- What learning approaches are selected? Are strategies taught?
- Does the teacher's book suggest teaching procedures?
- Are practice and testing activities provided? Is vocabulary recycled?
- How are learners encouraged to consolidate and widen their vocabulary outside the classroom?
- Does the coursebook contain useful visual material?
- Does the coursebook anticipate vocabulary needed for skills activities?

Finally, McCarten (2007: 19–20) provides the following summary of the role materials can play in vocabulary work:

> Materials can help students in two broad areas: First, they need to present and practise in natural contexts the vocabulary that is frequent, current, and appropriate to learners' needs. Second, materials should help students become better learners of vocabulary by teaching different techniques and strategies they can use to continue learning outside the classroom. And materials can help teachers in this in the following ways:

- Providing clearly marked vocabulary lessons
- Making the target vocabulary set stand out, including focused practice and regular review
- Giving lists of vocabulary to be learned for the lesson

Task 8.4

Apply the evaluation criteria suggested by Gairns and Redman (above) to the treatment of vocabulary in a coursebook you know or use.

8.3 MATERIALS FOR TEACHING GRAMMAR

INTRODUCTION

As we noted in Chapter 2, the place of grammar teaching in the language classroom has been a matter of intense debate for some time. It is somewhat ironic, then, that the place of grammar in *published* materials seems to be a matter of orthodoxy. Indeed, Stranks (2013) regards the preoccupation of coursebooks with grammar as 'obsessive', while Waters (2012) noted that the preoccupation of a particular best-selling coursebook with grammar, except for a few cosmetic changes, had actually *increased* over recent years despite continued theoretical uncertainty about the place of grammar teaching. Although we need to take into account contextual factors such as the age, needs and wants of the learners in reaching a decision as to whether to include work on grammar in our materials, we also need to take a position on whether materials which directly address grammar are *ever* useful and, if so, what kind of grammar materials might be useful for our purposes. Here it will be useful for readers to refer back to Chapter 2 and the consensus from SLA research that some kind of focus on grammar is beneficial to acquisition.

Task 8.5

Do *you* think materials should always have a grammar component? Refer back to arguments in Chapter 2 to justify your answer.

A GRAMMAR SYLLABUS

If you are writing materials for publication, you will probably find that the grammar syllabus is quite closely defined for you (see Chapter 9). However, if you are not writing for publication, you will be able to base your grammar syllabus on theoretically informed principles and customise them to your assessment of your target learners' needs, wants and learning preferences. You will, in this case, be interested, as both Swan (2006) and Stranks (2013) suggest, in the specific grammatical problems your target learners typically have. These problems may not actually be with the 'big grammatical topics' such as tenses or conditionals, but may lie in the area of what Timmis (2008) refers to as 'microgrammar', e.g. reporting patterns with specific verbs (e.g. *blame something on someone*); verb and preposition combinations (e.g. *depend on, rely on*); gerund/infinitive choices (e.g. *I hope to go, I don't mind going*);

and specific aspects of article use. If you are in control of the grammar syllabus, you will also be interested in the things your target learners want and need to say and the kind of structures which will best enable your learners to do this. This may or may not involve teaching inverted conditional structures such as *Had I assessed their needs, I would not have taught inverted conditionals.*

Two important questions materials designers need to ask, we would argue, when considering whether to include an item in a grammar syllabus, are:

1. What will this grammar structure enable the learners to do?
2. What evidence do I have that this structure causes problems for (these) learners?

It is important to note, however, that in framing such criteria we are not assuming that a syllabus is necessarily defined at the outset of the materials design process. As we have noted in Chapter 2, the syllabus may emerge from the texts and/or tasks selected for the materials: in this case the selection criteria outlined above will be applied retrospectively. Devising a grammar syllabus based on learners' needs, wants and L1 can be a daunting task, but there is no reason why existing syllabuses or documents such as the CEFR should not be used as an *inventory* of items to *select* from on the basis of the criteria we have outlined above.

Task 8.6
- Examine the grammar syllabus of a coursebook in relation to a specific group of learners.
- Rate the usefulness of each item on a scale:
  5   4   3   2   1
  (5 = extremely useful; 1 = not useful at all)

METHODOLOGY FOR GRAMMAR MATERIALS

Methodological options
We have noted a consensus that some kind of focus on grammar makes a difference. There is, however, no such consensus as to what kind of grammar teaching makes a difference (see also Chapter 2), as Swan (2006: 122–3) observes: 'Research on methodology is inconclusive, and has not shown detectable, lasting and wide-ranging effects for implicit versus explicit instruction, for inductive versus deductive learning or separated-out study of structure versus incidental focus on form during communicative activity.' While PPP appears to be the dominant methodology in coursebooks, a range of options is open to the materials writer. Among the options listed by Swan (2006) are:

- deductive teaching through explanations and examples
- inductive discovery activities
- decontextualised practice
- communicative practice
- incidental focus-on-form during communicative tasks

- teacher correction and recasts
- grammar games
- learning rules and examples by heart

We should note here Timmis's (2012b) distinction between proactive and reactive approaches: proactive grammar teaching is planned in advance and reactive teaching is in response to emerging problems or opportunities in the classroom. 'Incidental focus-on-form' and 'teacher correction and recasts' from Swan's (2006) list are essentially reactive and spontaneous and thus not really available to the materials writer, though they could well be mentioned as possibilities in a teacher's book in the case of published materials. Swan (2006) is, then, advocating an eclectic approach, but we must underline that it is *principled* eclecticism. Choices cannot be made at random: the specific approach taken will depend, as Swan (2006) observes, on 'the point being taught, the learner and the context'.

Present, practise, produce: criticism and rehabilitation

Despite coming under rather severe attack (e.g. Lewis 1993; Skehan 2003), PPP has proved a remarkably resilient language presentation paradigm in coursebooks (Tomlinson et al. 2001). Timmis (2012b: 121) outlines a typical PPP sequence:

> This procedure typically involves the presentation of the target structure in some kind of illustrative context and the explanation and/or elicitation of the form, meaning and use of the target structure. This is followed by controlled practice – where the learners manipulate the target item in drills or exercises – and free practice, where the focus is still on the target form, but the learners have more freedom over what to say.

There is a certain logic to this skill-building procedure and it is an easy structure to implement in materials. The question is, however, 'Does it work?' Let us examine first the case against PPP. SLA research (see Chapter 2) shows that the acquisition of a structure tends to be a partial, cumulative, gradual process. Most teachers, ourselves included, can relate stories of delivering PPP lessons which appear to work really well, only for the learner to be unable to use the structure in free conversation even immediately after the lesson. So should the principled materials writer jettison PPP? Not yet, and not completely, we would argue, even though we accept that PPP does not work well in the way it was intended to, i.e. producing immediate control of the target structure whenever needed. It may be, however, that, while this was not part of the original rationale for PPP, it has a *delayed effect* and primes the learner to acquire the structure from future input. Ellis (2006: 94) notes the potentially delayed advantages of intensive grammar teaching involving practice (e.g. PPP):

> Recent research (e.g. Spada and Lightbown 1999) indicates that even if learners are not ready to learn the targeted structure, intensive grammar teaching can help them progress through the sequence of stages involved in the acquisition of that structure.

While critics of PPP seem prepared to allow the possibility of delayed effect for other approaches to grammar teaching, e.g. noticing (see Chapter 2 and below), they seem unwilling to extend the same charity to PPP. We should also note Sheen's (2003) claim that *comparative* research has shown explicit teaching and practice approaches such as PPP are at least as effective as other approaches. It seems, then, that there is a case for keeping PPP in our eclectic repertoire; on the other hand, the case is nowhere near strong enough to justify its predominant position in published materials. We consider *when* it might be appropriate to use PPP in our materials later.

Beyond present, practise, produce

As materials writers, we need, then, to consider options other than PPP. We turn first to input-based approaches which focus on the relationship between 'input' – the language the learner is exposed to – and 'intake' – that part of the input which becomes part of the learner's potential productive repertoire (see also Chapter 2 for discussion of input and intake). Schmidt (1990) argued that the crucial link between input and intake was the process of 'noticing', whereby learners become *conscious* of the gap between what they are able to produce and the L2 input (see Chapter 2). The conclusion from this line of thinking is that materials need to encourage learners to pay conscious attention to *form* in input in order for the language they encounter, for example, in listening and reading texts to become available as output. Approaches which emphasise noticing from input have a good deal in common with C-R (Willis 1996) (see discussion and example in Chapter 2) and 'language awareness approaches' (Bolitho et al. 2003): there is an emphasis on drawing students' attention to a contextualised target feature and asking them to 'discover' its form, meaning and use inductively. With input-based approaches, learners are not necessarily required to produce the target form.

There are, however, approaches which require output as part of the grammar learning process rather than simply as grammar practice activities. The potential of output-based activities for promoting the learning of grammar is stressed by both Thornbury (2001) and Cullen (2008): such activities typically require learners to 'add grammar' to lexis, leading to the rather ugly term 'grammaring or grammaticisation tasks'. The theoretical rationale for such tasks is that the essential role of grammar is to act as a 'liberating force' (Cullen 2008); i.e. grammar liberates the speaker from a dependence on lexis and a dependence on context to convey meaning. Thornbury (2001: 21) outlines the essential design requirements for grammaring tasks:

> [they] will need to reduce the learner's dependence on the immediate context and on words alone and to provide an incentive to enlist grammar in order to make meanings crystal clear. At the same time, activities will need to provide learners with the right conditions – including sufficient processing time – so that they can marshal their grammaring skills. Finally, they will need clear messages as to how precise they have been: feedback must be explicit and immediate.

For Cullen (2008: 221), the essential features of grammaring tasks are 'learner choice over which grammatical structures to use; a process of "grammaticization" where the learners apply grammar to lexis; and opportunities to make comparisons and notice gaps in their use of grammar'.

Both writers give practical examples of activities which reflect the theory. Cullen (2008), for example, notes that some quite traditional activities can be turned to the service of 'grammaring', e.g. expanding newspaper headlines into short news paragraphs; combining short, non-complex sentences to form a linked paragraph; and using a picture story with word prompts to compose a short narrative.

Thornbury (1997) focuses particularly on reconstruction and reformulation tasks, noting dictogloss (a modified dictation where there is a delay between the teacher reading the text and the learners trying to reproduce it) as an example of a reconstruction technique, and the teacher rewriting a learner's script as an example of reformulation. We need to note that these particular activities can only be suggested by the materials writer rather than incorporated directly into materials.

Practice: quality not quantity

We need also to consider the role of practice. Swan (2005) notes that critics of approaches such as PPP, which involve practice, often caricature the kind of practice involved as if it necessarily has to be a meaningless, repetitive drill. The case for output as *practice* of a particular feature reflects the view of language as essentially a skill. The argument (DeKeyser 2003) is that learners can, through intensive *meaningful* practice, develop automatic control of structures which have initially been learned explicitly. It is important to emphasise here that the practice needs to be meaningful – practice is not just a matter of quantity, but also of *quality*.

Task 8.7

In which of the scenarios below do you think that the teacher is trying to teach grammar?

(a) T: What did you do at the weekend, Miguel?
     St: I goed to the cinema.
     T: Oh, you went to the cinema, did you? Which film did you see?
(b) The learner hands in a piece of written work. The teacher rewrites it so that it is grammatically correct and hands it back without further comment.
(c) The teacher writes a text and deliberately includes a lot of passives, but gives no explanation or further practice of the structure.
(d) The teacher constructs a task which requires the use of the past simple. The learners do the task in groups and the teacher makes no intervention. She asks one group to perform the task in front of the whole class and corrects any errors with the past simple.
(e) The teacher reads out a short text. He then asks the learners to write down as many words and phrases as they can remember. He repeats this process three or four times and then asks the learners, in groups, to reconstruct the text from the words and phrases they have written down. Finally, he gives the learners the original text and asks them to compare their reconstructed version with the original.

Task 8.8

Match activities (a) to (e) in Task 8.7 with the activity types below:

1. reconstruction
2. reformulation
3. input flooding
4. planned focus on form
5. recasting

PRINCIPLED ECLECTICISM

There is, then, a range of options open to the materials writer when designing materials to teach grammar. Eclecticism is easy to achieve, but we must return to the notion of *principled* eclecticism. On what basis are we to take decisions? The main criteria are outlined below (Timmis 2012b):

- **Age**: Explicit approaches are more likely to appeal to some adult learners than young learners because of their cognitive maturity. The age criterion does not, however, mean that we have to abandon planned grammatical development for young learners: implicit methods and covert practice of structures can be brought to bear where the pill of repetition is sugared in entertaining ways through, for example, songs, rhymes, stories and drama (Cameron 2001).
- **Level**: It seems reasonable to suppose that, as learners move up the levels, there will be a stronger tendency to use reactive approaches, since the learners are more likely to have encountered a particular item previously and perhaps even to have already received explicit instruction on the point (Timmis 2012b).
- **Learners' expectations**: We noted above (and we note in Chapter 9) that learners, teachers and publishers seem to expect grammar in the syllabus, and they probably also have expectations of how it will be taught, i.e. through explicit presentation and practice. While, as Timmis (2012a: 127) argues, 'a programme based only on meeting learners' expectation would produce *stasis*', materials which don't pay some attention to this expectation may not be welcomed by learners.
- **Learner abilities**: Spada and Lightbown (2008) suggest that learners' literacy in their L1 and knowledge of grammatical terminology will influence how far we can adopt explicit approaches. We also noted above that analytical learners may be better able to cope with inductive approaches.
- **Nature of the language point to be taught**: This aspect of the grammar teaching debate has arguably received too little attention. Willis (2003) argues that the conceptual difficulty of the grammar item in question should be a central criterion in deciding on which approach to adopt: proactive, explicit approaches for points which are conceptually straightforward and where the form can be taught quite quickly, e.g. past simple with *-ed* ending. Gradual C-R through input, however, is more suitable for points which are conceptually more subtle, e.g. the use of past simple versus present perfect.

One of the challenges in deciding on an approach to developing materials for grammar is the range of options available if one takes a broad view of what constitutes grammar teaching, as proposed by Ellis (2006: 84):

> *Grammar teaching* involves any instructional technique that draws learners' attention to some specific grammatical form in such a way that it helps them either to understand it metalinguistically and/or process it in comprehension and/or production so that they can internalize it.

In deciding on an appropriate option, materials developers then have to consider a range of factors, as we have seen above, in relation to the learners and the structure to be taught. What the research evidence supports, we would argue, is 'principled eclecticism'. There is no 'one-size-fits-all' approach to grammar materials: that is a challenge, but it also makes life interesting.

8.4 FURTHER READING ONE

McCarten, J. (2007). *Lessons from the Corpus, Lessons for the Classroom*. New York: Cambridge University Press.
McCarten (2007) points out that while spoken and written vocabulary have much in common, they also differ in some respects. Some of the specific features of spoken vocabulary, she notes, relate to the interactive nature of conversation. They are often to do with organising the speaker's contribution or organising the conversation as a whole; they are also important in building and maintaining relationships. McCarten describes and exemplifies a number of categories in the interactive vocabulary of conversation (noting, however that certain words or phrases may fall into more than one category):

- discourse markers
- responses
- monitoring expressions
- vague expressions
- hedging
- expressions of stance

The definitions and explanations below are extracts from McCarten (2007: 9–14):

- Discourse markers: 'A discourse marker is a word or phrase that organizes or manages the discourse in some way. In this case the type of discourse is conversation.'
- Responses: 'Words and expressions that people use to react or respond to what other people say, before they add their own contribution to the conversation.'
- Monitoring expressions: 'In conversation, speakers often involve the other participants to measure how the conversation is going. For example, a speaker may use expressions like "you know what I mean", or the shorter "you know", to check

if others in the conversation understand, sympathize with, or even agree with what he or she is saying.'

- Vague expressions: 'These include expressions that use very general, often informal words, instead of specific words to refer to things, activities, or situations. Some of the most frequent are the phrases "or something", "and things like that", "and stuff", "and everything", "or whatever", "and that kind of thing" and "and that sort of stuff".'

- Expressions of stance: 'Stance refers to how speakers express their attitude to what they say. So, for example, they may give information as a personal opinion and use expressions like "personally", "I think", "from my point of view", etc.'

- Hedging expressions: 'Speakers use hedging expressions when they want to avoid sounding blunt, too direct, too sure of themselves, or too "black and white".'

Task 8.9
Match the examples below (in bold) with definitions and explanations (a) to (f) above (all examples except 5 and 6 are taken from McCarten 2007):

Example 1
A: [. . .] they want to really publish it.
B: **Wow**.

Example 2
She's very sophisticated and she travels **and things like that**.

Example 3
He's very smart but he's also **kind of** young and naïve and quiet and **sort of** shy.

Example 4
A: [. . .] I won first prize.
B: Oh you always win.
A: I don't win.
B: Yes you do.
A: And **so anyway** the prize was ten dollars.

Example 5
Unfortunately, I have to go now.

Example 6
He's not the easiest person to get on with **if you know what I mean**.

Task 8.10
A means of broadening your ideas and techniques for the design of materials for vocabulary learning is to consider your own experiences as a language learner. How did you go about learning vocabulary? What kind of strategies did you use to help you learn vocabulary?

8.5 FURTHER READING TWO

Stranks, J. (2013). Materials for the teaching of grammar. In B. Tomlinson (ed.), *Developing Materials for Language Teaching*, 2nd edn (pp. 337–51). London: Bloomsbury.

This chapter is highly critical of the orthodox treatment of grammar in materials. Stranks's (2013) initial complaint is that grammar has a dominant role in coursebooks which seems to him obsessive. The next complaint in the chapter is that grammar work is 'randomly lexicalised', i.e. the vocabulary used to exemplify and practise structures is not the vocabulary typically used with that structure: Biber and Conrad (2010), for example, note that there are certain verbs which are typically used in the present continuous, e.g. *joking*, *bleeding* and *starving*. The grammar practice typically provided in coursebooks, Stranks argues, is too often highly controlled and decontextualised. Despite these complaints, however, he argues that materials writers do not have complete freedom to design grammar materials according to their own principles, but have to take into account 'the extent to which any adopted methodology meets the expectations of a) learners, b) teachers, c) the educational culture within which the learners and teachers work' (p. 339). Finally, Stranks observes that grammar should be exemplified through language which represents realistic use, and calls for production activities that allow learners to make meaningful utterances and to say things which they might conceivably want to say in the real world.

Task 8.11

From the summary of Stranks's chapter above, derive four or five evaluation criteria for grammar materials.

Task 8.12

Stranks maintains that grammar materials should use language that represents 'realistic use'. Looking at this chapter and others in the book, consider and list (brainstorming with others if possible) where such materials can be sourced, e.g. corpora, newspapers, social media and so on.

8.6 CONCLUSION

In concluding this chapter on issues involved with designing materials for vocabulary and grammar teaching, it is useful to summarise the main points that have been made in each section. With respect to Section 8.2 on developing materials for teaching **vocabulary**, these can be synthesised as follows:

- Efficient vocabulary learning is crucial to language learning.
- Corpus research has given us a clearer idea of the number of words learners need to learn.
- Corpus research has drawn attention to the importance of collocations and lexical chunks as well as individual words.
- Learners cannot normally be expected to learn enough vocabulary incidentally.

- Principled criteria, e.g. frequency, learnability and learners' interests, are needed to decide what vocabulary to teach.
- There is more to learning a word than simply learning its basic meaning. Learning a word thoroughly is an incremental process.
- Research has suggested that some popular techniques such as learning words in semantic sets are not effective; research has also suggested that 'old-fashioned' techniques such as translation or learning from lists are effective.
- Depth of processing is a key principle in vocabulary learning.

In Section 8.3, with regard to materials for **grammar** teaching:

- We noted that grammar is conventionally included in coursebooks and outlined three possible reasons for including grammar in materials: (1) it is what the market wants, (2) it facilitates communication and (3) it is educationally developmental.
- We referred back to Chapter 2 on SLA to remind ourselves of the consensus that some kind of grammar teaching seems to accelerate progress in accuracy.
- We suggested that an 'enabling view' of grammar forces us to consider what a particular grammar structure will do to help our learners communicate.
- We argued for 'principled eclecticism' whereby the approach to grammar teaching takes into account both the nature of the point to be taught and learner factors such as age, level and need. We also noted that quality of practice is more important than quantity of practice.

8.7 ADDITIONAL READINGS

Ellis, R. (2006). Current issues in the teaching of grammar: an SLA perspective. *TESOL Quarterly*, 40(1): 83–107.
As the title suggests, this article provides an overview of the debate about the best ways to approach the teaching of grammar. It summarises a lot of the empirical research which has been carried out and is a very good source of references if you want to follow up a particular aspect of the debate. You might also want to follow up the subsequent debate with Ron Sheen in a 'reader responds' article (Sheen 2006).

Folse, K. (2011). Applying L2 lexical research findings in ESL. *TESOL Quarterly*, 45(2): 362–9.
This is a concise and clear article about the why, what and how of vocabulary teaching. Folse refers to research which sometimes shows 'old-fashioned' methods to be more successful than current, popular methods.

Nation, P. (2013). Materials for teaching vocabulary. In B. Tomlinson (ed.), *Developing Materials for Language Teaching*, 2nd edn (pp. 351–65). London: Bloomsbury.
Nation focuses first on the need to plan vocabulary teaching and then refers to three 'conditions for learning': noticing, retrieving and elaboration. (Elaboration involves developing knowledge of a known word, e.g. by learning the noun form of a verb or

learning a slightly different sense of a word.) The chapter then describes input-based and output-based activities which can be used for vocabulary learning, followed by activities which focus on fluency development.

Sheen, R. (2003). Focus on form–: a myth in the making? *ELT Journal*, 57(3): 225–33. If you like a hard-hitting, controversial article, then this is one for you. Sheen argues that fashions moved towards focus on form with very little evidence to support them. He reports on an experiment he carried out which, he claims, showed that traditional focus on forms presentation was more effective than focus on form in helping learners to acquire a particular grammatical form.

NOTE

1. McCarten is referring to the most frequent words in the North American spoken corpus, which is part of the Cambridge International Corpus.

MATERIALS DESIGN: FROM PROCESS TO PRODUCT

9.1 INTRODUCTION

The question many people ask when required to write materials is, 'Where do I start?' In this chapter we hope to offer at least a rough map of the materials design journey from the starting point to the destination. It is important to note at the outset the distinction made by Timmis (2014) between 'unmediated' and 'mediated' materials writing. If you are writing unmediated materials, they will pass straight into the classroom without intervention from outside parties; indeed, writer and teacher may be one and the same person. If you are writing mediated materials, then, as we shall see, various intermediaries such as editors and government officials may influence the final form of the materials. This is particularly the case if you are writing commercial materials, but it may also be the case if you are writing in-house materials for a large institution. Amrani (2011: 268) stresses that if you are writing materials for publication, a lot of decisions may be taken out of your hands: 'Course content, approach and task design is often already established by exam syllabuses, guidelines or standards such as the Common European Framework.' Amrani (2011) also points out that the design specifications of a set of materials are often based on what publishers normally call a 'must haves list'. Such specifications could be seen as facilitating the writing process. However, as Timmis (2014) relates, it can be frustrating when such specifications emerge piecemeal *during* the writing process, which, from anecdotal evidence, is not an uncommon experience.

In this chapter, we are concerned mainly with mediated materials writing. Unlike in the rest of this book, there is an underlying assumption in this chapter that the reader is writing materials for commercial publication. However, we feel that, whether your intention is to write for publication or not, there is much to be learned from an understanding of the *process* of writing materials for publication, particularly in relation to the wide range of factors which potentially come into play when you are writing materials for users other than yourself and your class.

We will look at two aspects of the materials writing process: (1) typical production sequences, i.e. the stages writers may go through from conception to the finished product; and (2) the creative process, i.e. the mental processes and strategies writers adopt to create the materials.

9.2 THE PRODUCTION SEQUENCE

THE IDEALISED SEQUENCE

Drawing on the literature (e.g. St Louis et al. 2010; Prowse 2011; Tomlinson 2013b), we can identify the following possible stages in the production sequence:

1. Statement of beliefs
2. Needs analysis
3. Aims and objectives
4. Syllabus design
5. Drafting
6. Piloting
7. Production
8. Revision

It is important to note, however, that this is an idealised sequence and may be applied in a recursive rather than linear way. Many writers may, for example, omit stage 1. Aims and objectives may be reviewed after piloting. It may even be the case (Timmis 2014) that the entire sequence leads to a revision of the statement of beliefs.

STATEMENT OF BELIEFS

As we noted, an obvious question to ask about materials writing is 'Where do you start?' Tomlinson (2013b) takes an idealistic stance on this and argues that the starting point for writing materials should be a statement of the writer's core methodological principles and beliefs, a position echoed by St Louis et al. (2010: 249): 'Even before carrying out a needs analysis, materials developers need to have a clear idea of their view of language, learning and the learner as this will determine the manner in which activities will be designed.'

Such statements of principles and beliefs, Timmis (2014: 245) points out, can be particularly useful to ensure coherence if the materials are being written by a team:

> If you are writing materials for publication, particularly if you are writing as part of a team, you are probably going to need to draw up a set of design specifications and/or a set of methodological principles to ensure quality and consistency. You will also need a set of layout and presentation conventions.

In practice, however, such statements seem to be rare (Tomlinson 2013b), with most writers working to a *tacit* framework of beliefs (Hadfield 2014). We should also note, though we do not want publishers to dominate this particular section, that Timmis (2014) recounts the difficulties of reconciling such a framework with the requirements and statements of the publisher.

NEEDS ANALYSIS

There is clearly a case for a needs analysis of the target end-users to be carried out before the materials are designed (e.g. Richards 1995; St Louis et al. 2010; Jolly and Bolitho 2011; Stoller and Robinson 2014). An example of needs analysis to inform materials writing is provided by St Louis et al. (2010: 256) in the context of designing a remedial English course for first year university students in Venezuela. Their needs analysis comprised the following components:

- secondary school attended
- self-perception of competence in different skills/areas
- metacognitive strategies questionnaire (O'Neil and Abedi 1996)
- multiple choice grammar test

While such information should be of value in informing the course materials, we need to sound a cautionary note: how reliable are learners' self-perceptions of their competence, and why is grammar the only element of language competence tested? The cynical answer to the latter question is that grammar is tested because it *can* be tested quickly and cheaply: testing oral fluency through interviews, for example, is very time-consuming. In some cases, of course, when you are writing for a diverse and largely unknown population, as is the case with global coursebooks, it is simply not possible to carry out a needs analysis. On the other hand, if you are writing materials for a small ESP group – English for pilots, for example – then needs analysis will assume great significance.

AIMS AND OBJECTIVES

Let us assume, then, that we have a coherent set of methodological principles, either tacit or explicit, and an awareness of the needs of the target population: where next? Armed with this background information, we should be able to frame overarching aims and objectives for the materials, and it would also seem that we are now in a strong position to devise a syllabus (unless the syllabus has been imposed by the publisher or a ministry of education). This can appear a daunting task, but, reassuringly, it is rare to start from a *tabula rasa*. The following are some of the sources which can be consulted:

- needs analyses of the target group(s)
- exam requirements for the target group(s)
- other published materials for similar target groups
- the CEFR

At the time of writing, the CEFR, with its detailed specification of performance indicators for different levels, seems to be gaining currency as a syllabus source for coursebooks. The English Profile research project seeks to add further detail to these indicators. According to the website, http://www.englishprofile.org, English Profile is:

9.1

designed to create a 'profile' or set of Reference Level Descriptions for English. These will provide detailed information about what learners 'can do' in English at each of the six levels of the Common European Framework of Reference (CEFR), offering a clear benchmark for progress for English language learners.

Prowse (2011: 158) observes that in coursebook writing, 'the unstated assumption is that the syllabus precedes the creation', i.e. an a priori syllabus. The case has been made, however, as Prowse (2011) acknowledges, for reversing the traditional process and deriving the language syllabus from the texts included in the materials (Willis 2003; Tomlinson 2013b); indeed, we referred to the 'text-driven approach' in Chapter 2. There is not space here to do justice to the theoretical rationale for this approach to syllabus design (see Tomlinson 2013b and Timmis 2014 for further discussion), but it is worth drawing attention to two assumptions on which this approach rests:

1. Learners do not necessarily learn items in the order they are presented.
2. Learners will be more motivated to learn items they have experienced in context, particularly if they have been engaged in the texts.

Timmis (2014) notes two particular reservations about this approach: it may not offer the transparent accountability of the fixed a priori syllabus which seems to be sought by publishers, teachers and learners, and this emergent approach to syllabus design may only be suitable for the experienced teacher/writer (see Timmis 2014 for a detailed account of implementing a text-based approach in practice).

It is also possible to base a syllabus on tasks, though it can be difficult to ensure progression in such a syllabus unless we have clear criteria for task design and assessing task difficulty (Skehan 1998). Swan (2005) also points out the difficulty of ensuring systematic coverage of language in a task-based approach. The reservations about the *apparent* lack of system in a text-based approach also apply to a task-based approach.

In the case of both text-based and task-based syllabuses, the possibility exists of comparing the syllabus which has emerged from an analysis of the texts or tasks included in the materials against an inventory of items which need to be covered for institutional or exam purposes, and using this information to fill the gaps (Tomlinson 2013b). Good luck with selling this idea to publishers. It is interesting in this respect that Prowse (2011) observes that in making a book proposal to a publisher, he and his co-author include only a *grammar* syllabus at the outset, adding vocabulary, pronunciation, skills syllabuses etc. at a later stage. As we discussed in Chapter 8, the grammar syllabus has symbolic significance in published materials, as it seems to confer credibility and authority on them. A methodology very much in fashion at the time of writing, CLIL, as Prowse (2011) notes, offers a potentially radical approach to syllabus design, as, in its purest form at least, it is content or topics which determine the syllabus rather than language items.

DRAFTING

Armed with the results of needs analysis, with aims and objectives, and a syllabus, we should be in a good position to start writing. It is as well, however, to recall the words of the British prime minister in the Second World War, Winston Churchill, after a victory in battle: 'This is not the end. It is not even the beginning of the end. But it is perhaps the end of the beginning.'

We need to consider the process of drafting, piloting and revising, and the potential intervention of other stakeholders or intermediaries in the process such as editors, teachers, ministry officials and curriculum advisors. As Hadfield (2014) notes, surprisingly little has been written about the actual creative process of *writing* the materials, so we have chosen to focus in more detail on this in the next section (though we also address this briefly in the Further Reading sections of Chapter 3). It may be necessary to produce a number of drafts of the materials in response to feedback from stakeholders even before the materials pass to the piloting stage. For now, we will assume that ideas have been generated by spontaneous combustion and passed to the piloting stage, i.e. trying materials out in the classroom and either observing the materials in use yourself, as the materials writer, or soliciting feedback from teachers and/or learners.

PILOTING

Stoller and Robinson (2014: 265) carried out extensive piloting of their materials (writing materials for students of chemistry) and are strong advocates of the value of the process: 'Our systematic piloting efforts – over numerous years in various classroom settings, and with different stakeholder groups – helped us improve our textbook materials in innumerable ways . . .' They go on to list the various aspects of their materials which benefited from piloting (Stoller and Robinson 2014: 266):

- overall scope
- approach
- level
- organisation and sequencing of content
- organisation and sequencing of tasks
- ease of use and fit in different classroom settings

It seems reasonable to suppose that piloting will be of greater value the less the writer knows about the target end-users: it is easier to make informed guesses about the response to your materials from learners you know. Perkins (2008), for example, reports that the materials writer in her study attached particular value to feedback from piloting as he had little specialist knowledge of the target group, in this case adults with learning disabilities: he was able to benefit from precise information about which activities worked well and which did not. It is worth extending this notion of piloting to include feedback on the final product in use, as this too can be very revealing. Prowse (personal communication), for example, expressed astonishment that his materials were being used in ways quite different from those he had envisaged, when he consulted the users. Similarly, Timmis (2014) expressed surprise that Chinese teachers were getting the pupils to memorise the dialogues he had written for the coursebook, a possibility which had not crossed his mind.

While piloting seems at first sight to be a commonsense step, it should be noted that reservations have been expressed about its value. Among these are the following:

- How representative of the end-users is the feedback?
- Are problems observed in class due to the materials or the teacher?
- Does the feedback relate to the overall approach of the materials or simply to operational difficulties with particular activities?
- How many times should you pilot materials and how long should it take?

In the light of the above reservations, particularly the last question, it is not surprising that Amrani (2011) notes that publishers, under the pressure of production deadlines, are making less use of piloting and more use of reviewing. Reviewing normally involves sending the materials, or samples of the materials, to experienced practitioners or evaluators for feedback. If piloting is becoming less common, then Prowse's (2011: 166) reflection on the potential disconnection between materials writers and the classroom assumes extra significance: 'It would . . . be interesting to learn more about the relationship between writers and the classroom: how many still teach regularly, visit schools and observe classes, and work with groups of teachers.'

The role of stakeholders

Having piloted the materials and solicited the views of teachers and learners, or having at least canvassed the opinions of reviewers, you are now, you may be relieved to know, at 'the end of the beginning'. However, there is still a range of other stakeholders to consider. As Singapore Wala (2013: 63) notes: 'The materials development process is most often a multi-stage process with various stakeholders located at different points within the curriculum development framework wielding varied levels and extent of influence on the process and the output.' Feedback from stakeholders can be seen as a recursive phase in the sequence as it can occur and recur at any stage from the original proposal to the production phase.

Arguably, the most important stakeholder to take into account is the teacher who will be using your materials. Imagining your materials being used by a teacher with a different background from your own, in a context far different from your own, is a real challenge, as Mares (2003: 131) observes:

When I first began to write commercial materials, I was subconsciously writing for clones of myself, teachers who had chosen to take a further degree to better their understanding of teaching and learning, teachers who were familiar with the principles of language acquisition.

Singapore Wala (2013) also underlines that it is essential to take the needs and abilities of the end-user teachers into account, particularly their capacity and motivation to adopt innovation in materials.

In addition to teachers, Timmis (2014) refers to the following list of potential stakeholders:

- the internal leader of the writing team
- the publisher's editor
- the end-user teachers
- the local education authority
- the ministry of education
- project evaluators
- parents

We must not forget either the growing influence of the marketing team who, as Prowse (2011) observes, now wield considerable influence in the publishing process. While Timmis (2014) chronicles some of the frustrations of being forced to compromise in response to feedback from these agencies, Stoller and Robinson (2014: 266) take a more sanguine view of 'the value of input from various stakeholders that could inform the ongoing process of materials creation, revision and improvement'. Indeed, it should be said that Timmis (2014) expresses frustration more with the manner and timing of the publisher's intervention than with the feedback itself, conceding that, in the final analysis, the end-product probably benefited from the publisher's interventions. Two issues are particularly salient in Timmis's (2014) account of his negotiations with the publisher:

1. the publisher's insistence on a prominent grammar syllabus and explicit grammar teaching
2. questions of sociocultural appropriacy

In our experience, it is not uncommon for these particular issues to be the 'battleground' between authors and publishers. We dealt with the grammar debate more fully in Chapter 8, but we must address the question of sociocultural appropriacy here (see also Chapter 3). A well-known acronym among writers and publishers is PARSNIP, which represents topics to be avoided in materials:

Politics Alcohol Religion Sex Narcotics Isms Pork

Prowse (personal communication) suggests that PARSNIP is not applied as strictly as some critics suggest and that its application depends very much on the end-users of the book. Timmis (2014), however, relates how he had to excise references to alcohol and drug use in a text to be used with Southeast Asian teenagers, even though the text was actually a condemnation of these practices. He also relates how he was asked to remove a text about the Asian singer Coco Lee on the grounds that she had adopted Western values.

In implementing this content filter in this way, publishers will normally be acting, or at least claim to be acting, in the interests of the stakeholders listed above. The danger of imposing such a filter is that the materials can turn out bland and anodyne (Saraceni 2013), particularly if the filter is applied indiscriminately: Tomlinson (personal communication), for example, recalls being asked to remove the 'three little piggies' fairy tale from his materials on the grounds that it dealt with pork. It can be argued that the PARSNIP topics should not be outlawed in themselves; it is more a question of how you deal with them. One of the current authors, for example, recalls setting up an activity in a multilingual and multicultural adult class, where the non-Moslem students had to find out from the Moslem students what the five pillars of Islam were. The activity was successful, we would argue, because it exploited intercultural curiosity, but did not involve making *judgements* about anyone's beliefs: a case of peeling PARSNIPs perhaps.

The influence of stakeholders such as ministries is not, limited, however, to the censorship of content. In some cases, they may insist on the *inclusion* of certain kinds of content. Mukundan (2008) has drawn attention to the way coursebooks in Malaysia are enlisted to promote the state agenda, particularly the Five National Principles. The state policy to promote science and technology is reflected, for example, in a unit where a 13-year-old boy is taken to the National Science museum for his birthday, which, as Mukundan (2008) wryly notes, would not be high on the agenda of most 13-year-olds. Mukundan (2008) also points out that the state agenda to promote inter-racial harmony is reflected in units where representatives of different ethnic groups come together to resolve a problem. Similarly, Timmis (2014) relates how he was obliged to include reference to the country's national mission statement in every unit of the materials. Promoting inter-racial harmony and an interest in science are laudable goals, of course, but they can lead to very stilted materials when the agenda is too overt.

The influence of other stakeholders in the process, as exemplified above, is potentially huge, and it seems that compromise between the material writer's wishes and intentions and the desiderata of other stakeholders is inevitable. Feak and Swales (2014: 301) point to the importance of compromise (our italics):

> While the reasons for our comparative success are complex, we believe that in large part it has been due to our efforts to incorporate relevant research findings and *to calibrate the input of the many different stakeholders who have a vested interest in the final product.*

If, however, we take the view that 'a camel is a horse designed by a committee', we may worry about the results of compromise. In this respect, it is interesting that Timmis (2014: 258–9), in an attempt to distinguish between 'compromised principles' and 'principled compromise', draws up the following 'principles for compromise':

1. Is the feedback based on evidence from actual practice? If yes, seriously consider compromise.

2. How confident can you be that your principle is sound? If you are confident, refuse or minimise compromise.
3. Is the feedback based on *reliable* local knowledge? If yes, seriously consider compromise.
4. Can you incorporate the feedback, whether you like it or not, without serious detriment to the principles? If yes, seriously consider compromise.

PRODUCTION

The materials which have survived the drafting, revising, piloting, reviewing, and filtering and compromise process are now (finally!) ready to enter the production phase. At this stage, however, a new cast of players may enter the scene, among which are (Prowse 2011: 160):

- desk editor
- designer (often freelance)
- recording studio producer
- actors
- artists and photographers
- picture researchers
- copyright clearers
- proofreaders

Given the procedures we have described above, Prowse's (2011: 156) estimate of the timescale of a coursebook project is perhaps not surprising:

In the production process of a modern coursebook, which can take three to five years from initial idea to copies in the classroom, the actual creation of the lessons, paradoxically, can take up less time than all the other aspects of authorship [other activities = meetings, presentations, revisions, piloting . . .].

Task 9.1
We noted above that the CEFR is increasingly used to inform syllabus design for materials:

9.2

- Visit the CEFR website: http://www.coe.int/t/dg4/education/elp/elp-reg/Source/Key_reference/Overview_CEFRscales_EN.pdf
- Choose one of the levels (e.g. A2 or B1) and one of the four skills.
- Consider how useful these descriptors would be in informing the syllabus of your materials for your chosen level.

Task 9.2
How far do you think the content of materials should be governed by the PARSNIP acronym?

Task 9.3

We note above with reference to Singapore Wala (2013) that in writing materials, the needs and abilities of the end-user teachers should also be taken into account, particularly their capacity and motivation to adapt materials.

- Consider some materials you have created yourself or a selection of coursebook materials with respect to their 'adaptability', that is, their potential for adaptation and supplementation, and suggest some examples of this. You may like to refer to Chapter 4, Section 4.4, on this area.

9.3 THE PRODUCTION SEQUENCE IN ACTION

It is useful to look at some accounts of the writing process reported in the literature.

Richards (1995)

In Richards's process, we see a prominent role for teachers and a role for piloting, though a limited one, and the use of reviewers:

- Consultation with teachers on what they wanted
- Formation of a group of teacher-consultants (and seeking information from students)
- Pilot unit taught by teacher, observed by materials developers
- Consultation with teachers and students about the unit
- Incorporation of feedback into first draft
- First draft reviewed by publisher-appointed reviewers
- Second draft produced in response to reviewers' and editor's feedback
- Field-testing second draft, then further feedback

St Louis et al. (2010)

There are two distinctive features in the process outlined by St Louis et al. (2010). Firstly, step 5 (below) involves the analysis of the chosen texts with corpus software to determine their lexical density: this is a calculation of the number of different words in a text in relation to the number of total running words (see Chapter 7) and is, therefore, an indicator of text difficulty. Step 6 (below) includes quite specific criteria which the activities have to meet.

1. Reflect on our beliefs.
2. Carry out needs analysis.
3. Formulate achievable objectives.
4. Find input material.
5. Analyse the texts.
6. Create the activities (cater to students' individual learning styles; make use of different learning strategies; involve students' metacognitive skills; use students' prior knowledge; involve students affectively; allow students to express themselves creatively; encourage interaction; foster learner autonomy; build learner confidence).

Stoller and Robinson (2014)
This process, like that of St Louis et al. (2010), involves (step 3 below) the use of corpus software, in this case to try to determine the defining linguistic characteristics of different types of chemistry text. In this process, however, the corpus findings feed directly into the materials by determining which language items should be focused on (step 4 below).

1. articulating priorities and principles
2. scaffolding the instructional approach
3. selecting target genres, compiling corpora with full-length text exemplars, and analysing them using tools from CL and discourse, genre and move analyses
4. converting analytical findings into instructional materials
5. piloting and assessing materials
6. using feedback to improve materials

Prowse (2011: 159–60)
As Prowse's account of the process is unusually detailed, we have interspersed our comments on Prowse's account in italics for ease of reference:

1. Research into what is needed; identify gaps, weaknesses in other materials.
   This is in effect market research, though, judging from the remarkable similarity of many coursebooks, the conclusion must be that 'the market wants what it already has'.
2. Meeting with co-author to discuss and draft basic rationale: book and unit structure; grammar syllabus.
   Prowse remarks that this is a particularly time-consuming part of the process. We noted above that, in Prowse's case, only the grammar syllabus is submitted at this point.
3. Creation of draft unit (usually Unit 1).
4. Author and co-author continue to build up ideas for other syllabuses (e.g. vocabulary, writing, pronunciation) and build up a bank of authentic texts.
   Anecdotally, the collection of authentic texts at an early stage seems to be common practice among materials writers.
5. Meet design and art editor to discuss the 'look' of the book.
   It is particularly interesting that Prowse comments that the template for a page may be set before the writers start on the writing process proper.
6. After reports on draft unit and rationale, meeting with publisher and project manager.
   Prowse comments wryly: 'This is where sparks usually fly!'
7. First draft.
   Prowse comments: 'At the first draft stage we don't worry about writing to the page, detailed art briefs, recordings, keys, etc.'
8. Trialling of first draft.
   The first draft is sent out to about fourteen readers and triallers.
9. Meeting with publishers.

10. Second draft.

   Prowse comments that this is an intensive period of writing and at this stage, they are 'writing to the page', i.e. to the template given by the designer. It is also at this stage that the coursebook authors brief the authors of the accompanying workbook and teacher's book (it is common practice for these components to be written by different authors).

11. Third draft.

   It is at this stage that recordings are made and answer keys written.

12. Follow-up production work: design, cuts and rubrics.

We would appear to be at the end of the journey, but, from time to time, books will need to be revised and updated. Perhaps predictably in the light of our long discussion above, this is not as simple as it may seem, as Feak and Swales (2014: 299) note:

> All that appears to be needed [to revise an EAP textbook] is to update example texts, incorporate recent research findings, and fine-tune the tasks and explanations in the light of practitioner experience. However, it soon becomes clear that little is simple, given multiple stakeholders in the revision process.

Task 9.4

- Compose a short book proposal for a publisher. Include three or four statements of methodological principles and three or four USPs (unique selling points).
- Try to 'sell' your book idea to your fellow students in a 'Dragons' Den' scenario (*Dragons' Den* is a television series where entrepreneurs and inventors have to sell their idea to potential investors.)

Task 9.5

St Louis et al. (2010) note the following objectives for their materials:

- cater to students' individual learning styles
- make use of different learning strategies
- involve students' metacognitive skills
- involve students affectively
- foster learner autonomy

Choose at least two of these objectives and consider how they might be achieved practically in materials. It will be useful to refer back to Chapters 2, 6 and 7 for further details on these objectives and what they entail.

Task 9.6

9.3 Consider joining international forums for materials writing which encourage the exchange of ideas and foster creativity:

- The International Association of Teachers of English as a Foreign Language (IATEFL) has a materials writing special interest group (SIG): https://www.facebook.com/MaWSIG
- The C (Creativity) group founded by ELT materials writer and author Alan Maley: http://thecreativitygroup.weebly.com

9.4 THE CREATIVE PROCESS

While, as we have seen above, there are a number of accounts of stages in the materials writing process, Hadfield (2014: 321) observes that there is often little guidance 'as to how materials are to be written or how ideas are to be found'. The dearth of research in this area, noted also by Harwood (2010), is no doubt due in part to the difficulty of researching a materials writer's mental processes. There are, however, some accounts in expertise literature we can draw on. Perkins (2008), for example, researched how an individual materials writer (TW1) went about the materials writing task, using a research method known as 'think-aloud protocol' or 'concurrent verbalisation': the subject of the research (TW1) had to verbalise his thoughts while in the actual process of writing the materials.

A salient feature of TW1's approach to the task, Perkins (2008: 393) observes, was the cyclic nature of the design process:

It must be stressed that his style of writing was characteristically cyclic in nature. This meant that rather than him progressing through the design route in whole discrete steps, he instead tended to work through certain steps together in small repeated segments, sometimes returning to what he had previously done again and again in order to make changes or amendments for the sake of those principles which were important to the design of the book.

The cyclic or recursive nature of the design process is also emphasised by Hadfield (2014: 320). Drawing on introspective research into her own materials writing process, she draws attention to the tension between recursive and linear processes and between spontaneity and order:

Two oppositions are defined: that between the circuitous and recursive process described by the writers and various attempts to impose a more linear, orderly progression on the design process, and that between the apparently ad hoc spontaneous and intuitive process the writers describe and the call for design to be based on principled frameworks.

The recursive nature of the writing process in relation to the design of specific tasks is referred to by Samuda (2005: 397): 'Task design is a complex, highly recursive and often messy process, requiring the designer to hold in mind a vast range of task variables relating to the design-in-process.'

Hadfield (2014: 346) emphasises the non-linear nature of the design process in relation to the conceptualisation of activities:

Though writing activities entails similar considerations of aim, sequence of stages and groupings, there is no fixed order for these to be determined. In one activity the aim is clarified as a first step before writing; in another it is clarified and modified some time after the activity has been visualised in fairly concrete form.

The (apparently) spontaneous and intuitive nature of the materials writing process is underlined by Prowse (2011), on the basis of his discussions with a number of well-known ELT authors about their design processes. Hadfield (2014), however, stresses that the intuitive nature of materials writing should not be equated with an unprincipled approach, arguing that experienced materials writers draw on a *tacit* framework of principles.

The writer in Perkins' (2008) study regularly referred to other stakeholders in this particular project, as he was 'experienced enough to know when his experience was insufficient and was open to looking to outside sources for the materials writing guidance he needed when he deemed it necessary or desirable' (p. 397). TW1's experience was also evident, Perkins observes, in his consistent focus on the end-users of the book and on how the book would actually be used in class:

> Whilst writing, it was clear that TW1's focus was on the end users of the textbook and his efforts were directed in making the package of materials as user friendly as possible not only for students but also for teachers. Furthermore, it seemed that his experience as a teacher, teacher trainer and materials writer helped him to conceptualise how the book would ultimately be used by educators. (ibid.)

We see echoes in this 'conceptualisation of how the book would ultimately be used' of Kim's (2010) conclusion that experienced evaluators were able to visualise the context of use of the materials and relate their evaluation to the context. Similarly, Johnson (2003: 129) observed that experienced task designers have 'concrete visualisation capacity'. There are also echoes of Mares's (2003) reflection on the challenge of writing materials for different teachers in different contexts.

Hadfield (2014) refers to the process of taking stakeholders into account *during* the writing process as 'dialoguing' (which can take the form of an imagined dialogue with a given stakeholder about the content of the materials). She also refers to the process of visualising the context as 'imagining the scenario', again echoing Kim's (2010) conclusion that experienced evaluators are able to visualise the materials in use in a given context. Hadfield (2014) describes these mental activities as 'absolutely crucial to the process of materials design, since they push the writer into seeing the materials from others' viewpoints, analysing flaws, reworking material, and justifying decisions'. In similar vein, Perkins (2008) cites Johnson's (2003: 137) notion of 'maximum variable control' to describe how TW1 was able to keep various considerations in mind throughout the writing process. A further and perhaps surprising characteristic of experienced materials writers, Hadfield (2014) argues, is a willingness to abandon a particular idea even when considerable thought has been given to implementing it. This 'easy abandonment capacity' is also noted by Johnson (2003: 130) as a quality of experienced task designers.

Experienced materials writers, then, seem to have a number of qualities in common. They adopt a cyclic process in which they constantly return to and revise specific activities, and they are able to 'multi-task' mentally by considering the perspectives of other players in the process such as teachers, learners and publishers. The experienced materials writer can also fall back on various 'repertoires' (Perkins, personal communication), i.e. various mini-frameworks for the design of specific activities such as vocabulary or grammar tasks or ways of dealing with reading or listening texts. Reflecting on her own materials writing process, Hadfield (2014) adduced the set of principles below which seemed to guide her writing. We must keep in mind as we consider these principles Hadfield's (2014) observation that these were drawn only from her introspective analysis of a limited set of activities she had designed.

1. What is the aim of the theory?
2. How could this be translated into practice?
3. What should the aim of this activity be?
4. Does this activity fulfil the aim in the best way?
5. Is the activity focused on the aim, or are there distractions?
6. Is it engaging and appealing to both teachers and students?
7. Is the activity feasible – doable by students in terms of concept, ease of task and language level – and does it have the right level of challenge?
8. Is the staging in the best logical sequence?
9. Are students adequately prepared for the task?
10. Does the staging scaffold the students by providing achievable steps?
11. Are the groupings appropriate to the task, and do they provide variety and balance of interaction?
12. Does the activity have pace and momentum to maintain interest?
13. Does it create positive affect?
14. Does it, in the context of the book, chapter or section, provide appeal to different learning styles?
15. Will it result in student satisfaction with outcomes and a feeling of achievement?
16. Does it promote a good group dynamic?
17. Does it encourage creative use of language to encourage building of L2 identity?

Hadfield (2014) observes that this set of principles calls to mind Tomlinson's (2011b) framework of principles. We should note, however, that many of Hadfield's principles above, probably because they were adduced from specific activities, look more like task or activity design criteria than overall materials design principles (evident in the frequent use of the pronoun 'it'). Whether we regard these as design specifications or principles, we should note Hadfield's (2014) argument that experienced materials writers may be able to help novice materials writers by *articulating* the tacit principles or design criteria which underpin their work.

Task 9.7

Hadfield's seventeen-point list above is rather long and there is some overlap/repetition. Try to reduce the list to between eight and ten criteria which you would like to guide your materials writing.

Task 9.8

Perkins (2008) notes that writers typically use mini-frameworks to generate activities for specific areas such as the four skills or vocabulary/grammar work. A mini-framework for introducing vocabulary, for example, might involve a sequence such as: (1) match words and definitions, (2) gap-fill activity, (3) mark stress on the words and (4) drill the words for pronunciation.

- What frameworks are you aware of that can be applied to materials writing?

Task 9.9

Next time you produce a piece of material for classroom use, chart the development process. For techniques for doing this, see accounts in the chapters by Hadfield (2014) and Prowse (2011) which we have discussed above, as well as Johnson (2003). These writers describe techniques such as 'concurrent verbalisation' ('thinking aloud') (working in pairs makes this less artificial), recording discussions about the materials design process, retrospective verbal reports and keeping a reflective journal or log.

9.5 FURTHER READING ONE

We present below a well-known framework from the literature, Tomlinson's (2013) text-based framework. It is important to note that we are not offering an unqualified endorsement of this particular framework – see Timmis (2014) for the difficulties of implementing a text-based approach in practice. Our rationale is rather that this framework is user-friendly and, most importantly, has overt methodological principles. We also believe that one of the best ways of learning about materials writing is actually to do it.

Tomlinson, B. (2013c). Developing principled frameworks for materials development. In B. Tomlinson (ed.), *Developing Materials for Language Teaching*, 2nd edn (pp. 95–118). London: Bloomsbury.

In this chapter, Tomlinson describes a text-driven approach to materials development (from p. 99 onwards). In this framework, the materials writing process begins with **text collection** and **text selection**. The writer selects a spoken or written **text** with the potential to engage the target learners. The writer then devises **readiness activities** with the aim of helping learners 'achieve mental readiness for experiencing the text' (pp. 119–20). The next step in the process is to develop **experiential activities**, activities learners do while listening or reading. These activities encourage learners to enjoy the experience of the text rather than to study it. The materials writer then designs **intake response** activities which encourage learners to talk about what they have taken from the text. Intake response activities are followed by **development activities** in which learners use what they have taken from the text as a basis for oral or written language production. **Input response** tasks take learners back to the text to study the way language is used there: this may involve a focus on grammar, lexis, discourse or pragmatics. The framework is meant to be applied flexibly and allows the writer some freedom to change the sequence of activities or to omit certain activities.

Task 9.10
Apply this framework to a text of your choice to design materials for a specific group.

Task 9.11
Reflect on the process you adopted. How effective do you think the framework was in helping you generate materials? What are the strengths and weaknesses of this framework?

9.6 FURTHER READING TWO

Willis, J. (1996). *A Framework for Task-Based Learning*. London: Longman.
In Willis's TBL framework (p. 155), the main stages (which are explained below) are as follows:

1. Pre-task
2. Task cycle
    2.1 Task
    2.2 Planning
    2.3 Report
3. Language focus (related to language used in the task)
    3.1 Language analysis
    3.2 Language practice (of language from the analysis activities)

In this framework, Willis (1996) outlines the roles of *the teacher* and *the learners* at each stage:

1. **Pre-task**
    The teacher:
    □ introduces and defines the topic
    □ uses activities to help students recall/learn useful words and phrases
    □ ensures students understand task instructions
    □ may play a recording of others doing the same or a similar task
    The students:
    □ note down useful words and phrases from the pre-task activities and/or the recording
    □ may spend a few minutes preparing for the task individually

2. **Task cycle**

2.1 Task

The students:

☐ do the task in pairs/small groups – it may be based on a reading or listening text

The teacher:

☐ acts as monitor and encourages students

2.2 Planning

The students:

☐ prepare to report to the class how they did the task and what they discovered/ decided

☐ rehearse what they will say or draft a written version for the class to read

The teacher:

☐ ensures the purpose of the report is clear

☐ acts as language advisor

☐ helps students rehearse oral reports or organise written ones

2.3 Report

The students:

☐ present their spoken reports to the class, or circulate/display their written reports

The teacher:

☐ acts as chairperson, selecting who will speak next, or ensuring all students read most of the written reports

☐ may give brief feedback on content and form

☐ may play a recording of others doing the same or a similar task

3. **Language focus**

3.1 Language analysis

The students:

☐ do C-R activities to identify and process specific language features from the task, text and/or transcript

☐ may ask about other features they have noticed

The teacher:

☐ reviews each analysis activity carefully with the class

☐ brings other useful words, phrases and patterns to the students' attention

☐ may pick up on language from the report stage

3.2 Language practice

The teacher:

☐ conducts practice and analysis activities where necessary to build confidence

The students:

☐ practise words, phrases and patterns from the analysis activities

☐ practise other features occurring in the task, text or report stage

☐ enter useful language in their language notebooks

🖳
3.5 (See also the web page for a schema of the process as well as an outline of TBLT.)

Task 9.12

Design a task for a specific group using one of the following task types suggested by Willis (1996: 26–7): listing; ordering and sorting; comparing; problem-solving; sharing personal experiences; creative tasks.

Task 9.13

Discuss the strengths and weaknesses of this TBL cycle as a framework for materials development with reference to:

- coverage of language
- coverage of skills
- fluency, accuracy and complexity

9.7 CONCLUSION

We conclude this chapter by summarising its key points:

- There is a significant difference between writing materials for your own use and materials for use by others (or for publication).
- Materials writing is a multi-stage process involving planning (syllabus and methodology); drafting and writing; piloting and revising. This process is often recursive and some stages may be omitted.
- Documents such as the CEFR can help you to generate content.
- There are multiple stakeholders who can influence the writing process, e.g. publishers, education officials and teachers. This influence can affect all aspects of the materials, e.g. grammar content, visuals and cultural topics.
- The involvement of stakeholders inevitably involves compromise.
- Most materials writers seem to write to a tacit set of beliefs.
- Experienced materials writers seem to be able to visualise the materials in use and anticipate the reactions of various stakeholders.
- There are published frameworks for writing materials. These can help you get started, but none is perfect for all contexts.

9.8 ADDITIONAL READINGS

Bell, J. and Gower, R. (2011). Writing course materials for the world: a great compromise. In B. Tomlinson (ed.), *Materials Development in Language Teaching*, 2nd edn (pp. 135–51). Cambridge: Cambridge University Press.
This chapter offers a very useful insight into the process of producing published materials by two very experienced coursebook writers. The chapter is particularly interesting as it provides a detailed case study of the issues around compromise which we have discussed above.

Jolly, D. and Bolitho, R. (2011). A framework for materials writing. In B. Tomlinson (ed.) *Materials Development in Language Teaching*, 2nd edn (pp. 107–35). Cambridge: Cambridge University Press.

This chapter sets out a procedure for producing supplementary materials for a specific group. The authors set out a framework which involves five stages:

1. identification of a need or problem
2. exploration of the need or problem identified
3. contextual realisation (finding suitable ideas, contexts or texts)
4. pedagogical realisation (finding appropriate exercises and activities and composing instructions)
5. physical production of the materials

The framework is illustrated through four case studies.

Prowse, P. (2011). How writers write: testimony from authors. In B. Tomlinson (ed.), *Materials Development in Language Teaching*, 2nd edn (pp. 151–74). Cambridge: Cambridge University Press.

We have already referred to this chapter above, but it is interesting to read in full as it covers a number of topics not often discussed in the literature: working with a co-author, the creative process and working with publishers. It also involves an historical perspective as the same authors were interviewed about their working practice after an interval of fifteen years.

CONCLUSION

Our approach throughout this book has reflected our beliefs about, and approaches to, language teaching itself; we have taken a broadly inductive approach which has invited the reader to establish criteria by which to evaluate existing materials and to infer principles for developing them. In this concluding chapter, we synthesise these principles, and we point to some promising future directions in the field of materials development as it steadily builds a body of applied research.

Chapter 2 went to the core of materials development, as it were, looking to **SLA** research and theory for principles to underpin our learning materials: we also noted (with reference to central figures in SLA, Ellis (e.g. 2010), and in materials development, Tomlinson (e.g. 2013a, 2013b), that SLA is increasingly seen as the touchstone for our field. These principles, we discovered, applied not only to the input material itself and to adjustments to it, and to pedagogical frameworks we put on it, but also, of course, to the learner, whose receptivity to and engagement with the material are vital indicators of its efficacy.

In **Chapter 3** we explored the 'shifting sands' of **culture** and **context** – and in fact of the English language itself – upon which language learning materials have to be positioned, and we looked at the implications of this for materials publication. While recognising that ELT publishing faces a tension between global spread and local needs, we concluded that these can be reconciled by offering global textbooks that are flexible enough to admit local perspectives – including pedagogical ones – as well as 'local textbooks with global perspectives' (Ates 2012: 19). Localisation, we noted, has been flagged as one of the future directions for the field (e.g. Tomlinson 2013).

Chapter 4 dealt with materials **evaluation** and **adaptation**. We stressed in this chapter the importance of distinguishing between systematic and principled evaluation and adaptation, and ad hoc, intuitive processes of evaluation and adaptation. We emphasised that principled evaluation and adaptation depend on clearly articulated and coherent criteria which can be justified with reference to language learning theory. Most importantly, we argued that the process of developing evaluation criteria can contribute to teacher education by helping teachers to reflect on their beliefs and principles.

The use of **technology** in language teaching has forced a shift in our perception of what constitutes language learning *material*, and this was the focus of **Chapter 5**. *Interaction* has been at the core of our language pedagogy (in the West at least) since the inception of CLT, consolidated there by the affordances of (since the 2000s)

Web 2.0 and mobile technology. With these affordances, we demonstrate, traditional notions of authorship are broadened, and interaction in a sense 'becomes' the material. This means that the key pedagogical structure in this environment is *the task* which frames this interaction. This broader conceptualisation of materials will, we would predict, become just part of the normalisation of technology. Blended learning, the pedagogical realisation of this normalising, is on the rise (at the time of writing) (see, for example, McCarthy and Marsh forthcoming and Tomlinson and Whittaker 2013).

Chapter 6, the first chapter on materials for **skills**, starts with a couple of caveats. We are not entirely comfortable with the convenient division of the language skills into four, namely reading, listening, speaking and writing; what about communicative competence? What about intercultural competence? Nor would our preferred treatment of skills materials be as separate entities, since skills are almost always practised in combination. Nevertheless, like other authors (e.g. McDonough, Shaw and Masuhara 2013), we recognise this as a pedagogical and materials convention and begin, in Chapter 6, with **reading** and **listening**. Skills teaching has evolved in tandem with language pedagogy over the years, and we explore the prevailing *process* approach, in which materials are designed to encourage the acquiring of skills and strategies. We emphasise also that the resource (a printed text, a YouTube video clip and so on) does not dictate the skill; any combination of resource and skills is possible in our materials.

In **Chapter 7**, we discussed the so-called productive skills, **speaking** and **writing**. In relation to the former, we noted that speaking is a complex and demanding skill which needs systematic development which goes beyond simply providing activities to get students talking. We need both a syllabus of spoken discourse types and a syllabus of spoken language features. In relation to writing skills, we argued that the traditional product/process division is rather unhelpful and that both approaches have their place and can indeed be combined in a process genre approach. We concluded that the main role of materials in developing writing skills is to provide a stimulus to write and to provide scaffolding in terms of the kinds of organisational structure and discourse/lexical/grammatical features required to compose particular kinds of text.

Chapter 8 considered materials for teaching **vocabulary** and materials for teaching **grammar**. In both cases, we noted that corpora have a role to play in helping us decide which items to focus on in our materials. In relation to vocabulary, corpora have drawn our attention to the need to focus not just on single words, but also on collocations and chunks. We noted that 'depth of processing' is a key principle in vocabulary learning and that 'old-fashioned' techniques such as translation and learning from lists are not to be dismissed. In relation to grammar, we observed that taking an 'enabling' view of grammar, i.e. focusing on how grammar helps us say what we want to say, might be more fruitful than simply following the syllabuses that have become entrenched in coursebooks. We also made the case for 'principled eclecticism', i.e. matching our approach to the language point and the learners in question.

Chapter 9, subtitled 'From process to product', pulls the book together in a sense by offering a rough map of the **materials design** journey from the starting point to the destination. It first underlined the distinction between unmediated and mediated materials writing, stressing that mediated materials writing brings into the equation a range of potential stakeholders such as publishers, ministry officials and the end-user teachers. We outlined some typical stages in the materials writing process while noting that it is usually a recursive process. Indeed, we observed that among the characteristic qualities of experienced materials writers is the tendency to approach the task in a cyclical rather than linear manner. Other qualities of experienced materials writers are the ability to keep the end-users constantly in mind and the willingness to abandon ideas which are not bearing fruit. We noted that content frameworks such as the CEFR and writing frameworks such as Tomlinson's (2013) flexible framework can be very useful starting points for materials writing.

At the beginning of this book we asked *why* a book on materials development was needed. In the subsequent chapters, we demonstrated how language learning materials have to be carefully crafted to fit principles of SLA, language teaching contexts, language pedagogy, critical evaluation, authentic language data and pragmatic considerations. These areas are themselves all vital constituents of the field of language teaching, demonstrating that materials development is integral to the field, not ancillary to it. We would therefore argue for materials development to have a far more central place in language teacher education:

> language learning materials are such a key element in the teaching–learning encounter that consideration of their selection, use and design cannot be consigned to the periphery of a teacher education programme . . . materials evaluation and design should be a central (core) component of both pre-service and post-experience postgraduate programmes. (McGrath 2013: 100)

Considering the centrality of its concerns to language teaching, in fact, materials development training itself might be seen as the 'ultimate' teacher education tool. It empowers teachers by giving them control over their teaching materials and emancipates them from being constrained to work with those produced by 'the establishment'.

In conclusion, we maintain that since language learning materials are integral to the language teaching classroom, *not* providing training in materials development restricts language teachers to a superficial knowledge and understanding of the most essential instruments of their profession; the materials they work with.

Task 10.1

- Compare McGrath's (2013: 100) position on the place of materials development in teacher education, quoted just above, with the following:

> In Grossman and Thompson's (2008) study, [pre-service] trainees focused on creating materials from scratch rather than learning best how to exploit textbooks. This is profoundly unhelpful, given that the textbook occupies a central position in most classrooms. (Harwood 2014: 28–9)

- Reflect on your own position.

Task 10.2

• Reflect on and discuss these contrasting views:

> Every teacher is a materials developer. (Tomlinson 2003a: 1, citing a 1997 English Language Centre handout) The expertise required of materials writers is importantly different from that required of classroom teachers. (Allwright 1981: 6)

Task 10.3

> Whereas previously many language teachers . . . were lingua-cultural artisans who initiated students into many aspects of the host culture through tailor-made materials designed to improve their language proficiency, the new . . . ethic of corporate universities has transformed their professional identities into that of linguistic service technicians, charged with fixing broken language and mainlining a streamlined system of course delivery. (Hadley 2014: 209, citing Giroux 2004: 206)

• What do you understand by the terms 'lingua-cultural artisan' and 'linguistic service technician' as applied to language teachers/materials developers?
• Do you see the role of the teacher and/or materials developer as that of a 'lingua-cultural artisan' or that of a 'linguistic service technician'?
• Propose other descriptions of the relationship between teachers and materials.

BIBLIOGRAPHY

Abdul Latif, M. (forthcoming). Teaching grammar using inductive and communicative materials: exploring Egyptian EFL teachers' practices and beliefs. In H. Masuhara, B. Tomlinson and F. Mishan (eds), *Practice and Theory in Materials Development in Language Learning*. Newcastle upon Tyne: Cambridge Scholars Publishing.

Ableeva, R. and Stranks, J. (2013). Listening in another language: research and materials. In B. Tomlinson (ed.), *Applied Linguistics and Materials Development* (pp. 199–212). London: Bloomsbury.

Afflerbach, P., Pearson, D. and Scott, G. P. (2008). Clarifying differences between reading skills and reading strategies. *Reading Teacher*, 61(5): 364–73.

Akbari, R. (2007). Transforming lives: introducing critical pedagogy into ELT classrooms. *ELT Journal*, 62(3): 276–83.

Alderson, J. (1984). Reading in a foreign language: a reading problem or a language problem? In J. C. Alderson and A. H. Urquhart (eds), *Reading in a Foreign Language* (pp. 1–24). Harlow: Longman.

Al Khaldi, A. (2011). Materials development in Jordan: an applied linguistic challenge. Unpublished PhD thesis, Leeds Metropolitan University, UK.

Allan, R. (2009). Can a graded reader corpus provide 'authentic' input? *ELT Journal*, 63(1): 23–32.

Allwright, D. (1981). What do we want teaching materials for? *ELT Journal*, 36(1): 5–18.

Alptekin, C. (1996). Target-language culture in EFL materials. In T. Hedge and N. Whitney (eds), *Power, Pedagogy and Practice* (pp. 53–61). Oxford: Oxford University Press.

Alptekin, C. (2002). Towards intercultural communicative competence in ELT. *ELT Journal*, 56(1): 57–64.

Amrani, F. (2011). The process of evaluation: a publisher's view. In B. Tomlinson (ed.), *Materials Development in Language Teaching*, 2nd edn (pp. 267–95). Cambridge: Cambridge University Press.

Anderson, L. and Krathwohl, D. A. (2001). *A Taxonomy for Learning, Teaching and Assessing: A Revision of Bloom's Taxonomy of Educational Objectives*. New York: Longman.

Anderson, N. (2002). The role of metacognition in second language teaching and learning. ERIC Digest. Washington: ERIC Clearinghouse on Languages and Linguistics.

Arikan, A. (2004). Professional development programs and English language instructors: a critical-postmodern study. *Hacettepe University Journal of Education*, 27: 40–9. Retrieved 2 January 2015 from http://www.efdergi.hacettepe.edu.tr/200427ARDA%20ARIKAN.pdf

Arnold, J. (ed.) (1999). *Affect in Language Learning*. Cambridge: Cambridge University Press.

Arnold, J. and Brown, H. D. (1999). A map of the terrain. In J. Arnold (ed.), *Affect in Language Learning* (pp. 1–24). Cambridge: Cambridge University Press.

Ates, M. (2012). The English Textbook Writing Project in Turkey. *Folio*, 14(2): 18–21.

Au, K. (1998). Social constructivism and the school literacy learning of students of diverse backgrounds. *Journal of Literacy Research*, 30(2): 297–319.

Badger, R. and White, G. (2000). A process genre approach to teaching writing. *ELT Journal*, 54(2): 153–60.

Bandler, R. and Grinder, J. (1979). *Frogs into Princes*. Moab: Real People Press.

Bartlett, F. C. (1932). *Remembering*. Cambridge: Cambridge University Press. Reissued 1995.

Basturkmen, H. (2001). Descriptions of spoken language for higher level learners: the example of questioning. *ELT Journal*, 55(1): 4–12.

Bax, S. (2003). CALL: past, present and future. *System*, 31(2): 13–28.

Bell, J. and Gower, R. (2011). Writing course materials for the world: a great compromise. In B. Tomlinson (ed.), *Materials Development in Language Teaching*, 2nd edn (pp. 135–51). Cambridge: Cambridge University Press.

Benson, P. and Voller, P. (1997). *Autonomy and Independence in Language Learning*. London: Longman.

Berardo, S. (2006). The use of authentic materials in the teaching of reading. *Reading Matrix*, 6(2): 60–9.

Bernardini, S. (2000). Systematising serendipity: Proposals for concordancing large corpora with language learners. In L. Burnard and T. McEnery (eds), *Rethinking Language Pedagogy from a Corpus Perspective* (pp. 79–105). Frankfurt: Peter Lang.

Berns, N. (1995). English in Europe: Whose language, which culture? *International Journal of Applied Linguistics*, 5(1): 21–32.

Biber, D. and Conrad, S. (2010). *Corpus Linguistics and Grammar Teaching*. Retrieved 10 November 2014 from http://www.pearsonlongman.com/ae/emac/newsletters/may-2010-grammar.html

Biber, D., Conrad, S. and Reppen, R. (1998). *Corpus Linguistics: Investigating Language Structure and Use*. Cambridge: Cambridge University Press

Blake, R. (2008). *Brave New Digital Classroom: Technology and Foreign Language Learning*. Washington: Georgetown University Press.

Blake, R. (2014). Best practices in online learning: is it for everyone? In F. Rubio and J. Thoms (eds), *Hybrid Language Teaching and Learning: Exploring Theoretical, Pedagogical and Curricular Issues* (pp. 10–26). Boston: Heinle Cengage Learning.

Blau, E. (1982). The effect of syntax on readability for ESL students in Puerto Rico. *TESOL Quarterly*, 16: 517–28.

Bloom, B., Engelhart, M., Furst, E., Hill, W. and Krathwohl, D. (1956). *Taxonomy of Educational Objectives: The Classification of Educational Goals. Handbook I: The Cognitive Domain*. New York: David McKay.

Blyth, C. (2014). Opening up foreign language education with open educational resources: the case of *Français interactif*. In F. Rubio and J. Thoms (eds), *Hybrid Language Teaching and Learning: Exploring Theoretical, Pedagogical and Curricular Issues* (pp. 196–218). Boston: Heinle Cengage Learning.

Bolitho, R. (2008). Materials used in Central and Eastern Europe and the Former Soviet Union. In B. Tomlinson (ed.), *English Language Learning Materials: A Critical Review* (pp. 213–22). London: Continuum.

Bolitho, R., Carter, R., Hughes, R., Ivanic, R., Masuhara, H. and Tomlinson, B. (2003). Ten questions about language awareness. *ELT Journal*, 57(3): 251–9.

Bolster, A. (2014). Materials adaptation of EAP materials by experienced teachers: part I. *Folio*, 16(1): 16–22.

Bolster, A. (2015). Materials adaptation of EAP materials by experienced teachers: part II. *Folio*, 16(2).

Borg, S. (1999). Teachers' theories in grammar teaching. *ELT Journal*, 53(3): 157–67.

Boulton, A. (2009). Testing the limits of data-driven learning: language proficiency and training. *ReCALL*, 21(1): 37–54.

Bowler, B., Cunningham, S., Moor, P. and Parminter, S. (1999). *New Headway Pronunciation Course: Intermediate: Student's Practice Book*. Oxford: Oxford University Press.

Brazil, D. (1995). *A Grammar of Speech*. Oxford: Oxford University Press.

Brindle, M. (2012). A Wordle in your ear. *Folio*, 15(1): 25–7.

British Council Teaching English (2008). Retrieved 24 March 2013 from http://www. teachingenglish.org.uk/node/3036/results

Brown, G. and Yule, G. (1983). *Teaching the Spoken Language*. Cambridge: Cambridge University Press.

Bruthiaux, P. (2003). Squaring the circles: issues in modeling English worldwide. *International Journal of Applied Linguistics*, 13(2): 159–78.

Burden, K. (2002). Learning from the bottom up: the contribution of school based practice and research in the effective use of interactive whiteboards for the FE/HE sector. Paper presented at the Learning and Skills Research: Making an Impact Regionally conference, Doncaster, UK.

Burns, A. and Hill, D. (2013). Teaching speaking in a second language. In B. Tomlinson (ed.), *Applied Linguistics and Materials Development* (pp. 231–51). London: Bloomsbury.

Burton, G. (2012). Corpora and coursebooks: destined to be strangers forever? *Corpora*, 7: 91–108.

Bygate, M. (2001). Speaking. In R. Carter and D. Nunan (eds), *The Cambridge Guide to TESOL* (pp. 14–20). Cambridge: Cambridge University Press.

Byram, M. (1997). *Teaching and Assessing Intercultural Competence*. Clevedon: Multilingual Matters.

Byram, M., Morgan, C. and Colleagues (1994). *Teaching-and-Learning Language-and-Culture*. Clevedon: Multilingual Matters.

Byrne, D. (1988). *Teaching Writing Skills*. London: Longman.

Cameron, L. (2001). *Teaching Languages to Young Learners*. Cambridge: Cambridge University Press.

Canagarajah, S. (1999). *Resisting Linguistic Imperialism in Language Teaching*. Oxford: Oxford University Press.

Carter, R. (2004). *Language and Creativity: The Art of Common Talk*. London: Routledge.

Chambers, E. and Gregory, M. (2006). *Teaching and Learning English Literature*. London: Sage.

Chapelle, C. (2003). *English Language Learning and Technology*. Amsterdam: John Benjamins.

Chapelle, C. (2009). The relationship between second language acquisition theory and computer-assisted language learning. *Modern Language Journal*, 93: 741–53.

Chapelle, C. (2010). The spread of computer-assisted language learning. *Language Teaching*, 43(1): 66–74.

Chen, Y-S. and Shao-Wen Su, S-W. (2012). A genre-based approach to teaching EFL summary writing. *ELT Journal*, 66(2): 184–92.

Chomsky, N. (1988). *Language and Problems of Knowledge*. Cambridge, MA: MIT Press.

Clavel-Arriotia, B. and Fuster-Márquez, M. (2014). The authenticity of real texts in advanced English language textbooks. *ELT Journal*, 68(2): 124–34.

Clement, R., Gardner, R. C. and Smythe, P. C. (1977). Motivational variables in second language acquisition: a study of francophones learning English. *Canadian Journal of Behavioural Science*, 9: 123–33.

Cobb, T. (1999). Breadth and depth of vocabulary acquisition with hands-on concordancing. *Computer Assisted Language Learning*, 12: 345–60.

Cohen, A. and Ishihara, N. (2013). Pragmatics. In B. Tomlinson (ed.), *Applied Linguistics and Materials Development* (pp. 113–26). London: Bloomsbury.

Coleman, H. (1986). Evaluating teachers' guides: do teachers' guides guide teachers? *JALT Journal*, 8: 17–36.

Conrad, S. (2000). Will corpus linguistics revolutionize grammar teaching in the 21st century? *TESOL Quarterly*, 34(3): 548–60.

Conrad, S. (2004). Corpus linguistics, language variation, and language teaching. In J. Sinclair (ed.), *How to Use Corpora in Language Teaching* (pp. 67–85). Amsterdam: John Benjamins.

Conzett, J. (2000). Integrating collocation into a reading and writing course. In M. Lewis (ed.), *Teaching Collocation: Further Developments in the Lexical Approach* (pp. 70–87). Hove: Language Teaching.

Cook, G. (1995). Theoretical issues: transcribing the untranscribable. In G. Myers and G. Leech (eds), *Spoken English on Computer* (pp. 35–53). New York: Longman.

Cook, G. (1998). 'The uses of reality': a reply to Ron Carter. *ELT Journal*, 52(1): 57–63.

Cook, V. (2003). Materials for adult beginners from an L2 user perspective. In B. Tomlinson (ed.), *Developing Materials for Language Teaching* (pp. 275–91). London: Continuum.

Cortazzi, M. and Jin, L. (1999). Cultural mirrors: materials and methods in the EFL classroom. In E. Hinkel (ed.), *Culture in Second Language Teaching* (pp. 196–219). Cambridge: Cambridge University Press.

Coupland, N. (2001). Introduction: sociolinguistic theory and social theory. In N. Coupland, S. Sarangi and C. Candlin (eds), *Sociolinguistics and Social Theory* (pp. 1–26). Harlow: Pearson Education.

Coxhead, A. (2000). The academic word list: a corpus-based word list for academic purposes. In B. Kettemann and G. Marko (eds), *Teaching and Learning by Doing Corpus Analysis: Proceedings of the Fourth International Conference on Teaching and Language Corpora* (pp. 73–90). New York: Rodopi.

Craik, F. I. M. and Lockhart, R. S. (1972). Levels of processing: a framework for memory research. *Journal of Verbal Learning and Verbal Behavior*, 11: 671–84.

Craven, M. (2008). *Real Listening and Speaking*. Cambridge: Cambridge University Press.

Criado, R. and Sanchez, A. (2009). English language teaching in Spain: do textbooks comply with the official methodological regulations? A sample analysis. *International Journal of English Studies*, 9(1): 1–28.

Crookes, G. and Schmidt, R. (1991). Motivation: reopening the research agenda. *Language Learning*, 41: 469–512.

Crossley, S. A., Louwerse, M. M., McCarthy, P. M. and McNamara, D. S. (2007). A linguistic analysis of simplified and authentic texts. *Modern Language Journal*, 91: 15–30.

Crystal, D. (2001). *Language and the Internet*. Cambridge: Cambridge University Press.

Crystal, D. (2003). *The Cambridge Encyclopedia of the English Language*, 2nd edn. Cambridge: Cambridge University Press.

Csikszentmihalyi, M. (1997). *Finding Flow: The Psychology of Engagement with Everyday Life*. New York: Basic Books.

Cullen, R. (2008).Teaching grammar as a liberating force. *ELT Journal*, 62(3): 221–30.

Cullen, R. and Kuo, I-C. (2007). Spoken grammar and ELT course materials: a missing link? *TESOL Quarterly*, 41(2): 361–86.

Cunningham, S. and Moor, P. (1998). *Cutting Edge Intermediate Student's Book*. Harlow: Pearson Education.

Cunningham, S. and Moor, P. (2005). *New Cutting Edge Upper Intermediate Student's Book*, 2nd edn. Harlow: Pearson Education.

Cunningsworth, A. (1995). *Choosing Your Course Book*. Cambridge: Cambridge University Press.

Cutting, J. (2014). *Understanding Language*. Edinburgh: Edinburgh University Press.

Darian, S. (2001). Adapting authentic materials for language teaching. *English Teaching Forum Online*, 39(2).

Dat, B. (2008). ELT materials used in Southeast Asia. In B. Tomlinson (ed.), *English Language Learning Materials: A Critical Review* (pp. 263–81). London: Continuum.

Dat, B. (2013). Materials for developing speaking skills. In B. Tomlinson (ed.), *Developing Materials for Language Teaching*, 2nd edn (pp. 407–29). London: Bloomsbury.

Davis, D. R. (2006). World Englishes and descriptive grammars. In B. Kachru, Y. Kachru and C. L. Nelson, *The Handbook of World Englishes* (pp. 509–25). Oxford: Blackwell.

de Andres, V. (1999). Self-esteem in the classroom or the metamorphosis of butterflies. In J. Arnold (ed.), *Affect in Language Learning* (pp. 87–102). Cambridge: Cambridge University Press.

de Bot, K. (1996). Review article: the psycholinguistics of the output hypothesis. *Language Learning*, 46(3): 529–55.

Deardorff, D. (ed.) (2009). *The Sage Handbook of Intercultural Competence*. Los Angeles: Sage.

Deci, E. L. and Ryan, R. M. (1985). *Intrinsic Motivation and Self-Determination in Human Behaviours*. New York: Plenum.

DeKeyser, R. (2003). Implicit and explicit learning. In C. Doughty and M. Long, *The Handbook of Second Language Acquisition* (pp. 313–48). Malden: Blackwell.

Delialioglu, O. and Yildirim, Z. (2007). Students' perceptions on effective dimensions of interactive learning in a blended learning environment. *Journal of Educational Technology and Society*, 10(2): 133–46.

Dellar, H. (2004). What have corpora ever done for us? Retrieved 17 March 2013 from http://www.developingteachers.com/articles_tchtraining/corporapf_hugh.htm

Dellar, H. (2007). *Advanced Innovations*. Andover: Heinle Cengage Learning.

Dellar, H. and Walkley, A. (2007). *Innovations Advanced*. Andover: Heinle Cengage Learning.

Dellar, H. and Walkley, A. (2010). *Outcomes*. Andover: Heinle Cengage Learning.

Dendrinos, B. (1992). *The EFL Textbook and Ideology*. Athens: N. C. Grivas.

Dewaele, J-M. (2009). Individual differences in second language acquisition. In W. Ritchie and T. Bhatia (eds), *The New Handbook of Second Language Acquisition* (pp. 623–46). Bingley: Emerald Group.

Dewey, J. (2007). English as a lingua franca and globalization: an interconnected perspective. *International Journal of Applied Linguistics*, 17(3): 332–54.

Dörnyei, Z. (1998). Motivation in second and foreign language learning. *Language Teaching*, 31: 117–35.

Dörnyei, Z. (2001). *Teaching and Researching Motivation*. London: Pearson Education.

Dörnyei, Z. (2009). The L2 motivational self system. In Z. Dörnyei and E. Ushioda (eds), *Motivation, Language Identity and the L2 Self* (pp. 9–42). Bristol: Multilingual Matters.

Doughty, C. and Long, M. (2003). The scope of enquiry and goals of SLA. In C. Doughty and M. Long (eds), *The Handbook of Second Language Acquisition* (pp. 3–16). Malden: Blackwell.

Doyle, R. (1993). *Paddy Clarke Ha Ha Ha*. London: Secker and Warburg.

Dudeney, G., Hockly, N. and Pegrum, M. (2013). *Digital Literacies*. Harlow: Pearson Education.

Duke, N., Pearson, P. D., Strachan, S. L. and Billman, A. K. (2011). Essential elements of fostering and teaching reading comprehension. In S. J. Samuels and A. E. Farstrup (eds), *What Research Has to Say About Reading Instruction*, 4th edn (pp. 51–93). Newark: International Reading Association.

Dushku, S. and Thompson, P. (2012). An example of corpus-informed materials development: 'Campus Talk' – advanced oral communication textbook for international students. Paper presented at the TESOL Convention, Philadelphia, USA.

Eapan, L. (2014). Issues in English textbook construction for primary schools in multilingual contexts. *Folio*, 16(1): 9–11.

Edge, J. (1987). From Julian Edge. *ELT Journal*, 41(4): 308–9.

Ediger, A. (2001). Teaching children literacy skills in a second language. In M. Celce-Murcia (ed.), *Teaching English as a Second or Foreign Language*, 3rd edn (pp. 153–69). Boston: Heinle & Heinle.

Egbert, J. (ed.) (2010). *CALL in Limited Technology Contexts*. San Marcos: CALICO

Ellis, R. (1994). *The Study of Second Language Acquisition*. Oxford: Oxford University Press.

Ellis, R. (1997). *Second Language Acquisition*. Oxford: Oxford University Press.

Ellis, R. (2004). Individual differences in second language learning. In A. Davies and C. Elder (eds), *The Handbook of Applied Linguistics* (pp. 525–51). Malden: Blackwell.

Ellis, R. (2006). Current issues in the teaching of grammar: an SLA perspective. *TESOL Quarterly*, 40(1): 83–107.

Ellis, R. (2008). *The Study of Second Language Acquisition*, 2nd edn. Oxford: Oxford University Press.

Ellis, R. (2010). Second language acquisition research and language teaching materials. In N. Harwood (ed.), *English Language Teaching Materials: Theory and Practice* (pp. 33–57). Cambridge: Cambridge University Press.

Ellis, R. (2011). Macro- and micro-evaluations of task-based teaching. In B. Tomlinson (ed.), *Materials Development in Language Teaching*, 2nd edn (pp. 212–36). Cambridge: Cambridge University Press.

Ellis, R., Loewen, S., Elder, C., Erlam, R., Philp, J. and Reinders, H. (2009). *Implicit and Explicit Knowledge in Second Language Learning, Testing and Teaching*. Bristol: Multilingual Matters.

Ellison, L. (2001). *The Personal Intelligences: Promoting Social and Emotional Learning*. Thousand Oaks: Corwin Press.

English Language Centre (1997). Unpublished handout from the English Language Centre, Duran, South Africa.

Eoyang, E. (1999). The worldliness of the English language: a lingua franca past and future. *ADFL Bulletin*, 31(1): 26–32.

Eskey, D. E. (2005). Reading in a second language. In E. Hinkel (ed.), *Handbook of Research in Second Language Teaching and Learning* (pp. 563–80). Mahwah: Erlbaum.

Evans, G. (2012). A materials evaluation toolkit. Unpublished MA dissertation, Leeds Metropolitan University, UK.

Everett, D. (2008). *Don't Sleep, There Are Snakes*. London: Profile Books.

Feak, C. and Swales, J. (2014). Tensions between the old and the new in EAP textbook revision: a tale of two projects. In N. Harwood (ed.), *English Language Teaching Textbooks: Content, Consumption, Production* (pp. 299–319). Basingstoke: Palgrave Macmillan.

Felix, U. (2008). The unreasonable effectiveness of CALL: what have we learned in two decades of research? *ReCALL*, 20: 141–61.

Field, J. (2008). *Listening in the Language Classroom*. Cambridge: Cambridge University Press.

Finkbeiner, M. and Nicol, J. (2003). Semantic category effects in second language word learning. *Applied Psycholinguistics*, 24: 369–83.

Folse, K. (2004). Myths about teaching and learning second language vocabulary: what recent research says. *TESL Reporter*, 37(2): 1–13.

Folse, K. (2011). Applying L2 lexical research findings in ESL teaching. *TESOL Quarterly*, 45(2): 362–9.

Forehand, M. (2012). Bloom's Taxonomy. Retrieved 18 March 2014 from http://projects.coe. uga.edu/epltt/index.php?title=Bloom%27s_Taxonomy

Foster, P. and Skehan, P. (1996). The influence of source of planning and focus of planning on task-based performance. *Language Teaching Research*, 3(3): 215–47.

Fox, G. (1998). Using corpus data in the classroom. In B. Tomlinson (ed.), *Materials Development in Language Teaching* (pp. 25–43). Cambridge: Cambridge University Press.

Freeman, D. (2014). Reading comprehension questions: the distribution of different types in global EFL textbooks. In N. Harwood (ed.), *English Language Teaching Textbooks: Content, Consumption, Production* (pp. 72–110). Basingstoke: Palgrave Macmillan.

Gadd, N. (1998). Towards less humanistic English teaching. *ELT Journal*, 52(3): 223–34.

Gagliardi, G. and Maley, A. (eds) (2010). *EIL, ELF, Global English: Teaching and Learning Issues*. Bern: Peter Lang.

Gairns, R. and Redman, S. (1986). *Working with Words: A Guide to Teaching and Learning Vocabulary*. Cambridge: Cambridge University Press.

Galloway, N. and Mariou, E. (2014). Global Englishes. In J. Cutting, *Understanding Language* (pp. 43–69). Edinburgh: Edinburgh University Press.

Gardner, H. (1983). *Frames of Mind*. New York: Basic Books.

Gardner, R. C. (1995). Interview with Jelena Mihaljevic Djigunovic. *Stranijezici*, 24: 94–103.

Ghosn, I-K. (2013). Language learning for young learners. In B. Tomlinson (ed.), *Applied Linguistics and Materials Development* (pp. 61–74). London: Bloomsbury.

Gill, S. (2000). Against dogma: a plea for moderation. *IATEFL Issues*, 154: 18–19. Retrieved 7 September 2011 from http://www.thornburyscott.com/tu/gill.htm

Gilmore, A. (2004). A comparison of textbook and authentic interactions. *ELT Journal*, 58(4): 363–74.

Gilmore, A. (2007). Authentic materials and authenticity in foreign language learning. *Language Teaching*, 40(2): 97–118.

Gilmore, A. (2011). 'I prefer not text': Developing Japanese learners' communicative competence with authentic materials. *Language Learning*, 61(3): 786–819.

Giroux, H. (2004). Teachers as transformative intellectuals. In A. Canestrari and B. Marlowe (eds), *Educational Foundations: An Anthology of Critical Readings* (pp. 205–14). Thousand Oaks: Sage.

Godwin-Jones, R. (2011). Emerging technologies: challenging hegemonies in online learning. *Language Learning and Technology*, 16(2): 4–13.

Goh, C. (2007). *Teaching Speaking in the Language Classroom*. Singapore: SEAMO.

Gor, K. and Long, M. (2009). Input and second language processing. In W. Ritchie and T. Bhatia (eds), *The New Handbook of Second Language Acquisition* (pp. 445–72). Bingley: Emerald Group.

Grabe, W. (2009). *Reading in a Second Language: Moving from Theory to Practice*. Cambridge: Cambridge University Press.

Grant, N. (1987). *Making the Most of Your Textbook*. Harlow: Longman.

Gray, J. (2010b). *The Construction of English: Culture, Consumerism and Promotion in the ELT Global Coursebook*. Basingstoke: Palgrave Macmillan.

Gregg, K. (1984). Krashen's monitor and Occam's razor. *Applied Linguistics*, 5: 79–100.

Grgurović, M., Chapelle, C. A. and Shelley, M. C. (2013). A meta-analysis of effectiveness studies on computer technology-supported language learning. *ReCALL*, 25: 165–98.

Grigg, T. (1986). The effects of task, time and rule knowledge on grammar performance for three English structures. *University of Hawaii Working Papers in ESL*, 5(1): 37–60.

Grossman, P. and Thompson, C. (2008). Learning from curriculum materials: scaffolds for new teachers. *Teaching and Teacher Education*, 24: 2014–26.

Gruba, P. and Hinkelman, D. (2012). *Blending Technologies in Second Language Classrooms*. Basingstoke: Palgrave Macmillan.

Guiora, A., Beit-Halllahmi, R., Brannon, R., Dull, C. and Scovel, T. (1972). The effects of experimentally induced changes in ego states on pronunciation ability in second language: an exploratory study. *Comprehensive Psychiatry*, 13: 421–8.

Hadfield, J. (2014). Chaosmos: spontaneity and order in the materials design process. In N. Harwood (ed.), *English Language Teaching Textbooks: Content, Consumption, Production* (pp. 320–60). Basingstoke: Palgrave Macmillan.

Hadley, G. (2002). Sensing the winds of change: an introduction to data-driven learning. *RELC Journal*, 33(2): 99–124.

Hadley, G. (2014). Global textbooks in local contexts: an empirical investigation of effectiveness. In N. Harwood (ed.), *English Language Teaching Textbooks: Content, Consumption, Production* (pp. 205–40). Basingstoke: Palgrave Macmillan.

Hampel, R. (2006). Rethinking task design for the digital age: a framework for language teaching and learning in a synchronous online environment. *ReCALL*, 18(1): 105–21.

Hartley, B. and Viney, P. (1978). *Streamline English Departures*. Oxford: Oxford University Press.

Hartley, B. and Viney, P. (1979). *Streamline English Connections*. Oxford: Oxford University Press.

Hartley, B. and Viney, P. (1985). *Streamline English Directions*. Oxford: Oxford University Press.

Hartley, B. and Viney, P. (1987). *Streamline English Destinations*. Oxford: Oxford University Press.

Harwood, N. (2002). Taking a lexical approach to teaching: principles and problems. *International Journal of Applied Linguistics*, 12(2): 139–55.

Harwood, N. (ed.) (2010). *English Language Teaching Materials: Theory and Practice*. Cambridge: Cambridge University Press.

Harwood, N. (ed.) (2014). *English Language Teaching Textbooks: Content, Consumption, Production*. Basingstoke: Palgrave Macmillan.

Healy, A. F. and Bourne L. E., Jr (eds) (1998) *Foreign Language Learning: Psycholinguistic Studies on Training and Retention*. Mahwah: Erlbaum.

Hedge, T. (2005). *Writing*. Oxford: Oxford University Press.

Hedge, T. and Whitney, N. (eds) (1996). *Power, Pedagogy and Practice*. Oxford: Oxford University Press.

Hewings, M. and Thaine, C. (2012). *Cambridge Academic English Students' Book Advanced*. Cambridge: Cambridge University Press.

Hill, J. (2000). Revising priorities: from grammatical failure to collocational success. In M. Lewis (ed.), *Teaching Collocation: Further Developments in the Lexical Approach* (pp. 47–69). Hove: Language Teaching.

H: . 006). Current perspectives on teaching the four skills. *TESOL Quarterly*, 40(1):

11). The digital generation. *ELT Journal*, 65(3): 322–5.

3a). Technology for the language teacher: mobile learning. *ELT Journal*, 67(1):

Hockly, N. (2013b). Moving with the times: mobile literacy and ELT. Paper presented at the IATEFL Conference, 9–13 April, Liverpool, UK.

Hockly, N. (2014). Digital technologies in low-resource ELT contexts. *ELT Journal*, 68(1): 79–84.

Hoffman, E. (1989). *Lost in Translation: A Life in a New Language*. New York: Penguin.

Holliday, A. R. (1994). *Appropriate Methodology and Social Context*. Cambridge: Cambridge University Press.

Howatt, A. P. and Widdowson, H. G. (2004). *A History of English Language Teaching*. Oxford: Oxford University Press.

Hu, G. (2002). Potential cultural resistance to pedagogical imports: the case of communicative language teaching in China. *Language, Culture and Curriculum*, 15(2): 93–105.

Huang, L-S. (2011). Corpus-aided language learning. *ELT Journal*, 65(4): 481–4.

Hughes, A. (2013). The teaching of reading in English for young learners: some considerations and next steps. In B. Tomlinson (ed.), *Applied Linguistics and Materials Development* (pp. 183–98). London: Bloomsbury.

Hughes, R. (2002). *Teaching and Researching Speaking*. Harlow: Pearson.

Hughes, R. (2010). Materials to develop the speaking skill. In N. Harwood (ed.), *English Language Teaching Textbooks: Content, Consumption, Production* (pp. 207–24). Cambridge: Cambridge University Press.

Humphries, S. (2012). From policy to pedagogy: exploring the impact of new communicative textbooks on the classroom practice of Japanese teachers of English. In C. Gitsaki and R. B. Baldauf, Jr (eds), *Future Directions in Applied Linguistics: Local and Global Perspectives* (pp. 488–507). Newcastle: Cambridge Scholars.

Hyland, K. (2003). *Second Language Writing*. Cambridge: Cambridge University Press.

Hyland, K. (2007) Genre pedagogy: language, literacy and L2 writing instruction, *Journal of Second Language Writing*, 16: 148–64.

Hyland, K. (2013). Materials for developing writing skills. In B. Tomlinson (ed.), *Developing Materials for Language Teaching*, 2nd edn (pp. 391–407). London: Bloomsbury.

Hymes, D. (1972). On communicative competence. In J. Pride and J. Holmes (eds), *Sociolinguistics* (pp. 269–93). Harmondsworth: Penguin.

Islam, C. and Mares, C. (2003). Adapting classroom materials. In B. Tomlinson (ed.), *Developing Materials for Language Teaching* (pp. 86–100). London: Continuum.

Jenkins, J. (2005). Implementing an international approach to English pronunciation: the role of teacher attitudes and identity. *Tesol Quarterly*, 39(3): 535–43.

Jenkins, J. (2006). Global intelligibility and local diversity: possibility or paradox? In R. Rubdy and M. Saraceni (eds), *English in the World: Global Rules, Global Roles* (pp. 32–9). London: Continuum.

Jenkins, J. (2007). *English as a Lingua Franca: Attitude and Identity*. Oxford: Oxford University Press.

Jenkins, J. (2010). ELF still at the gate: attitudes towards English. In J. Jenkins and R. Cagliero (eds), *Discourses, Communities and Global Englishes* (pp. 101–14). Bern: Peter Lang.

Jenks, D., Stone, P. and Navarro, D. (2012). Material gains: the benefits of collaborative and creative materials development. *Folio*, 14(2): 14–17.

Johns, T. (1991). Should you be persuaded: two examples of data-driven learning. *English Language Research Journal*, 4: 1–16.

Johnson, K. (2003). *Designing Language Teaching Tasks*. Basingstoke: Palgrave Macmillan.

Johnson, K. (ed.) (2005). *Expertise in Second Language Learning and Teaching*. Basingstoke: Palgrave Macmillan.

Johnson, K., Kim, M., Ya-Fang, L., Nava, A., Perkins, D., Smith, A., Soler-Canela, O. and

Lu, W. (2008). A step forward: investigating expertise in materials evaluation. *ELT Journal*, 62(2): 157–63.

Johnstone Young, T. and Walsh, S. (2010). Which English? Whose English? An investigation of 'non-native' teachers' beliefs about target varieties. *Language, Culture and Curriculum*, 23(2): 123–37.

Jolly, D. and Bolitho, R. (2011). A framework for materials writing. In B. Tomlinson (ed.), *Materials Development in Language Teaching*, 2nd edn (pp. 107–35). Cambridge: Cambridge University Press.

Jones, C. (2007). Spoken gramma: is 'noticing' the best option? *Modern English Teacher*, 16(4): 155–60.

Jones, R. E. (2001). A consciousness-raising approach to the teaching of conversational storytelling. *ELT Journal*, 55(2): 155–63.

Kachru, B. (1982). *The Other Tongue: English Across Cultures*. Oxford: Pergamon.

Kachru, B. (1985). Standards, codification and sociolinguistic realism: the English language in the outer circle. In R. Quirk, H. G. Widdowson and Y. Cantù (eds), *English in the World: Teaching and Learning the Language and Literatures* (pp. 11–30). Cambridge: Cambridge University Press.

Kachru, Y. and Nelson, C. L. (2006). *World Englishes in Asian Contexts*. Hong Kong: Hong Kong University Press.

Kadepurkar, H. (2009). Coursebook development: An Indian perspective. *Folio*, 13(2): 20–1.

Kaltenböck, G. and Mehlmauer-Larcher, B. (2006). Computer corpora and the language classroom: on the potential and limitations of computer corpora in language teaching. *ReCALL*, 17(1): 65–84.

Kay, S. and Jones, V. (2000). *Inside Out*. Oxford: Macmillan.

Kay, S. and Jones, V. (2009). *New Inside Out Intermediate Student's Book*. Oxford: Macmillan.

Kessler, J. (ed.) (2008). *Processability Approaches to Second Language Development and Second Language Learning*. Newcastle: Cambridge Scholars.

Kiddle, T. (2013). Developing digital language learning materials. In B. Tomlinson (ed.), *Developing Materials for Language Teaching*, 2nd edn (pp. 189–206). London: Bloomsbury.

Kim, M. (2010). Expertise in EFL coursebook evaluation. Unpublished PhD thesis, University of Lancaster, UK.

Koda, K. (2004). *Insights into Second Language Reading: A Cross-Linguistic Approach*. Cambridge: Cambridge University Press.

Kolb, D. A. (1984). *Experiential Learning: Experience as the Source of Learning and Development. Vol. 1*. Englewood Cliffs: Prentice Hall.

Koprowski, M. (2005). Investigating the usefulness of lexical phrases in contemporary coursebooks. *ELT Journal*, 59(4): 322–32.

Kramsch, C. (1993). *Context and Culture in Language Teaching*. Oxford: Oxford University Press.

Krashen, S. (1982). *Principles and Practice in Language Acquisition*. New York: Pergamon.

Krashen, S. (1985). *The Input Hypothesis*. New York: Longman.

Krashen, S. (1993). *The Power of Reading; Insights from the Research*. Englewood: Libraries Unlimited.

Krashen, S. (2009). Hypotheses about free voluntary reading. In J. Mukundan (ed.), *Readings on ELT Materials III* (pp. 181–4). Selangor Darul Ehsan: Pearson Malaysia.

Kukulska-Hulme, A. and Shield, L. (2008). An overview of mobile assisted language learning: from content delivery to supported collaboration and interaction. *ReCALL*, 20: 271–89.

Kumaravadivelu, B. (1996). Maximising learning potential in the communicative classroom.

In T. Hedge and N. Whitney (eds), *Power, Pedagogy and Practice* (pp. 241–53). Oxford: Oxford University Press.

Kumaravadivelu, B. (2006). TESOL methods: changing tracks, challenging trends. *TESOL Quarterly*, 40(1): 59–81.

Kumaravadivelu, B. (2008). *Cultural Globalisation and Language Education*. New Haven: Yale University Press.

Kuo, I. V. (2006). Addressing the issue of teaching English as a lingua franca. *ELT Journal*, 60(3): 213–21.

Lambert, W. (1974). Culture and language as factors in learning and education. In F. Aboud and R. Meade (eds), *Cultural Factors in Learning and Education* (pp. 91–122). Bellingham: Fifth Western Washington Symposium on Learning.

Larsen-Freeman, D. (1991). *An Introduction to Second Language Acquisition Research*. London: Longman.

Larsen-Freeman, D. (2000). Second language acquisition and applied linguistics. *Annual Review of Applied Linguistics*, 20: 165–81.

Laufer, B. and Hulstijn, J. (2001). Incidental vocabulary acquisition in a second language: the construct of task-induced involvement. *Applied Linguistics*, 21(1): 1–26.

Laufer, B. and Shmueli, K. (1997). Memorizing new words: does teaching have anything to do with it? *RELC Journal*, 28: 89–108.

Lazar, G. (1994). Using literature at lower levels. *ELT Journal*, 48(2): 115–24.

Learned, J. E., Stockdill, D. and Moje, E. B. (2011). Integrating reading strategies and knowledge building in adolescent literacy instruction. In S. J. Samuels and A. E. Farstrup (eds), *What Research Has to Say about Reading Instruction*, 4th edn (pp. 159–87). Newark: International Reading Association.

Leow, R. (1993). To simplify or not to simplify: a look at intake. *Studies in Second Language Acquisition*, 15(3): 333–55.

Levelt, W. J. M. (1989). *Speaking: From Intention to Articulation*. Cambridge, MA: MIT Press

Lewis, M. (1993). *The Lexical Approach*. Hove: Language Teaching.

Lewis, M. (ed.) (2000). *Teaching Collocation: Further Developments in the Lexical Approach*. Hove: Language Teaching.

Li, D. (1998). 'It's always more difficult than you plan and imagine': teachers' perceived difficulties in introducing the communicative approach in South Korea. *TESOL Quarterly*, 32,(4): 677–703.

Littlejohn, A. P. (2011). The analysis of language teaching materials: inside the Trojan horse. In B. Tomlinson (ed.), *Materials Development in Language Teaching*, 2nd edn (pp. 179–212). Cambridge: Cambridge University Press.

Littlewood, W. (2004). The task-based approach: some questions and suggestions. *ELT Journal*, 58(4): 319–26.

Littlewood, W. (2006). Communicative and task-based language teaching in East Asian classrooms. Revised version of a plenary paper presented at the International Conference of the Korean Association for Teachers of English, June, Seoul, Korea. Retrieved 1 October 2014 from http://www.zanjansadra.ir/attaches/30062.pdf

Littlewood, W. (2009). Process-oriented pedagogy: facilitation, empowerment, or control? *ELT Journal*, 63(3): 246–54.

Liu, Y., Mishan, F. and Chambers, A. (forthcoming). Pilot study on investigating EFL teachers' perceptions of task-based language teaching: the context of higher education in China.

Lockhart, R. and Craik, H. (1990). Levels of processing: a retrospective commentary on a framework for memory research. *Canadian Journal of Psychology*, 44(1): 87–112.

Long, M. (1983). Linguistic and conversational adjustments to non-native speakers. *Studies in Second Language Acquisition*, 5(2): 177–93.

Long, M. (1991). A feeling for language: the multiple values of teaching literature. In J. Brumfit and R. Carter (eds), *Literature and Language Teaching* (pp. 42–59). Oxford: Oxford University Press.

Long, M. (1993). Assessment strategies for SLA theories. *Applied Linguistics*, 14: 225–49.

Long, M. (1996). The role of the linguistic environment in second language acquisition. In W. Ritchie and T. Bhatia (eds), *Handbook of Second Language Acquisition* (pp. 413–68). San Diego: Academic Press.

Long, M. H. and Larsen-Freeman, D. (1991). *An Introduction to Second Language Acquisition Research*. London: Longman.

Lozanov, G. (1978). *Suggestology and Outlines of Suggestopedy*. New York: Gordon & Breach.

MacAndrew, R. and Martinez, R. (2002). *Taboos and Issues*. Boston: Heinle.

Maley, A. (2011). Squaring the circle: reconciling materials as constraint with materials as empowerment. In B. Tomlinson (ed.), *Materials Development in Language Teaching*, 2nd edn (pp. 379–403). Cambridge: Cambridge University Press.

Maley, A. (2013). Vocabulary. In B. Tomlinson (ed.), *Applied Linguistics and Materials Development* (pp. 95–113). London: Bloomsbury.

Maley, A. and Prowse, P. (2013). Reading. In B. Tomlinson (ed.), *Applied Linguistics and Materials Development* (pp. 165–82). London: Bloomsbury.

Mares, C. (2003). Writing a coursebook. In B. Tomlinson (ed.), *Developing Materials for Language Teaching* (pp. 130–40). London: Continuum.

Mariani, L. (1997). Teacher support and teacher challenge in promoting learner autonomy. *Perspectives*, 23(2): 1–10.

Martin, J. R. (1984). Language, register and genre. In F. Christie (ed.), *Children Writing: Reader* (pp. 21–9). Geelong: Deakin University Press.

Martinez, R. and Schmitt, N. (2012). A phrasal expressions list. *Applied Linguistics*, 33(3): 299–320.

Masuhara, H. (2003). Materials for developing reading skills. In B. Tomlinson (ed.), *Developing Materials for Language Teaching* (pp. 340–63). London: Continuum.

Masuhara, H. (2011). What do teachers really want from coursebooks? In B. Tomlinson (ed.), *Materials Development in Language Teaching*, 2nd edn (pp. 236–67). Cambridge: Cambridge University Press.

Masuhara, H., Haan, N., Yi, Y. and Tomlinson, B. (2008). Adult EFL courses. *ELT Journal*, 62(3): 294–312.

Masuhara, H., Tomlinson, B. and Mishan, F. (forthcoming). *Practice and Theory in Materials Development in Language Learning*. Newcastle upon Tyne: Cambridge Scholars Publishing.

Mayer, R. (2005). Introduction to multimedia learning. In R. Mayer (ed.), *The Cambridge Handbook of Multimedia Learning* (pp. 1–16). Cambridge: Cambridge University Press.

McCarten, J. (2010). Corpus-informed coursebook design. In A. O'Keeffe and M. McCarthy (eds), *The Routledge Handbook of Corpus Linguistics* (pp. 413–28). London: Routledge.

McCarthy, M. (2003). Talking back: 'small' interactional response tokens in everyday conversation. *Research in Language and Social Interaction*, 36(1): 37–63.

McCarthy, M. (2004). *Touchstone*: from corpus to coursebook. Retrieved 1 October 2014 from http://salsoc.com/downloads.php?action=show&id=13

McCarthy, M. and Carter, R. (1995). Spoken grammar: what is it and how should we teach it? *ELT Journal*, 49(3): 207–17.

McCarthy, M. and Marsh, D. (forthcoming). *Blended Learning: Perspectives for Language Learning and Teaching*. Cambridge: Cambridge University Press.

McCarthy, M. and McCarten, J. (2010). Bridging the gap between corpus and coursebook: the case of conversation strategies. In F. Mishan and A. Chambers (eds), *Perspectives on Language Learning Materials Development* (pp. 11–32). Bern: Peter Lang.

McCarthy, M. and McCarten, J. (2012). Corpora and materials design. In K. Hyland, M. H. Chau and M. Handford (eds), *Corpus Applications in Applied Linguistics* (pp. 225–41). London: Continuum.

McCarthy, M., McCarten, J. and Sandiford, H.(2005). *Touchstone 2*. New York: Cambridge University Press.

McCarthy, M., McCarten, J. and Sandiford, H. (2006). *Touchstone*. New York: Cambridge University Press.

McCarthy, M., McCarten, J. and Sandiford, H. (2008). *Touchstone*. Cambridge: Cambridge University Press.

McDonough. J. and Shaw, C. (1993). *Materials and Methods in ELT*. Oxford: Blackwell.

McDonough, J., Shaw, C. and Masuhara, H. (2013). *Materials and Methods in ELT*, 3rd edn. Malden: John Wiley and Sons.

McEnery, T. and Xiao, R. (2011). What corpora can offer in language teaching and learning. In E. Hinkel (ed.), *Handbook of Research in Second Language Teaching and Learning. Vol. 2* (pp. 364–80). London: Routledge.

McGrath, I. (2002). *Materials Evaluation and Design for Language Teaching*. Edinburgh: Edinburgh University Press.

McGrath, I. (2006). Teachers' and learners' images for coursebooks: implications for teacher development. *ELT Journal*, 60(2): 171–80.

McGrath, I. (2013). *Teaching Materials and the Roles of EFL/ESL Teachers*. London: Bloomsbury.

McKay, S. (2002). English as an international language. In S. McKay, *Teaching English as an International Language: Rethinking Goals and Perspectives*. New York: Cambridge University Press.

McNamara, N. (2011). Exploring experiences with technology: a psychological perspective. In L. Murray, E. Riordan and T. Hourigan (eds), *Quality Issues in ICT Integration: Third Level Disciplines and Learning Contexts* (pp. 179–94). Newcastle: Cambridge Scholars.

Medgyes, P. (1996). Native or non-native: who's worth more? In T. Hedge and N. Whitney (eds), *Power, Pedagogy and Practice* (pp. 31–42). Oxford: Oxford University Press.

Meskill, C. (2007). 20 minutes into the future. In J. Egbert and E. Hanson-Smith (eds), *CALL Environments*, 2nd edn (pp. 423–36). Alexandria, VA: TESOL.

Min, H. T. (2008). EFL vocabulary acquisition and retention: reading plus vocabulary enhancement activities and narrow reading. *Language Learning*, 58(1): 73–115.

Mishan, F. (2005). *Designing Authenticity into Language Learning Materials*. Bristol: Intellect.

Mishan, F. (2010a). Task and task authenticity: paradigms for language learning in the digital era. In F. Mishan and A. Chambers (eds), *Perspectives on Language Learning Materials Development* (pp. 149–71). Bern: Peter Lang.

Mishan, F. (2010b). Withstanding washback: thinking outside the box in materials development. In B. Tomlinson and H. Masuhara (eds), *Research for Materials Development in Language Learning: Evidence for Best Practice* (pp. 353–68). London: Continuum.

Mishan, F. (2013a). Demystifying blended learning. In B. Tomlinson (ed.), *Developing Materials for Language Teaching*, 2nd edn (pp. 207–23). London: Bloomsbury.

Mishan, F. (2013b). Studies of pedagogy. In B. Tomlinson (ed.), *Applied Linguistics and Materials Development* (pp. 269–86). London: Bloomsbury.

Mishan, F. (forthcoming). Re-conceptualising materials for the blended language learning environment. In M. McCarthy and D. Marsh (eds), *Blended Learning: Perspectives for Language Learning and Teaching*. Cambridge: Cambridge University Press.

Mishan, F. and Chambers, A. (eds) (2010). *Perspectives on Language Learning Materials Development*. Bern: Peter Lang.

MobiThinking (n.d.). Retrieved 26 October 2014 from http://mobiforge.com

Modiano, M. (2000). Rethinking ELT. *English Today*, 16: 28–34.

Modirkhameneh, S. and Samadi, M. (2013). Personalizing the teaching of reading and vocabulary through the Diglot-Weave technique. *Folio*, 15(2): 14–17.

Mol, H. and Tin, T. B. (2008). EAP materials in Australia and New Zealand. In B. Tomlinson (ed.), *English Language Learning Materials: A Critical Review* (pp. 74–99). London: Continuum.

Moskowitz, G. (1978). *Caring and Sharing in the Foreign Language Class: A Sourcebook on Humanistic Techniques*. Boston: Heinle & Heinle.

Motteram, G. (2011). Developing language-learning materials with technology. In B. Tomlinson (ed.), *Materials Development in Language Teaching*, 2nd edn (pp. 303–27). Cambridge: Cambridge University Press.

Motteram, G. (2013). *Innovations in Learning Technologies for English Language Teaching*. London: British Council.

Mukundan, J. (2008). Agendas of the state in developing world English language textbooks. *Folio*, 12(2): 17–19.

Mukundan, J. (2009). *ESL Textbook Evaluation: A Composite Framework*. Cologne: Lambert Academic.

Munandar, M. and Ulwiyah, I. (2012). Intercultural approaches to the cultural content of Indonesia's high school ELT textbooks. *Cross-Cultural Communication*, 8(5): 67–73.

Murphy, T. (2011). *Essential Grammar in Use*, 2nd edn, French edn. Cambridge: Cambridge University Press.

Murphy, T. and García Clemente, F. (2008). *Essential Grammar in Use*, 3rd edn, Spanish edn. Cambridge: Cambridge University Press.

Myskow, G. and Gordon, K. (2010). Focus on purpose: using a genre approach in an EFL writing class. *ELT Journal*, 64(3): 283–92.

Nakahama, Y., Tyler, A. and van Lier, L. (2001). Negotiation of meaning in conversational and information gap activities: a comparative discourse analysis. *TESOL Quarterly*, 35(3): 377–405.

Nation, I. S. and Newton, J. (2009). *Teaching ESL/EFL Listening and Speaking*. New York: Routledge.

Nation, P. (2012). Teaching vocabulary. In M. Eisenmann and T. Summer (eds), *Basic Issues in EFL Teaching and Learning* (pp. 93–104). Heidelberg: Winter.

Nault, D. (2006). Going global: rethinking culture teaching in ELT contexts. *ELT Contexts, Language, Culture and Curriculum*, 19(3): 314–28.

Norton, J. (2009). Developing speaking skills: how are current theoretical and methodological approaches represented in course books? Paper presented at the 43rd IATEFL Conference, Cardiff, UK.

Nunan, D. (1987). Communicative language teaching: making it work. *ELT Journal*, 4(2): 136–45.

Oblinger, D. (2003). Boomers and gen-Xers millennials: understanding the new students. *Educause Review*, 38(4): 37–47. Retrieved 30 April 2013 from http://net.educause.edu/ir/library/pdf/erm0342.pdf

O'Dell, F. (1997). Incorporating language into the syllabus. In N. Schmitt and M. McCarthy (eds), *Vocabulary: Description, Acquisition and Pedagogy* (pp. 258–79). Cambridge: Cambridge University Press.

O'Keeffe, A., McCarthy, M. and Carter, R. (2007). *From Corpus to Classroom.* Cambridge: Cambridge University Press.

O'Neil, H. F. and Abedi, J. (1996). Reliability and validity of a state metacognitive inventory: potential for alternative assessment. *Journal of Educational Research*, 89(4): 234–45.

Oxenden, C. and Latham-Koenig, C. (1999). *English File Student's Book.* Oxford: Oxford University Press.

Oxenden, C. and Latham-Koenig, C. (2008a). *New English File Intermediate Student's Book.* Oxford: Oxford University Press.

Oxenden, C. and Latham-Koenig, C. (2008b). *New English File Upper Intermediate Student's Book.* Oxford: Oxford University Press.

Oxford, R. (1999). Anxiety and the language learner: new insights. In J. Arnold (ed.), *Affect in Language Learning* (pp. 58–67). Cambridge: Cambridge University Press.

Oxford, R. and Crookall, D. (1989). Research on language learning strategies: methods, findings, and instructional issues. *Modern Language Journal*, 73: 404–19.

Papathanasiou, E. (2009). An investigation of two ways of presenting vocabulary. *ELT Journal*, 6(4): 313–22.

Paran, A. (2012). Language skills: questions for teaching and learning. *ELT Journal*, 66(4): 450–8.

Parker, C-A. (2012). The relevance of Received Pronunciation in teaching phonemics for Irish English teachers. Unpublished MA thesis, University of Limerick, Ireland.

Peacock, M. (1997). The effect of authentic materials on the motivation of EFL learners. *ELT Journal*, 51(2): 144–54.

Peacock, M. (1998). Usefulness and enjoyableness of teaching materials as predictors of on-task behavior. *TESL-EJ*, 3(2).

Perkins, D. (2008). Expertise in ELT textbook writing: what a case study of an experienced materials designer at work can reveal about materials development. In M. Pawlak (ed.), *Investigating Language Learning and Teaching* (pp. 387–401). Poznań: Adam Mickiewicz University.

Phillipson, R. (1992). *Linguistic Imperialism.* Oxford: Oxford University Press.

Phillipson, R. (1996). ELT: the native speaker's burden. In T. Hedge and N. Whitney (eds), *Power, Pedagogy and Practice* (pp. 23–30). Oxford: Oxford University Press.

Pica, T., Young, R. and Doughty, C. (1987). The impact of interaction on comprehension. *TESOL Quarterly*, 21(4): 737–58.

Pienemann, M. (1984). Psychological constraints on the teachability of languages. *Studies in Second Language Acquisition*, 6: 186–214.

Pigada, M. and Schmitt, N. (2006). Vocabulary acquisition from extensive reading: a case study. *Reading in a Foreign Language*, 18(1): 1–28.

Pintrich, P. (2002). The role of metacognitive knowledge in learning, teaching, and assessing. *Theory into Practice*, 41(4): 219–25.

Pit Corder, S. (1974). The significance of learners' errors. In J. Richards (ed.), *Error Analysis: Perspectives in Second Language Acquisition* (pp. 19–30). London: Longman.

Popovici, R. and Bolitho, R. (2003). Personal and professional development through writing: the Romanian Textbook Project. In B. Tomlinson (ed.), *Developing Materials for Language Teaching* (pp. 505–17). London: Continuum.

Prabhu, N. (1987). *Second Language Pedagogy.* Oxford: Oxford University Press.

Prensky, M. (2001). Digital natives, digital immigrants. *On the Horizon*, 9(5): 1–6. Retrieved 2 May 2013 from http://www.scribd.com/doc/9799/Prensky-Digital-Natives-Digital-Immigrants-Part1

Prensky, M. (2009). *H. sapiens* digital: from digital immigrants and digital natives to digital wisdom. *Innovate* 5(3). Retrieved 28 April 2013 from http://www.innovateonline.info/index.php?view=article&id=705

Prince, P. (1996). Second language vocabulary learning: The role of context versus translations as a function of proficiency. *Modern Language Journal*, 80: 478–93.

Prodromou, L. and Mishan, F. (2008). Materials used in Western Europe. In B. Tomlinson (ed.), *English Language Learning Materials: A Critical Review* (pp. 193–212). London: Continuum.

Prowse, P. (2011). How writers write: testimony from authors. In B. Tomlinson (ed.), *Materials Development in Language Teaching*, 2nd edn (pp. 151–73). Cambridge: Cambridge University Press.

Pulverness, A. (1999). Context or pretext? Cultural content and the coursebook. *Folio*, 5(2): 5–9.

Pulverness, A. (2003). Materials for cultural awareness. In B. Tomlinson (ed.), *Developing Materials for Language Teaching* (pp. 426–38). London: Continuum.

Pulverness, A. and Tomlinson, B. (2013). Materials for cultural awareness. In B. Tomlinson (ed.), *Developing Materials for Language Teaching*, 2nd edn (pp. 443–60). London: Bloomsbury.

Raimes, A. (1983). *Techniques in Teaching Writing*. New York: Oxford University Press.

Redston, C. and Cunningham, G. (206). *face2face*. Cambridge: Cambridge University Press.

Redston, C. and Cunningham, G. (2013a). *face2face Intermediate Student's Book*. Cambridge: Cambridge University Press.

Redston, C. and Cunningham, G. (2013b). *facetoface Upper Intermediate Student's Book*. Cambridge: Cambridge University Press.

Reid, J. (2001). Writing. In R. Carter and D. Nunan (eds), *The Cambridge Guide to TESOL* (pp. 28–34). Cambridge: Cambridge University Press.

Reigeluth, C. (1999). *Instructional-Design Theories and Models: A New Paradigm of Instructional Theory*. New York: Routledge.

Reinders, H. and White, C. (2010). The theory and practice of technology in materials development and task design. In N. Harwood (ed.), *English Language Teaching Materials: Theory and Practice* (pp. 58–80). Cambridge: Cambridge University Press.

Reinhardt, J. (2010). The potential of corpus-informed L2 pedagogy. *Studies in Hispanic and Lusophone Linguistics*, 3(1): 239–51.

Renandya, W. A. and Farrell, T. S. (2011). 'Teacher, the tape is too fast!' Extensive listening in ELT. *ELT Journal*, 65(1): 52–9.

Riazi, A. M. (2003). What do textbook evaluation schemes tell us? A study of the textbook evaluation schemes of three decades. In W. Renyanda (ed.), *Methodology and Materials Design in Language Teaching: Current Perceptions and Practices and their Implications* (pp. 52–69). Singapore: SEAMEO.

Richards, J. (1995). Easier said than done: an insider's account of a textbook project. In A. Hidalgo, D. Hall and G. Jacobs (eds), *Getting Started: Materials Writers on Materials Writing* (pp. 95–135). Singapore: SEAMEO.

Richards, J. (2001). The role of instructional materials. In J. Richards, *Curriculum Development in Language Teaching* (pp. 251–85). Oxford: Oxford University Press.

Richards, J. and T. Rodgers. (2001). *Approaches and Methods in Language Teaching*, 2nd edn. New York: Cambridge University Press.

Rinvolucri, M. (2002). *Humanising Your Coursebook*. Peaslake: Delta.

Risager, K. (2007). *Language and Culture Pedagogy*. Clevedon: Multilingual Matters.

Ritchie, W. and Bhatia, T. (eds) (2009). *The New Handbook of Second Language Acquisition*. Bingley: Emerald Group.

Römer, U. (2004). Comparing real and ideal language learner input: the use of an EFL textbook corpus in corpus linguistics and language teaching. In G. Aston, S. Bernardini and D. Stewart (eds), *Corpora and Language Learners* (pp. 151–68). Amsterdam: John Benjamins.

Römer, U. (2006). Pedagogical applications of corpora: some reflections on the current scope and a wish list for future developments. *ZAA (Zeitschrift fur Anglistik und Amerikanistik)*, 54(2): 121–34.

Rossner, R. (1988). Materials for communicative language teaching and learning. *Annual Review of Applied Linguistics*, 8: 140–63.

Rubdy, R. (2003). Selection of materials. In B. Tomlinson (ed.), *Developing Materials for Language Teaching* (pp. 37–58). London: Continuum.

Rubdy, R. and Saraceni, M. (eds) (2006). *English in the World: Global Rules, Global Roles*. London: Continuum.

Rumelhart, D. E. (1977) Understanding understanding. In G. Mandler, W. Kessen, A. Ortony and F. I. M. Craik (eds), *Memories, Thoughts, and Emotions: Essays in Honor of George Mandler* (pp. 257–66). Hillsdale: Erlbaum.

Samuda, V. (2005). Expertise in pedagogic task design. In K. Johnson (ed.), *Expertise in Second Language Learning and Teaching* (pp. 230–54). Basingstoke: Palgrave Macmillan.

Saraceni, C. (2013). Adapting coursebooks: a personal view. In B. Tomlinson (ed.), *Developing Materials for Language Teaching*, 2nd edn (pp. 49–63). London: Bloomsbury.

Saville-Troike, M. (2003). Extending 'communicative' concepts in the second language curriculum: a sociolinguistic perspective. In D. L. Lange and R. N. Paige (eds), *Culture as the Core: Perspectives on Culture in Second Language* (pp. 3–18). Greenwich, CT: Information Age.

Scarborough, D. (1984). *Reasons for Listening*. Cambridge: Cambridge University Press.

Scheffler, P. (2009). Rule difficulty and the usefulness of instruction. *ELT Journal*, 63(3): 5–12.

Schmidt, R. (1990). The role of consciousness in second language learning. *Applied Linguistics*, 11(2): 129–58.

Schmitt, N. (2010). *Researching Vocabulary: A Vocabulary Research Manual*. Basingstoke: Palgrave Macmillan.

Schmitt, N. and Schmitt, D. (1995). Vocabulary notebooks: Theoretical underpinnings and practical suggestions. *English Language Teaching Journal*, 49(2): 133–43.

Schneider, V. I., Healy, A. F. and Bourne, L. E., Jr (1998). Contextual interference effects in foreign language vocabulary acquisition and retention. In A. F. Healy and L. E. Bourne, Jr (eds), *Foreign Language Learning: Psycholinguistic Studies on Training and Retention* (pp. 77–90). Mahwah: Erlbaum.

Schumann, J. (1978b). *The Pidginization Process: A Model for Second Language Acquisition*. Rowley: Newbury House.

Schumann, J. H. (1999). A neurobiological perspective on affect and methodology in second language learning. In J. Arnold (ed.), *Affect in Language Learning* (pp. 28–42). Cambridge: Cambridge University Press.

Schwartz, H. (2009). Facebook: the new classroom commons? *Chronicle of Higher Education: Chronicle Review*, 28 September.

Scott, M. (2013). Wordsmith tools, version 6.0.

Scotton, C. and Bernsten, J. (1988). Natural conversations as a model for textbook dialogue. *Applied Linguistics*, 9(3): 372–84.

Seidhofer, B. (2006). English as a LINGUA FRanca in the expanding circle: what it isn't. In R. Rubdy and M. Saraceni (eds), *English in the World: Global Rules, Global Roles* (pp. 40–50). London: Continuum.

Shanahan, D. (1997). Articulating the relationship between language, literature and culture: towards a new agenda for foreign language teaching and research. *Modern Languages Journal*, 81(2): 164–74.

Shawer, S., Gilmore, D. and Banks-Joseph, S. (2008). Student cognitive and affective development in the context of classroom-level curriculum development. *Journal of the Scholarship of Teaching and Learning*, 8(1): 1–28.

Sheen, R. (2003). Focus on form: a myth in the making? *ELT Journal*, 57(3): 225–33.

Sheen, R. (2006). Comments on R. Ellis's 'Current issues in the teaching of grammar: an SLA perspective': a reader responds. *TESOL Quarterly*, 40(4): 828–32.

Sheldon, L. (1988). Evaluating ELT textbooks and materials. *ELT Journal*, 42(4): 237–46.

Shimada, K. (2009). The globalisation and individuality of EFL composition textbooks in Japan. *Folio*, 13(2): 29–31.

Shin, D. and Nation, P. (2008). Beyond single words: the most frequent collocations in spoken English. *ELT Journal*, 62(4): 339–48.

Shirky, C. (2010). Does the internet make you smarter? *Wall Street Journal*, June 4. Retrieved 6 January 2015 from http://www.wsj.com/articles/SB10001424052748704025304575284973472694334

Sidaway, R. (2006). The genre-based approach to teaching writing. *English*, spring, 24–7.

Siegel, J. (2014). Exploring L2 listening instruction: examinations of practice. *ELT Journal*, 68,(1): 22–30.

Sikafis, N. and Sougari, A-M. (2010). Between a rock and a hard place: an investigation of EFL teachers' beliefs on what keeps them from integrating global Englishes in their classrooms. In C. Gagliardi and A. Maley (eds), *EIL, ELF, Global English: Teaching and Learning Issues* (pp. 301–20). Bern: Peter Lang.

Sinclair J. M. (1987). Collocation: a progress report. In R. Steele and T. Threadgold (eds), *Language Topics: Essays in Honour of Michael Halliday* (pp. 319–31). Amsterdam: John Benjamins.

Sinclair, J. and Renouf, A. (1988). A lexical syllabus for language learning. In R. Carter and M. McCarthy (eds), *Vocabulary and Language Teaching* (pp. 140–60). Harlow: Longman.

Singapore Wala, D. (2003). A course book is what it is because of what it has to do. In B. Tomlinson (ed.), *Developing Materials for Language Teaching* (pp. 58–71). London: Continuum.

Singapore Wala, D. (2013). Publishing a coursebook: the role of feedback. In B. Tomlinson (ed.), *Developing Materials for Language Teaching*, 2nd edn (pp. 63–89). London: Bloomsbury.

Skehan, P. (1998). *A Cognitive Approach to Language Learning*. Oxford: Oxford University Press.

Skehan, P. (2003). Task-based instruction. *Language Teaching*, 36(1): 1–14.

Skehan, P. and Foster, P. (1997) Task type and processing conditions as influences on foreign language performance. *Language Teaching Research*, 1(3): 185–211.

Slaouti D. (2013). Technology in ELT. in J. McDonough, C. Shaw and H. Masuhara (eds), *Materials and Methods in ELT*, 3rd edn (pp. 79–105). Oxford: Wiley-Blackwell.

Smiley, J. and Masui, M. (2008). Materials in Japan: coexisting traditions. In B. Tomlinson (ed.), *English Language Learning Materials: A Critical Review* (pp. 245–62). London: Continuum.

Soars, L. and Soars, J. (1986). *Headway Intermediate Student's Book*. Oxford: Oxford University Press.

Soars, L. and Soars, J. (1996). *New Headway Intermediate Student's Book*. Oxford: Oxford University Press.

Soars, L. and Soars, J. (2003a). *New Headway Intermediate Student's Book*, 3rd edn. Oxford: Oxford University Press.

Soars, L. and Soars, J. (2003b). *New Headway Advanced Student's Book*. Oxford: Oxford University Press.

Soars, L. and Soars, J. (2005). *New Headway Upper-Intermediate Student's Book*, 3rd edn. Oxford: Oxford University Press.

Soars, L. and Soars, J. (2009). *New Headway Intermediate Student's Book*, 4th edn. Oxford: Oxford University Press.

Sokmen, A. (1997). Current trends in vocabulary teaching. In N. Schmitt and M. McCarthy (eds), *Vocabulary: Description, Acquisition and Pedagogy* (pp. 237–57). Cambridge: Cambridge University Press.

Spada, N. and Lightbown, P. (1999). Instruction, first language influence, and developmental readiness in second language acquisition. *Modern Language Journal*, 83: 1–22.

Spada, N. and Lightbown, P. (2008). Form-focused instruction: isolated or integrated? *TESOL Quarterly*, 42(2): 181–207.

Spiro, J. (2013). *Changing Methodologies in TESOL*. Edinburgh: Edinburgh University Press.

St Louis, R., Trias, M. and Pereira, S. (2010). Designing materials for a twelve-week remedial course for pre-university students: a case study. In F. Mishan and A. Chambers (eds), *Perspectives on Language Learning Materials Development* (pp. 249–70). Bern: Peter Lang.

Stapleton, P. and Radia, P. (2010). Tech-era L2 writing: towards a new kind of process. *ELT Journal*, 64(2): 175–83.

Stokes, A. (2012). ICT: the age factor. *Loud and Clear*, 31(2): 2.

Stoller, F. and Robinson, M. (2014). An interdisciplinary textbook project: charting the paths taken. In N. Harwood (ed.), *English Language Teaching Textbooks: Content, Consumption, Production* (pp. 262–99). Basingstoke: Palgrave Macmillan.

Stranks, J. (2013). Materials for the teaching of grammar. In B. Tomlinson (ed.), *Developing Materials for Language Teaching*, 2nd edn (pp. 337–51). London: Bloomsbury.

Swain, M. (1985). Communicative competence: some roles of comprehensible input and comprehensible output in its development. In S. Gass and C. Madden (eds), *Input in Second Language Acquisition* (pp. 165–79). Rowley: Newbury House.

Swain, M. (1995). Three functions of output in second language learning. In G. Cook and B. Seidelhofer (eds), *Principle and Practice in Applied Linguistics: Studies in Honor of H. G. Widdowson* (pp. 125–44). Oxford: Oxford University Press.

Swales, J. M. (1990). *Genre Analysis: English in Academic and Research Settings*. Cambridge: Cambridge University Press.

Swales, J. and Feak, C. B. (2009). *Abstracts and the Writing of Abstracts*. Ann Arbor: University of Michigan Press.

Swales, J. and Feak, C. B. (2010). From text to task: Putting research on abstracts to work. In M. F. Ruiz-Garrido, J. C. Palmer-Silveira and I. Fortanet-Gómez (eds), *English for Professional and Academic Purposes* (pp. 167–80). Amsterdam: Rodopi.

Swan, M. (2005). Legislation by hypothesis: the case of task-based instruction. *Applied Linguistics,* 26(3): 376–401.

Swan, M. (2006). Teaching grammar: does grammar teaching work? *Modern English Teacher*, 15(2): 5–13.

Sybing, R. (2011). Assessing perspectives on culture in EFL education. *ELT Journal*, 65(4): 467–9.

Tan, M. (2003). Language corpora for language teachers. *Journal of Language and Learning* 1(2). Retrieved 12 May 2014 from http://www.jllonline.co.uk/journal/jllearn/1_2/tan1.html

Tasseron, M. (forthcoming). How teachers use the global ELT coursebook. In H. Masuhara,

B. Tomlinson and F. Mishan (eds), *Practice and Theory in Materials Development in Language Learning*. Newcastle upon Tyne: Cambridge Scholars Publishing.

Taylor, L. (1997). *International Express Intermediate*. Oxford: Oxford University Press.

Thomas, M. (2009). *Handbook of Research on Web 2.0 and Second Language Learning*. Hershey: IGI Global.

Thomas, M (ed.) (2011). *Deconstructing Digital Natives: Young People, Technology and the New Literacies*. London: Routledge.

Thomas, M. and Reinders, H. (2010). *Task-Based Language Learning and Teaching with Technology*. London: Continuum.

Thompson, G. (1996). Some misconceptions about communicative language teaching. *ELT Journal*, 50(1): 9–15.

Thornbury, S. (1997). Reformulation and reconstruction: tasks that promote 'noticing'. *ELT Journal*, 51(4): 326–35.

Thornbury, S. (2000a). Deconstructing grammar. In A. Pulverness (ed.), *IATEFL 2000: Dublin Conference Selections* (pp. 59–67). Canterbury: IATEFL.

Thornbury, S. (2000b). A dogma for EFL. *IATEFL Issues*, 153(1–2). Retrieved 24 September 2011 from http://www.thornburyscott.com/tu/Dogma%20article.htm

Thornbury, S. (2001). *Uncovering Grammar*. Oxford: Macmillan Heinemann.

Thornbury, S. and Slade, D. (2006). *Conversation: From Description to Pedagogy*. Cambridge: Cambridge University Press.

Timmis, I. (2002). Native-speaker norms and international English: a classroom view. *ELT Journal*, 56(3): 240–9.

Timmis, I. (2005). Towards a framework for teaching spoken grammar. *ELT Journal*, 59(2): 117–25.

Timmis, I. (2008). The lexical approach is dead: long live the lexical dimension! *Modern English Teacher*, 17(3): 5–10.

Timmis, I. (2012a). Spoken language research and ELT: where are we now? *ELT Journal*, 66(4): 514–22.

Timmis, I. (2012b). Language in use: grammar. In M. Eisenmann and T. Summer (eds), *Basic Issues in EFL Teaching and Learning* (pp. 135–46). Heidelberg: Winter.

Timmis, I. (2013). Spoken language research: the applied linguistic challenge. In B. Tomlinson (ed.), *Applied Linguistics and Materials Development* (pp. 79–95). London: Bloomsbury.

Timmis, I. (2014). Writing materials for publication: questions raised and lessons learned. In N. Harwood (ed.), *English Language Teaching Textbooks: Content, Consumption, Production* (pp. 241–61). Basingstoke: Palgrave Macmillan.

Tims, C., Redstone, C. and Cunningham, G. (2005). *face2face Pre-Intermediate*, Polish edn. Cambridge: Cambridge University Press.

Tinkham, T. (1997). The effects of semantic and thematic clustering on the learning of second language vocabulary. *Second Language Research*, 13(2): 138–63.

Tomalin, B. (2000). Using films in ELT. Paper presented at IATEFL conference, Dublin, Ireland.

Tomlinson, B. (2001). Materials development. In R. Carter and D. Nunan (eds), *The Cambridge Guide to Teaching English to Speakers of Other Languages* (pp. 66–72). Cambridge: Cambridge University Press.

Tomlinson, B. (ed.) (2003a). *Developing Materials for Language Teaching*. London: Continuum.

Tomlinson, B. (2003b). Materials evaluation. In B. Tomlinson (ed.), *Developing Materials for Language Teaching* (pp. 15–36). London: Continuum.

Tomlinson, B. (2003c). Developing principled frameworks for materials development. In B. Tomlinson (ed.), *Developing Materials for Language Teaching* (pp. 107–29). London: Continuum.

Tomlinson, B. (2008). *English Language Learning Materials: A Critical Review*. London: Continuum.

Tomlinson, B. (2010). Principles of effective materials development. In N. Harwood (ed.), *English Language Teaching Materials: Theory and Practice* (pp. 81–108). Cambridge: Cambridge University Press.

Tomlinson, B. (2011a). Introduction: principles and procedures of materials development. In B. Tomlinson (ed.), *Materials Development in Language Teaching*, 2nd edn (pp. 1–31). Cambridge: Cambridge University Press.

Tomlinson, B. (ed.) (2011b). *Materials Development in Language Teaching*, 2nd edn. Cambridge: Cambridge University Press.

Tomlinson, B. (2012). State of the art review: materials development for language learning and teaching. *Language Teaching*, 45(2): 143–79.

Tomlinson, B. (ed.) (2013a). *Applied Linguistics and Materials Development*. London: Bloomsbury.

Tomlinson, B. (2013b). *Developing Materials for Language Teaching*, 2nd edn. London: Bloomsbury.

Tomlinson, B. (2013c). Developing principled frameworks for materials development. In B. Tomlinson (ed.), *Developing Materials for Language Teaching*, 2nd edn (pp. 95–118). London: Bloomsbury.

Tomlinson, B. (2014). Looking out for English. *Folio*, 16(1): 5–9.

Tomlinson, B. and Masuhara, H. (2004). *Developing Language Course Materials*. Singapore: SEAMO.

Tomlinson, B. and Masuhara, H. (eds) (2010). *Research for Materials Development in Language Learning: Evidence for Best Practice*. London: Continuum.

Tomlinson, B. and Masuhara, H. (2013). Adult coursebooks. *ELT Journal*, 67(2): 233–49.

Tomlinson, B. and Whittaker, C. (2013). *Blended Learning in English Language Teaching: Course Design and Implementation*. London: British Council.

Tomlinson, B., Dat, B., Masuhara, H. and Rubdy, R. (2001). EFL courses for adults. *ELT Journal*, 55(1): 80–101.

Tran-Hoang-Thu (2010). Teaching culture in the EFL/ESL classroom. Paper presented at the Los Angeles Regional Conference, California Teachers of English to Speakers of Other Languages, 11 September, Fullerton, USA. Retrieved 29 March 2013 from http://files.eric.ed.gov/fulltext/ED511819.pdf

Tremblay, P. F. and Gardner, R. C. (1995). Expanding the motivation construct in language learning. *Modern Language Journal*, 79: 505–20.

Ur, P. (1996). *A Course in Language Teaching: Practice and Theory*. Cambridge: Cambridge University Press

Vogel, T. (2001). Learning out of control: some thoughts on the World Wide Web in learning and teaching foreign languages. In A. Chambers and G. Davies (eds), *ICT and Language Learning: A European Perspective* (pp. 133–42). Lisse: Swets & Zeitlinger.

Vygotsky, L.S. (1978). *Mind in Society: The Development of Higher Mental Processes*. Cambridge, MA: Harvard University Press.

Vygotsy, L. S. (1981). The genesis of higher mental functions. In J. V. Wertsch (ed.), *The Concept of Activity in Soviet Psychology* (pp. 144–88). Armonk: M. E. Sharpe.

Walter, C. (2007). First- to second-language reading comprehension: not transfer, but access. *International Journal of Applied Linguistics*, 17(1): 14–37.

Wang, L-Y. (2005). A study of junior high school teachers' perceptions of the liberalization of the authorized English textbooks and their experience of textbook evaluation and selection.

Unpublished MA dissertation, National Yunlin University of Science and Technology, Taiwan.

Waring, R. (1997). The negative effects of learning words in semantic sets: a replication. *System*, 25(2): 261–74.

Waters, A. (2007a). ELT and 'the spirit of the times'. *ELT Journal*, 61(4): 353–9.

Waters, A. (2007b). Ideology, reality and false consciousness in ELT. *ELT Journal*, 61(4): 367–8.

Waters, A. (2009). Advances in materials design. In M. Long and C. Doughty (eds), *The Handbook of Language Teaching* (pp. 311–27). Oxford: Blackwell.

Waters, A. (2012). Trends and issues in ELT methods and methodology. *ELT Journal*, 66(4): 440–9.

Weber, J-J. (2001). A concordance and genre-informed approach to essay writing. *ELT Journal*, 55(1): 14–20.

White, R. (1988). *The ELT Curriculum: Design, Innovation and Management*. Oxford: Blackwell.

Widdowson, H. G. (1998). Context, community, and authentic language. *TESOL Quarterly*, 32(4): 705–16.

Widdowson, H. G. (2000). On the limitations of linguistics applied. *Applied Linguistics*, 21(1): 3–25.

Wilkins, D. (1972). *Linguistics in Language Teaching*. Cambridge, MA: MIT Press.

Wilkins, D. (1976). *Notional Syllabuses: A Taxonomy and its Relevance to Foreign Language Curriculum Development*. Oxford: Oxford University Press.

Williams, M. and Burden, R. (1997). *Psychology for Language Teachers*. Cambridge: Cambridge University Press.

Williams, R. (1986). 'Top ten' principles for teaching reading. *ELT Journal*, 40(1): 42–5.

Willis, D. (2003). *Rules, Patterns and Words: Grammar and Lexis in ELT*. Oxford: Oxford University Press.

Willis, J. (1996). *A Framework for Task-Based Learning*. London: Longman.

Willis, J. and Willis, D. (1996). *Challenge and Change in Language Teaching*. Oxford: Heinemann.

Yano, Y., Long, M. and Ross, S. (1994). The effects of simplified and elaborated texts on foreign language reading comprehension. *Language Learning*, 44: 198–219.

Young, D. (1999). Linguistic simplification of SL reading material: effective instructional practice? *Modern Language Journal*, 83(3): 350–66.

Yu, L. (2001). Communicative language teaching in China: progress and resistance. *TESOL Quarterly*, 35(1): 194–8.

Yuen, K-M. (2011). The representation of foreign cultures in English textbooks. *ELT Journal*, 65(4): 458–66.

Zacharias, N. T. (2005). Teachers' beliefs about internationally-published materials: a survey of tertiary English teachers in Indonesia. *RELC Journal*, 36: 23–37.

Zeng, Y. (2007). Metacognitive instruction in listening: a study of Chinese non-English major undergraduates. Unpublished MA dissertation, National Institute of Education, Nanyang Technological University, Singapore.

Zhang, X. (2013). Foreign language listening anxiety and listening performance: conceptualizations and causal relationships. *System*, 41(1): 164–77.

Zimmerman, C. (1997). Do reading and interactive vocabulary instruction make a difference? An empirical study. *TESOL Quarterly*, 31: 121–40.

Zlatkovska, E. (2010). WebQuests as a constructivist tool in the EFL teaching methodology class in a university in Macedonia. *CORELL: Computer Resources for Language Learning*, 3: 14–24.

INDEX